MORE ADVANCE LOVE FOR **FEAST**

"I trust Lindsay Anderson and Dana VanVeller to tell great stories, keep me entertained, and teach me something about Canadian food that I wouldn't have learned anywhere else. Inspiring recipes are the crux of this cookbook, but the personal narratives are what make you want to read it cover to cover."

CAREY POLIS, editor of *BonAppetit.com*

"*Feast* is a book that pulls the blinders off and lets us see the complexity of Canadian regional gastronomy. It's a book like this that makes me want to truly wander and appreciate this amazing country for all it has to offer."

HUGH ACHESON, James Beard Award–winning chef and author of *The Broad Fork*

"A beautiful culinary adventure through Canada that you can take from your home kitchen. It will make you want to cook, explore, and maybe even book a ticket to go see those Manitoba polar bears for yourself!"

MOLLY YEH, blogger and author of *Molly on the Range*

"*Feast* showcases the diversity of our landscape and at the same time gives insight into the wild ingredients, products, climates, and cultures that coexist in our country. Congrats to Lindsay and Dana—what an incredible journey."

DANIEL BURNS, chef/owner of Tørst and co-author of *Food & Beer*

"With passion and humour, Lindsay and Dana capture the essence of our country's diverse food culture and present it in an inspiring cookbook. *Feast* will forever change how you view Canadian cuisine."

AIMÉE WIMBUSH-BOURQUE, blogger and author of *Brown Eggs and Jam Jars*

"Join Lindsay and Dana as they reveal a bounty that will scoot you into the kitchen to cook up a real Canadian feast. A must-read for anyone interested in food as it's enjoyed in Canada."

ELIZABETH BAIRD, author of *Classic Canadian Cooking*

FEAST

F
E
CHEWAN
AIK
TRÉSOR

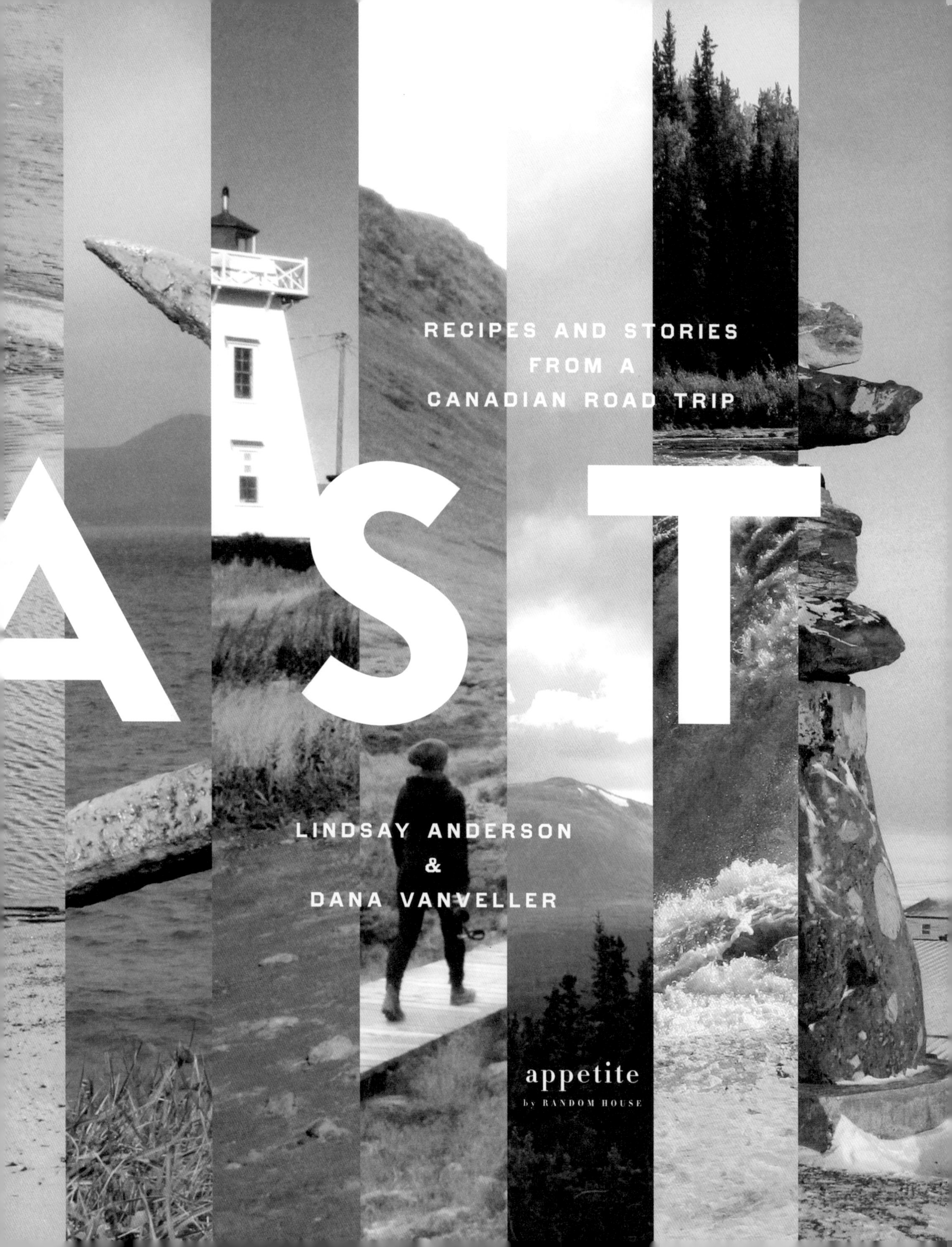

A S T

RECIPES AND STORIES
FROM A
CANADIAN ROAD TRIP

LINDSAY ANDERSON
&
DANA VANVELLER

appetite
by RANDOM HOUSE

For my Grandpa, Harry Disbrow,
one of the most curious and encouraging of souls.
—LA

For my Pake and Beppe,
still my favourite food producers.
—DV

Library and Archives of Canada Cataloguing in Publication is available upon request.

ISBN: 978-0-14-752971-8
eBook ISBN: 978-0-14-752972-5

Cover concept: Lindsay Anderson and Dana VanVeller
Cover illustration: CS Richardson
Printed and bound in China

Published in Canada by Appetite by Random House®, a division of Penguin Random House LLC.

www.penguinrandomhouse.ca

10 9 8 7 6 5 4 3 2 1

appetite by RANDOM HOUSE | Penguin Random House

FEAST CONTAINS:

Foreword

Oh, how I love a road trip! And, better yet, a Canadian road trip. But Lindsay and Dana have taken this concept one step further: a few years ago, they set out on the ultimate edible road trip across all of Canada.

When I first heard about these two young, talented, and adventurous food writers who were about to explore the country, and celebrate food and all that is Canadian, I immediately knew that I had to meet them one day to hear all the stories of their many adventures.

But keeping in mind that Lindsay and Dana may not have the chance to meet the entire country and regale them with their tales, they have done the next best thing: they have written a book that is a road map of their journey—their dream come true. I have learned a great deal from their stories, and from the people they met along the way.

Our Canadian food culture is rich, diverse, and remarkable, and in *Feast*, you'll find the history, tradition, and storytelling to match. As you turn the pages, you will be instantly transported to the ten provinces and three territories that Lindsay and Dana visited, each so unique and brilliant. They have captured the beauty of this magnificent country through their photographs and words. In this book, we get to celebrate Canadian food alongside Lindsay, Dana, and their friends—chefs, food producers, farmers, First Nations elders, grandmothers and many more wonderful Canadians who have shared their recipes with us. And these recipes are so good that I've decided I want to cook them all.

I have such respect for all of our Canadian farmers, fishermen, ranchers, and growers who work across this entire country and give us incredible products to cook with and enjoy. And I have such respect for these two women who have shared their sense of humour, knowledge, and passion for Canadian cuisine. This is one amazing road trip, and an amazing book! I love this beautiful country so much, but if I ever forget, *Feast* will be an excellent reminder.

—Chef Lynn Crawford

Introduction

We have been asked, time and time again, why we decided to do a road trip and write about Canadian food culture. Our answers are always a little vague, and that's because we can't remember exactly how it all started. We think the first conversation began during a camping trip in Squamish, British Columbia, while eating chips and lounging on a fallen log in the river—the kind of moment when dreams get tossed around. On that trip, we spoke of the ways in which our lives would soon be open-ended; contracts were finishing, leases were up, and it seemed that by the next summer, we'd be poised for adventure. Over the next few weeks, those initial musings of "Wouldn't it be interesting if . . . ?" transitioned to "Why not?" Why *not* plan a trip across the country and see what it is, exactly, that Canadians eat?

Of course, there were *plenty* of reasons not to, money being the biggest, but that didn't stop us from researching. We simultaneously became obsessed with and terrified of our potential project, quickly realizing how enormous an undertaking it would be. How would we manage to get to all 10 provinces and 3 territories? How would we pay for it? And perhaps most importantly, would anybody even care enough to read about it? Crazy as it was, the idea stuck. Discussions continued, we found the courage to purchase our domain, www.edibleroadtrip.com, and that was it. We'd now invested a whopping $20 in this thing, and you can't just throw that kind of money away!

With a name and a yet-to-be-constructed website, we were committed, thus initiating hundreds of hours of planning, all fuelled by endless cups of tea and bars of dark chocolate. We researched routes, funding options, cookstoves, campgrounds, restaurants, farmers, brewers, distillers, fishers, website templates, Twitter handles, gas prices, Indiegogo videos, and more. After months spent researching, writing proposals, emailing contacts, and fundraising, our departure date neared and we were left feeling nervous that we were two overly ambitious idiots.

Ultimately, we decided this: If we fundraised and still had only enough money to get from British Columbia to Saskatchewan, that would be fine. We'd just work for a while and live life on the prairies. If we got ourselves to Newfoundland and ran out of money again, that would be fine, too. We'd work in St. John's and get to know George Street. That was the upside of being young and mortgage-free; we could figure it out as we went. Idiots have such freedom!

The miraculous thing is that it all worked out. In fact, we travelled one month longer than we initially planned, and while we didn't always live glamorously, we didn't run out of money, either. With funds from our Indiegogo campaign and sponsorship from various tourism boards, we eventually made it to all 10 provinces and 3 territories over 5 months, travelling a total of 36,767 kilometres (22,846 miles), mostly in Dana's small white car. Most miraculous of all? After spending nearly 24 hours a day together for 150 days, our friendship didn't suffer. In fact, it had grown much stronger.

Together, we found ourselves in places we never expected to be, like crossing a frozen lake in Nunavut to get to the hockey rink for a Beer Dance, one of us leading the other because her glasses had become too painfully cold to keep on her face. We stared at each other through the metal porthole of an old wrecked ship on a beach on Haida Gwaii, British Columbia, and woke up at 2 am in a Northern Ontario campground to find ourselves in a flooded tent. These moments either had us exclaiming "This is AMAZING!" or "What were we thinking? Why are we here? WHOSE IDEA WAS THIS ANYWAY!?"

Our road trip adventures took us to every part of the country over three seasons (though Nunavut in November definitely felt like winter). We trekked around under the midnight sun in the Yukon. We saw polar bears and ate muskox in Manitoba. We discovered pastries called "nun's farts" and tomato wine in Quebec, and we ate spoonfuls of local sturgeon caviar off the backs of our hands in New Brunswick. Though some days were all fun and others pushed us to the brink of tears, they could rarely, if ever, be considered ordinary.

Here's one of the beautiful things we discovered about travelling through Canada: though we stayed within one national border, moving from region to region was like travelling to many different countries. In fact, our idea of this nation became far less cohesive than it previously was, and we were totally okay with that; it was just one more reason to love it here. While landscapes and accents sometimes changed by the hour, what remained consistent was kindness. We were struck by how friendly and hospitable people were as we travelled, from coast to coast and up to the Great White North. If you take nothing else away from this book, please remember this: there are many wonderful things to eat in Canada, and Canadians are genuinely nice folks.

In addition to teaching us many new things, our journey affirmed something we'd already suspected: that this country needs to reassess its weird identity problem when it comes to cuisine. People still love to say "There is no such thing as Canadian food, just poutine and Nanaimo bars." Of course, we are passionate supporters of both gravy-covered fries and anything sweet, but a statement like that doesn't do this place justice. It's true that no one dish represents every last part of Canada, but how could it, and why would we want it to? Canada is huge! There are simply too many cultures and kilometres to find one convenient answer, and that's okay—it's a complicated country. But there *is* such a thing as Canadian food, and it's broad and diverse and so, so compelling. This is evidenced by the groundbreaking work of Kate Aitken, Julian Armstrong, Elizabeth Baird, Pierre Berton, Derek Dammann, Michele Genest, Andrew George, Chris Johns, Jamie Kennedy,

Normand Laprise, Rose Murray, Martin Picard, Anita Stewart, and the many others who've written about our national cuisine.

It's no surprise, then, that we came back with a great many stories to tell, just as we'd hoped. So many, in fact, that it took us nearly a year to finish documenting all the places we'd seen and people we'd met. During that time, we won Best Culinary Travel Blog in *Saveur* magazine's 2014 Best Food Blog Awards, which was an honour we are incapable of describing. Though at first it was the ultimate pipe dream, we always thought our road trip stories would make a good foundation for a book, and we were thrilled when Robert McCullough and the team at Appetite by Random House agreed. This cookbook is a collection of over 110 recipes, 90 of which were contributed by an eclectic group of chefs, bakers, farmers, producers, bloggers, home cooks, and others we met during our trip or were able to connect with later because of it. Each of them not only donated a recipe to this project, but also shared their time, knowledge, and passion for Canadian cuisine. The remaining recipes, like the Caesar (page 274) and Arctic Apple Fritters (page 199), were developed by us, both because we love cooking and we wanted an excuse to recipe-test cocktails and doughnuts multiple times.

This book is by no means meant to be the Comprehensive Encyclopedia of Canadian Food—we'd need at least six more volumes before we could even consider calling it that. It is, however, a celebration of the people, places, and history we encountered during our five-month trek, and of a country we think is unbelievably cool.

We hope these recipes and stories are a way for you to explore places in Canada you have not yet visited—or perhaps are too smart to try and reach in a two-wheel-drive hatchback. Either way, thanks so much for reading, and happy cooking!

Using This Book

CHOOSING YOUR INGREDIENTS

In this book, several ingredients get used constantly, like flour, sugar, salt, and oil. You'll find the details of which varieties to use in each recipe, but here are some basic recommendations. The easiest way to make good food is by starting with good ingredients, and generally speaking, the easiest way to find good ingredients is by shopping in season at farmers' markets. While we recommend using local, organic, and/or sustainably raised food whenever you can, we also recognize that these things tend to cost a bit more money. Our way around that is by purchasing more of the inexpensive staples (kale! lentils! fruit!) and less of the more expensive ones, like meat and cheese. Here are some tips for purchasing ingredients:

Fruits and Vegetables Unless you have an amazingly effective greenhouse, we don't recommend trying to make Panzaprese (page 166) in the dead of winter. Instead, make it during the summer when market tables are nearly buckling under the weight of all those gorgeously ripe tomatoes and fresh herbs. Not only will your food taste infinitely better, but eating seasonally is often more convenient and in line with what your body is craving. Salads will cool you down in the middle of a July heat wave, while stews, rich with root vegetables, will warm you up mid-winter.

Spices When it comes to spices, buy *fresh*. Yes, they are dried, but no, that doesn't mean they will last forever. If you can, buy spices like cloves and cumin whole, then grind them with a mortar and pestle or spice grinder (or a coffee grinder used exclusively for spices) as you need them. Otherwise, buy pre-ground spices in small packages you can use up within several months. Buying bulk is never a good idea, as the spices will lose flavour and become stale over time, meaning your future baking and cooking projects will lack the depth they otherwise could have had.

Salt Considering just how many types are available to consumers and how much they can vary in volume, salt is probably the most important example of an ingredient that people take for granted, but which can really make a difference depending on what you use. Unless otherwise indicated, for recipes in this book we used Diamond Crystal Kosher Salt, which weighs 3 grams per teaspoon, has medium-sized crystals, and is relatively easy to find. If you're using another type of salt altogether, just be mindful that you may want to add a little more or a little less to your dish, depending on the size of the crystals. If you have the package, check the nutritional information label, where you will usually find how much the salt weighs per teaspoon. Try to measure a similar weight to what is listed in the recipe, which may not always be the same number of teaspoons shown in the ingredients list.

Eggs We recommend using free-range eggs for your cooking and baking. Not only were they laid by happier chickens, but they also will taste and look better. A barely yellow egg yolk is so much less satisfying than one that's vibrantly orange! One thing to remember, however, is that unless paprika was added to the chickens' feed, free-range egg yolks will usually be lighter in the winter when chickens don't have as much access to pasture.

Free-Range Meat We once met a cattle rancher who said "I always encourage people to buy 20 percent less meat and spend 20 percent more on the meat they do purchase." Yes, that's a man who raises meat for a living telling people to buy less of it. It makes sense, though. As with any other ingredient, the quality of the meat you buy will affect the overall flavour of a dish, so meat that's raised with consideration of the animal's welfare is bound to make your food taste better. Besides the flavour aspect, there's also the fact that you'll be supporting producers who prioritize ethical and environmentally friendly practices.

For this book, we bought most of our meat from one of our favourite butcher shops—Windsor Meats on East Hastings Street in Vancouver. The folks there went out of their way to accommodate us, never once batting an eye when we'd stroll in and say "Today we need ground elk, a rabbit, oxtail, and some wild boar, please."

Sustainable Seafood Shopping for seafood can be a confusing and intimidating process, as it's not always clear where it came from or whether it was sourced in an environmentally friendly way. If you have a sustainable seafood shop in your city (like the Daily Catch in Vancouver or Hooked in Toronto, for example), you can buy from there without having to worry. If you don't, here are a few tips to help you find good seafood:

★ When visiting a seafood shop, ask the fishmonger where the fish/crab/lobster/etc. you're buying came from and how it was sourced.

★ Buy locally. If you can buy seafood fresh off a small, reputable boat, do! This way you can ask the fishers directly about what they're selling, and you'll know the seafood wasn't harvested with a big industrial trawler.

★ Take advantage of programs like Ocean Wise, SeaChoice, and the Marine Stewardship Council to help you decide which seafood to buy when in a grocery store.

★ Finally, do some research. It can be complicated out there, but knowledge is power!

ALTERNATIVE INGREDIENTS

We want you to think of this book as a true Canadian cliché—friendly, diverse, and accommodating! Canada is an enormous place with vastly different landscapes, languages, and cultures. What does that mean when it comes to cooking? Well, we're aware that ingredients available to someone in Smuts, Saskatchewan, may not be so readily available to a person in Heart's Content, Newfoundland, and vice versa. (Smuts is now a prairie ghost town, but the people in Heart's Content are still there and presumably still content to be close to their neighbouring communities of Heart's Desire and Heart's Delight.) Grocery stores tend to carry a much greater variety than they used to, but that doesn't mean everyone will be able to easily find birch syrup, for example. Throughout the book, we've provided alternative ingredients that can be used in place of ones you may not be able to find. Here are some common examples, with their alternatives:

★ Birch syrup: A 1:1 mix of maple syrup and molasses

★ Labrador tea: One-third of the amount called for of dried sage and/or rosemary

★ Black garlic: Equivalent amount of roasted garlic tossed with a balsamic reduction (1 tsp per head of garlic)

★ Red Fife flour: Spelt or stone-ground whole wheat flour

★ Goat yogurt: Sour cream

★ Bison, elk, reindeer, muskox, moose: Lean beef

★ Lingonberries/partridgeberries: Cranberries

★ Spruce or fir tips: Equivalent amount of chopped flat-leaf parsley, unless otherwise stated

Before you use the alternatives, we encourage you to try to source the originals first—it may take you to a grocery store or butcher shop you'd never thought to visit, or even better, out into the woods! A number of recipes feature foraged ingredients, many of which require very little foraging experience. If you're interested in doing more research on what wild foods are available to you, we highly recommend books like Beverley Gray's *The Boreal Herbal* or David Arora's classic *Mushrooms Demystified*.

WEIGHT VS VOLUME FOR FLOUR

You'll see that we've indicated which type of flour to use in each recipe. For any recipes calling for all-purpose flour, we used unbleached, all-purpose white flour (sometimes organic and sometimes not). For whole grain flours (like spelt or Red Fife), we used flours that were stone-ground or stone-milled as opposed to industrially ground versions in which the germ has been removed and then added back in.

While most cooks in Canada use the cup/teaspoon measurement system, there are some (usually professionals) who go by weight instead. We've provided volume measurements for most ingredients, but one of the trickier ones to calculate is flour.

Many factors go into determining the exact weight of 1 cup of flour. Elevation, the hydration of the flour itself, whether someone has scooped it from the bag or carefully spooned it into the measuring cup . . . all of these things, and more, can greatly affect the overall weight. Because people tend to scoop their flour from the bag, this packs the flour into the cup slightly, making it a bit heavier. We've determined our weight for 1 cup of flour (150 g) based on that method. This measurement may be slightly higher than what other cookbooks or professional websites say, but this seemed like the most logical, consistent standard that would also account for the cooking habits of home cooks.

Note: Where measuring flour by weight is beneficial to the recipe, you'll find it and the other ingredients in grams; otherwise, we measure flour by volume.

BASIC TECHNIQUES

Blind Baking When a pie or tart recipe calls for a blind-baked crust, it means the pastry needs to be partially or fully baked before the filling goes into it. To do so, first preheat the oven to the temperature the recipe indicates. Roll out the pastry and line the pie plate/tart shell with it, forming the edges as you'd like them to appear in the finished product (fluted, crimped with a fork, etc.). Next, line the entire pie plate with parchment or tinfoil, placing it in a shape that mimics the pastry itself. Be sure to cover the pastry crust with the parchment or tinfoil, otherwise it may brown too quickly or unevenly. Fill the bottom of the pie plate with either reusable ceramic baking weights or a solid layer of dried beans, which will keep the parchment or tinfoil in place. Bake in the preheated oven for the amount of time indicated in the recipe, or until the crust has turned golden brown. Remove from the oven and let cool.

Making Fresh Pasta Mix the dry ingredients together in a large bowl. Make a well in the centre and add the wet ingredients. Start mixing in the centre of the well and work your way outward, slowly creating a stiff dough—this will take quite a bit of work, so it's preferable to use an electric stand mixer with a dough hook. When ready, the dough should be smooth but quite firm. If the dough is too dry, add 1 Tbsp (15 mL) of olive oil and/or an egg yolk. Let the dough rest for at least 1 hour under a damp tea towel. You can rest it overnight, wrapped in plastic wrap in the refrigerator, but remove it and let it come to room temperature before you roll it.

Use a pasta roller, or a rolling pin and some serious elbow grease, to roll out the rested dough. Working in small portions (about one-sixth of your dough at a time), press it into flat rectangular pieces and roll it through the machine multiple times, working from the widest setting (1) to the smallest setting (8 or 9). Cut the pieces in half crosswise if they're getting too long to manage. As the pieces are ready, dust them generously with flour. Either keep them in sheet form (for lasagna or ravioli) or cut them into strands using the cutting roller on the machine or a knife, and toss with more flour before placing them on a floured baking sheet. Keep covered with a slightly damp tea towel.

Cooking Sachets A cooking sachet is a small, heatproof bag that allows you to infuse a stock or a sauce with a few ingredients that are used during the cooking process but that don't appear in the final dish. You can purchase a reusable cooking sachet from a kitchen store or make your own small bag with cheesecloth and twine. Tie the sachet to one of the pot handles when you first place it in; this way, it'll be easier to retrieve.

CANNING BASICS

We've collected a diverse assortment of food preservation recipes for this book—some of which require canning—and you can reference this general guide when making any of them. Even if you're the type who generally cooks "by feel" and adapts recipes as you go, we recommend sticking as closely as possible to the instructions in canning recipes to ensure proper preservation—it's a science, after all! Fresh, high-quality produce makes the best preserves, so buy the good stuff and process it as quickly as possible once you're home.

EQUIPMENT Before you start canning, we recommend that you gather a few helpful tools. Avoid using equipment made from copper, aluminum, or iron, as these can cause discolouration in your final product. You should have:

A canning pot or large stockpot with a rack It's important to use something that will keep the jars from hitting the bottom of the pot. You can buy canning racks that are designed to fit stockpots, or you can line the bottom of your pot with a few canning rings. Some cooling racks for baked goods will even fit.

Mason jars, lids, and rings Make sure the jars are free from cracks and chips, particularly around the rim, and make sure the lids are new; otherwise, they may not seal. The rings can be reused many times.

A wide-mouth funnel and a ladle These make transferring the preserves to the jar much easier, with much less spillage!

A lid wand This tool has a magnetized end that makes it easier to collect lids from their warm water bath. The other end doubles as a stir stick to remove any air bubbles from the preserves.

Tongs and a jar lifter Tongs are great for lifting empty jars out of the boiling water, and a rubberized jar lifter is essential for lifting full, processed jars out of the water.

A few clean tea towels You'll want these for wiping spillage from the jars, to provide a place to store sanitized jars that need to be filled, and for hot jars to cool post-processing.

Don't worry if you don't have all of these pieces of equipment, though most are inexpensive and worth the investment if you plan on canning regularly. We've canned both with the full set-up and using more "primitive" tools. While the latter slows down the process, it's still a great time, especially if you have a few buddies with which to share the experience.

METHOD Typically, you should fill your canner three-quarters full of water before starting any canning project. Start heating the water immediately, as it takes a while to come to a boil.

Prepare and sterilize the equipment Start by washing the jars, lids, rings, and equipment in hot, soapy water and rinsing thoroughly. Once the jars are cleaned, sterilize them by submerging them in a boiling hot water bath for 10 minutes. Once they are sterilized, turn off the heat and leave the jars in the hot water until just before you fill them. To sterilize the lids and rings, place them in a smaller pot of water and bring to a gentle simmer (not a boil). Simmer for 10 minutes, then lower the heat and keep the lids and rings submerged and warm until just before you need them.

When you're ready to fill the jars, lift them out of the water using tongs, tip out the excess water from the jars, and line them up on a clean tea towel where they can be filled while still hot. Keep the full canner of hot water, as this is what you'll use to process the filled jars.

Fill the jars Once the preserve is ready, transfer it to the still hot sterilized jars using a ladle and a wide-mouth funnel. Produce expands when it's boiled, so it's important not to fill your jars to the brim. Pay attention to the specific amount of headspace each recipe calls for, which is the amount of unfilled space between the top of the preserve and the rim of the jar. Usually, the required headspace is at least ½ inch (1 cm). Using a chopstick or a lid wand, gently stir the preserve to release any air bubbles, and wipe any spillage from the rim with a clean cloth. Using tongs or a lid wand, top the jar with a lid, then twist on a canning ring, stopping when you meet resistance so the ring isn't too tight (known as "fingertip tight").

Process in a water bath Submerging the jars in a boiling water bath is an essential step in food preservation. The hot water heats the food to a temperature that kills any yeasts, bacteria, and moulds that could grow in your food. It also forces oxygen out of the jars (which is why it's important that the canning rings aren't too tight), creating a strong vacuum seal.

Using a jar lifter, put the full jars back into the hot water bath and set the heat to boil. Make sure there are 1 to 2 inches (2.5 to 5 cm) of water covering the tops of the jars. Keep the jars submerged for the full amount of time specified in the recipe, starting the timer once the water is actively boiling.

Let cool Once processed, remove the jars from the water bath using a jar lifter and place on a clean towel on the countertop. Within a few minutes of removing the jars, you'll likely start hearing the popping sound of the jars creating a vacuum seal. Don't worry if this doesn't happen right away, as it sometimes takes longer than you'd think. Let the jars cool for 12 to 24 hours before handling them. Once cool, check that all the jars have sealed by pressing down on the centre of each lid. The lid should be firmly concave and not bounce back when pressed. At this point, wipe the jars with a damp cloth, remove the rings and store them for another canning project, add labels, and store the jars in a cool, dark place. Place any jars that didn't seal in the refrigerator and enjoy them within a few weeks.

Most canned goods are generally best consumed within a year but will often last even a few months longer.

55587

Day Breakers

BREAKFAST & BRUNCH

RED FIFE CRÊPES

WITH SAUTÉED PLUMS

Did you know Lindsay wrote her master's thesis on Red Fife flour? It's true! You're probably thinking, "That's very nerdy." You might also be wondering, "What is Red Fife?" It's one of Canada's original heritage grains, and its arrival in this country is steeped in foggy, Scottish folklore. Though it fell from favour as other grains arrived on the scene, it's now experiencing a renaissance, particularly in the Prairies. We decided to give it a try in crêpes and discovered the flour's nutty flavour goes well with buttermilk and honey. If you can't find Red Fife, seek out another finely-milled whole grain instead, like spelt. If you can, it's best to make this batter the night before.

SERVES 4 TO 6

CRÊPES

- 2 Tbsp (30 mL) honey
- 2 Tbsp (30 mL) unsalted butter, plus extra for frying
- 3 eggs
- 1 cup (250 mL) buttermilk
- 2 Tbsp (30 mL) cold water
- 3/4 cup (185 mL) Red Fife flour, or stone-ground spelt or whole wheat flour
- 1/4 tsp (1 mL) salt

PLUMS

- 1 Tbsp (15 mL) unsalted butter
- 1/4 tsp (1 mL) ground cardamom
- 1/4 tsp (1 mL) salt
- 2 Tbsp (30 mL) honey
- 1/2 tsp (2.5 mL) whisky or vanilla extract
- 4 to 6 medium red or purple plums (about 450 g), pitted and sliced

FOR SERVING

Maple syrup, plain yogurt, or whipped cream

For the crêpes, measure the honey into a large bowl. Over medium-low heat, melt the butter in a saucepan until it turns golden brown, about 4 to 5 minutes, then immediately pour over the honey. Whisk to combine. Whisk in the eggs, followed by the buttermilk and cold water. Add the flour and salt and whisk thoroughly to combine. Cover and let rest in the refrigerator for at least 1 hour, or overnight if possible. The next day, take the batter out of the refrigerator about 30 minutes before you'd like to use it.

When you're ready to fry the crêpes, put about 1 tsp (5 mL) of butter into the pan (you'll need about that much to fry each crêpe), and heat over medium-low heat. Ensure the butter has been spread out evenly and, once it's bubbling, measure about 1/4 cup (60 mL) of batter into the pan. Working quickly, pick up the pan and tip it in a circular motion so the batter spreads out thinly and evenly across the pan's surface (don't worry if it's not perfect). Set the pan back down on the element and let the crêpe cook until you see its edges are dry and turning brown and the centre is rippling from the heat below. Carefully flip. The second side will need to cook for only about 45 seconds before you can slide it onto a plate, add more butter to your pan, and start on the next one. If they aren't being eaten right away, keep the crêpes warm in a 170°F (77°C) oven until it's time to serve. You should end up with about 10 to 12 large crêpes. FYI: Because they're whole wheat, these crêpes are a little more delicate than ones made entirely with white flour. Be gentle, but also don't worry if they tear a little while warm.

For the plums, heat the butter in a medium pan over medium heat. After 3 to 4 minutes, or once the butter is actively bubbling, stir in the cardamom, salt, and honey. Add the whisky or vanilla and stir quickly. Add the plums and toss to coat. Let them cook for 2 to 3 minutes. Give them a stir, then let them cook for 2 minutes more, or until they're soft but not falling apart. Remove from the heat and let cool in the pan for 5 minutes. Serve warm over the crêpes with maple syrup and plain yogurt or whipped cream.

EGGS GALIANO

Baked eggs in tomato sauce, generally known as "shakshuka," originates in Tunisia, not the southern Gulf Island of Galiano. However, while it doesn't have historical ties to British Columbia's coast, it does have important emotional significance for us. It's a dish we made while staying at a friend's cabin—*the cabin of our dreams*—on Galiano Island as we celebrated a big new job Lindsay had just been hired for. Our pal Heather joined us, and for a weekend we hiked, sunned, drank wine, and ate; we were the three happiest fools you've ever met. This is our version of shakshuka: a hearty, colourful dish that's become a favourite brunch staple. Be sure to serve it with plenty of fresh bread to sop up the sauce.

SERVES 4 TO 6

1 link (about 5.5 oz or 150 g) good-quality cured chorizo, cut into ½-inch (1 cm) chunks
1 tsp (5 mL) olive oil
1 medium red onion (about 160 g), ¾ finely diced, ¼ thinly sliced
1 small red bell pepper (about 170 g), diced
3 cloves garlic, thinly sliced
½ tsp (2 mL) ground cumin
One 28-ounce (796 mL) can whole tomatoes, with juice
¾ tsp (3 mL) salt
6 to 8 eggs
1 avocado (about 150 g)
¼ cup (60 mL) crumbled feta
¼ cup (60 mL) chopped fresh cilantro

FOR SERVING

1 loaf sourdough or other fresh bread, sliced and toasted

Preheat the oven to 375°F (190°C).

In a large, ovenproof skillet (preferably well-seasoned cast iron), sauté the chorizo over medium heat, stirring frequently. After about 8 minutes, once the chorizo looks crispy, remove it with a slotted spoon, keeping as much oil as possible in the pan. Add the olive oil (and add more if the chorizo didn't release much fat). Add the diced red onion, bell pepper, and garlic. Sauté about 10 minutes, or until the onions and pepper have softened. Stir in the cumin, then add the tomatoes and salt. Bring to a boil, lower the heat, and simmer for about 10 minutes, stirring occasionally. Add the chorizo. Let simmer until the sauce has thickened, about 10 to 15 minutes. Taste and season further if desired.

With the pan still over medium heat, use a spoon to make 6 (or 8) evenly spaced shallow divots in the sauce, and carefully crack an egg into each one. Transfer the pan to the preheated oven and bake for 8 minutes. While the eggs are baking, peel, pit, and dice the avocado, then set aside. Remove the pan from the oven and sprinkle the feta evenly over the surface, then return to the oven for about 3 to 5 more minutes (a non-cast iron skillet will take a little longer). Remove from the oven when the egg whites are just set but the yolks are still runny—you'll want to keep a close eye on it toward the end. Top with the sliced red onion, chopped avocado, and cilantro. Big slices of toasted sourdough, drizzled with olive oil and sprinkled with salt, are the perfect accompaniment.

PRAIRIE CHERRY GALETTE

WITH LEMON & THYME

Kimberley Phaneuf is the sweet lady behind the Flour Shoppe: Bread and Pastry Studio in Regina, a home-based business that bakes up custom cakes and dozens of pastries each week for the city's farmers' market. She uses local ingredients whenever possible, including Saskatchewan's best-kept secret: sour cherries. A galette is a kind of free-form pie, and we were excited about this recipe from the moment she sent it to us—even more so once it had come out of the oven. This is a great dish for brunch, but could just as easily be topped with whipped cream or ice cream and served as dessert. Also, if it makes your morning easier, you can make the dough for the crust a day ahead!

SERVES 6 TO 8

CRUST

- 1 cup (150 g) whole wheat flour (see note on page 6)
- 1¼ cups (188 g) all-purpose flour
- ⅓ cup (35 g) almond flour
- ¼ cup (50 g) white sugar
- 1¼ tsp (4 g) salt
- 1 cup (227 g) cold unsalted butter, diced
- 2 egg yolks
- ¼ cup (60 mL) ice water

FILLING

- ¾ cup (150 g) white sugar
- 2 Tbsp (14 g) cornstarch
- 1 Tbsp (6 g) lemon zest
- 2 Tbsp (2.5 g) finely chopped fresh thyme or lemon thyme
- 2 pounds (910 g) fresh or frozen sour cherries, pitted

1 egg yolk, lightly beaten
2 Tbsp (30 mL) cream or whole milk
White sugar, for sprinkling, if desired

FOR SERVING

- Ice cream or whipped cream

Note: If using frozen cherries, let thaw and drain, but do not press out any extra juice.

In a food processor, pulse the flours, sugar, and salt a few times until blended. Add the butter and pulse until it has broken down to pea-sized pieces (a few larger pieces are okay).

Whisk together the egg yolks and ice water and pour over the flour mixture. Pulse a few times, just until the dough comes together, adding more water only if it appears dry.

On a lightly floured surface, gently knead the dough three to four times, then pat it into a disc (or two, if making smaller galettes) and wrap in plastic. Let it rest and chill in the refrigerator for at least 2 hours (or up to 24) before rolling.

When you're ready to roll out the galette, remove the dough from the refrigerator and let it sit at room temperature until slightly softened, about 10 to 15 minutes.

Dust the countertop with flour and line a baking sheet with parchment paper. Roll the dough out in a circular shape to about ¼-inch (6 mm) thickness. Don't worry if it looks a little wonky, it's rustic! Once rolled, transfer the dough to the prepared baking sheet.

To make the filling, add the sugar, cornstarch, lemon zest, and thyme to a large bowl and mix together. Add the cherries and stir to combine.

Pour the cherry mixture onto the centre of the prepared crust, leaving a 2½-inch (6½ cm) border around the edges. Fold the edges of the crust over the cherries toward the centre—this will keep your filling contained. Chill in the refrigerator for 20 to 30 minutes.

While the galette chills, preheat the oven to 400°F (200°C). When ready, whisk together the egg yolk and cream and brush over the crust edges. Sprinkle with sugar, if desired. Bake the galette until the crust is golden (check the bottom by lifting slightly with an offset spatula) and the cherries are bubbling, about 30 to 40 minutes. If the crust is browning too quickly, make a "collar" with tinfoil and place over the edges to protect them from the heat. Once cooked, remove the galette from the oven and let cool for 10 to 15 minutes before slicing.

Slice and serve warm, garnished with ice cream or whipped cream.

British Columbia

We began our trip in British Columbia, Canada's westernmost province. From north to south, it's a place that changes dramatically, containing an almost bizarre number of ecosystems and weather patterns. In a matter of days, you can move from the desert climate of Osoyoos to the lush Great Bear Rainforest on the northwest coast.

In June 2013, we bid goodbye to our friends and trekked out to Spring Island, which lies off the coast of Vancouver Island near the remote First Nations community of Kyuquot. We spent five days kayaking, hiking, and eating fresh seafood with West Coast Expeditions, a company that sets up camp each summer and welcomes guests from around the world. There were sea otters tumbling through kelp, puffins zipping past overhead, and as many bald eagles as there are crows in East Vancouver. We lived in a perpetual state of awe.

On Vancouver Island, we enjoyed nine versions of the Nanaimo bar in Nanaimo, lunch in the idyllic Cowichan Bay, and high tea in Victoria. Back on the mainland, we drove north to admire the mountains in Whistler and Pemberton, then headed east to the Okanagan, a place that's impossibly bountiful.

In Lindsay's hometown of Prince George, we arrived at the same time as trucks filled with tree planters, people for whom Lindsay spent four summers cooking out at camp. In fact, it was through tree planters that we met, so we give them credit for this entire friendship, road trip, and book!

Farther north still, we ferried for seven hours from Prince Rupert to Haida Gwaii, where we camped on the beach and gathered huckleberries and sea asparagus each morning to have with breakfast. We tried herring roe for the first time, walked through an overgrown graveyard hidden in the forest, and sat on huge boulders beneath the cliffs at Tow Hill, with Alaska visible in the distance.

With the whole country ahead of us, and with much of our trip still unplanned and underfunded, we could have been nervous wrecks during those first few weeks in British Columbia. The Pacific has a powerful ability to calm nerves, however, as do the maze-like vineyards of the Okanagan and dense forests of the north. We left the province feeling capable and brave and fit for adventure on our first-ever territorial visit . . .

BARLEY PANCAKES

WITH BLUEBERRY SAUCE

Julie Van Rosendaal is a Calgary-based food writer, food stylist, cookbook author, and food columnist for the CBC. Basically, she's *exactly* the person you want in charge of your breakfast. These pancakes celebrate a highly underrated prairie ingredient—barley—and are hearty, filling, and easy to whip up.

SERVES 4

PANCAKES

2 cups (500 mL) finely ground barley flour
2 tsp (10 mL) baking powder
1/8 tsp salt
2 cups (500 mL) whole milk
2 eggs
2 Tbsp (30 mL) canola oil, plus extra for cooking

BLUEBERRY SAUCE

2 cups (500 mL) fresh or frozen blueberries
2 Tbsp (30 mL) white sugar
1 Tbsp (15 mL) freshly squeezed lemon juice

FOR SERVING

Maple syrup

To make the pancakes, add the barley flour, baking powder, and salt to a medium bowl and whisk together. Add the milk, eggs, and oil and whisk until just combined.

Set a heavy skillet over medium-high heat, then drizzle with oil and wipe it around the pan with a paper towel. Once the pan is hot, turn down the heat to medium-low, pour in about one-eighth of the batter, and cook until bubbles start to break through and the surface looks matte. Flip with a thin spatula and cook until golden on the other side. Repeat with the remaining batter—you should end up with about eight large pancakes.

To make the blueberry sauce, add the berries and sugar to a small pot and simmer until the berries pop and become saucy, about 5 minutes (2 to 3 minutes longer if using frozen berries). Add the lemon juice and more sugar if desired.

Serve the pancakes warm, topped with the blueberry sauce and maple syrup.

BANNOCK TWO WAYS

While researching bannock, we came across a fantastic online resource called *Bannock Awareness*. Put together by Michael Blackstock of the Kamloops Forest Region, it describes a history of bannock within First Nations' pre-contact culture, offering a different story than that which suggests bannock arrived exclusively with Scottish traders. Before wheat flour arrived, wild plants, corn, and nuts were ground into a sort of flour and then cooked in ways that could be considered an early form of the bread-like staple.

Here we've provided two recipes for our favourite kinds of bannock. The first (our go-to while camping) comes from Greg Mazur and is more of a drop biscuit style. The second is a rolled version and comes from Doreen Crowe, a restaurant owner in the Alderville First Nation in Ontario. Our friend Chris went to her restaurant almost daily with his parents, and grew up with this bannock.

EACH RECIPE SERVES 4 TO 6

GREG'S BELLA COOLA BANNOCK

2 cups (500 mL) all-purpose flour
1 Tbsp (15 mL) baking powder
1 Tbsp (15 mL) white sugar
1/8 tsp salt
2 Tbsp (30 mL) unsalted butter
1 egg
1/4 to 1/2 cup (60 to 125 mL) whole milk
Oil, for frying

FOR SERVING

Maple syrup
Flaky sea salt

Combine the flour, baking powder, sugar, and salt. Using a pastry cutter or knife, cut in the butter until the pieces are pea-sized. Mix in the egg, then pour in about 1/4 cup (60 mL) of milk. Mix together just until a dough forms, adding more milk if needed. Divide the dough into 10 to 12 biscuit-sized pieces. In a large frying pan, pour in about 1/4 inch (6 mm) of oil and heat over medium-high. When the oil is hot, fry the bannock—being careful not to crowd them—until golden brown. Serve immediately with maple syrup and flaky sea salt.

DOREEN CROWE'S BANNOCK

2 cups (500 mL) all-purpose flour, plus extra for rolling
2 1/2 tsp (12 mL) baking powder
1/2 tsp (2 mL) salt
3/4 to 1 cup (185 to 250 mL) water, to start
Oil, for frying

In a large bowl, mix the flour, baking powder, salt, and water together to form a dough. If the dough is a bit dry, add more water 1 Tbsp (15 mL) at a time. Turn the dough out onto a floured surface and roll out into a 9- × 12-inch (23 × 30 cm) rectangle about 1/4-inch (6 mm) thick. Cut into approximately 3- × 3-inch (8 × 8 cm) squares. Heat about 1/4 inch (6 mm) of oil in a large frying pan over medium-high heat, and fry the bannock—being careful not to crowd them—until golden brown, about 2 minutes on each side. Serve warm.

B33R WAFFLES

WITH SALTED BUTTER

While we were writing our book proposal, Lindsay worked at 33 Acres, a craft brewery in Vancouver's Mount Pleasant neighbourhood. The perks were plentiful: it's a beautifully bright space, *the beer is free for staff*, and their waffles for weekend brunch are simply unbeatable. While you can use any kind of beer for this recipe, we prefer using a brew that's malty and roasty over one that's hoppy and bitter; try a stout, porter, or 33 Acres of Darkness, the brewery's version of a black lager. Thanks to Josh, Dustin, and Brewmaster Dave for sharing your brews and breakfast!

SERVES 4

2 cups (500 mL) all-purpose flour
1/4 cup (60 mL) lightly packed brown sugar
1 Tbsp (15 mL) baking powder
1/8 tsp salt
2 eggs, yolks and whites separated
1 1/4 cups (310 mL) buttermilk
1/2 cup (125 mL) beer or milk
1 tsp (5 mL) vanilla extract
1/4 cup (60 mL) unsalted butter, melted and partially cooled

FOR SERVING

Salted butter
Maple syrup

Lightly brush or spray your waffle iron with oil, and preheat it. Mix the flour, sugar, baking powder, and salt in a large bowl.

In a medium bowl, combine the egg yolks, buttermilk, beer, vanilla, and butter. In a separate bowl, beat the egg whites with an electric mixer until soft peaks form.

Pour the beer mixture into the dry ingredients, and combine. Add in any additional ingredients you desire (see note), and stir to incorporate. Gently fold the egg whites into the batter, just until blended.

Ladle about 3/4 cup (185 mL) of batter onto the hot waffle iron and let cook about 3 to 5 minutes, or until golden brown. Serve hot with a generous pat of salted butter and plenty of maple syrup.

Optional additions to the batter: A pinch of dried or fresh rosemary or thyme; 1 tsp (5 mL) of lime, lemon, or orange zest; 1/2 cup (125 mL) toasted shredded coconut; or a handful of fresh berries.

SALTY ROSEMARY GRANOLA

WITH HEMP HEARTS & PISTACHIOS

Though we are never at a loss for good granola on the West Coast (there are granola makers galore in Vancouver), we wanted to make something that showcases a central Canadian ingredient: hemp hearts. Saskatchewan and Manitoba are the country's biggest producers of these earthy little "superfood" seeds, which *are* legal and *won't* make you high. They will, however, provide you with plenty of omega-3 fatty acids, minerals, all the essential amino acids, protein, and more. They're amazing when paired with pistachios, rosemary, and pumpkin seeds, but you can swap out the nuts and seeds for whichever ones you'd like. Just don't skimp too much on the salt.

MAKES APPROXIMATELY 5 CUPS

2 cups (500 mL) old-fashioned rolled oats
1 cup (250 mL) unsweetened, large flake coconut
1 cup (250 mL) shelled unsalted pistachios, roughly chopped
1 cup (250 mL) pumpkin seeds
¼ cup (60 mL) hemp hearts
1 to 1½ tsp (5 to 7 mL) salt
3 Tbsp (45 mL) extra virgin coconut oil
¼ cup (60 mL) maple syrup
¼ cup (60 mL) honey
1 Tbsp + 1 tsp (20 mL) finely chopped fresh rosemary

Preheat the oven to 325°F (160°C).

In a large bowl, mix the oats, coconut, pistachios, pumpkin seeds, hemp hearts, and salt, and set aside. In a small pot, melt the coconut oil, syrup, honey, and rosemary together over medium heat. Swirl occasionally to infuse the rosemary flavour into the mixture. Remove from the heat and pour over the dry ingredients. Mix well.

Divide the granola evenly over two baking sheets, and bake in the preheated oven for about 20 minutes, stirring the granola and rotating the pans in the oven halfway through. Bake until golden brown, checking on it every 5 minutes or so—the coconut can go from perfectly toasted to burnt rather quickly! Remove from the oven, let cool completely, and store in an airtight container for up to 4 weeks. It won't last that long, though. Trust us.

FRIED EGG, CHARRED AVOCADO & LEMON TAHINI BREAKFAST SANDWICH

Sidewalk Citizen Bakery is owned by Aviv Fried and Michal Lavi, who moved to Calgary from Israel as undergrads over a decade ago. After Michal became a geologist/filmmaker and Aviv finished a master's degree in biomedical engineering, they decided to start a bakery—a risky undertaking, but one they felt passionately about. When Aviv and Michal officially ventured into the bread business on their own, Lindsay was their very first employee. Now they have two brick-and-mortar locations, *dozens* of staff (including head chef Colin Metcalfe), and a huge following in Calgary. This sandwich is a marvellous example of their culinary roots in Israel and prodigious knack for combining big flavours.

SERVES 4

ISRAELI SALAD

- 2 mini cucumbers (about 115 g), finely diced
- 4 small tomatoes (about 200 g), seeded and finely diced
- 2 Tbsp (30 mL) finely diced red onion
- 2 small cloves garlic, minced
- 1 Tbsp + 1 tsp (20 mL) red wine vinegar
- 1 tsp (5 mL) salt

LEMON TAHINI MAYO

- 6 Tbsp (90 mL) mayonnaise
- 2 Tbsp (30 mL) tahini
- 2 Tbsp (30 mL) freshly squeezed lemon juice
- 2 small cloves garlic, minced
- 2 tsp (10 mL) lemon zest
- 2 Tbsp (30 mL) finely chopped fresh cilantro
- 2 tsp (10 mL) salt
- 2 Tbsp (30 mL) toasted sesame seeds

CHARRED AVOCADOS

- 2 avocados (about 150 g each), halved and pits removed
- 2 tsp (10 mL) olive oil
- 2 tsp (10 mL) Korean chili flakes (*gochugaru*) or crushed red pepper flakes
- 2 tsp (10 mL) salt
- 1 Tbsp + 1 tsp (20 mL) freshly squeezed lime or lemon juice

FRIED EGGS

- 2 Tbsp (30 mL) olive oil
- 4 eggs
- 2 tsp (10 mL) za'atar
- 1 tsp (5 mL) salt

FOR SERVING

- More fresh cilantro, for garnish
- 4 brioche buns, sliced in half

For the Israeli salad, place all of the ingredients into a bowl and toss to combine. Make this at least 1 hour ahead to let the flavours come together. Set aside in the refrigerator until needed.

For the lemon tahini mayo, place all the ingredients in a bowl and whisk until well combined. Set aside.

For the charred avocados, set the oven to broil on high heat. Brush the oil over the cut surfaces of the avocados. When the oven is hot, broil the top of the avocado halves until dark brown, about 5 to 8 minutes, then remove from the oven. Sprinkle the tops with the chili flakes and salt. Scoop out the avocado flesh and drizzle with the lime juice and any leftover olive oil. Set aside until needed. While the oven is on, toast the buns.

To fry the eggs, warm the olive oil in a non-stick pan over medium heat. Once the pan is hot, crack the eggs into the hot oil and season the tops with za'atar and salt. The eggs will bubble up and get brown on the bottom. Remove from the pan once the whites are set but the yolks are still runny, about 3 to 5 minutes.

Generously spread the lemon tahini mayo evenly over the cut sides of each bun. Next, place half an avocado, slightly mashing it with a fork, on the bottom of each bun, followed by a fried egg and about a quarter of the Israeli salad. Garnish with plenty of fresh cilantro, finish with the top half of the buns, and serve immediately.

MONTREAL-STYLE BAGELS

In doing research for the book, we came across a website called the Wandering Chew, run by two friends named Sydney Warshaw and Kat Romanow. Their goal is to create new Jewish food experiences in Montreal with events like Mexican Jewish and Iraqi Jewish pop-up dinners and their "Beyond the Bagel" walking tour. After poring over their website, we knew two things: we wanted to be friends with them, and they had to be in the book! Much to our delight, Kat and Sydney said they'd be happy to contribute, and they developed this recipe for bagels, a Jewish food near the top of the Montreal culinary canon. For anyone who doesn't live near St-Viateur Bagel or Fairmount Bagel but wishes they did, these are for *you*.

MAKES 12 BAGELS

1½ cups (375 mL) warm water
1 Tbsp (9 g) active dry yeast
5 Tbsp (63 g) white sugar
3 Tbsp (45 mL) vegetable oil
2 Tbsp (30 mL) maple syrup
1 egg, beaten
4 cups (600 g) all-purpose flour, plus extra for sprinkling (see note on page 6)
1½ tsp (4.5 g) salt
12 cups (3 L) water for boiling
⅓ cup (80 mL) honey or malt syrup
⅓ cup (24 g) sesame seeds (or enough to cover the bagels)
⅓ cup (24 g) poppy seeds (or enough to cover the bagels)

FOR SERVING

Cream cheese
Montreal Steak-Spiced Gravlax (page 36)

In a large bowl or the bowl of a stand mixer, combine the water and yeast. Let it sit for about 5 minutes, or until the yeast is activated—you'll know it's activated once the mixture becomes frothy.

Add the sugar, vegetable oil, maple syrup, and egg to the bowl and mix the ingredients, by hand or with a stand mixer, until the sugar is dissolved. Mix the flour and salt together, then add it to the wet mixture 1 cup at a time. You should have a dough that's sticky but holds together.

Turn out the dough onto a floured counter, sprinkle more flour on top, and start to knead. Sprinkling over more flour as necessary, knead the dough until it's smooth and elastic, then place it in a lightly oiled bowl and cover with a tea towel or plastic wrap. Let the dough rise in a draft-free place for 30 minutes.

Just as the dough is almost finished rising, put the 12 cups (3 L) of water and the honey in a large pot. Bring to a boil.

Preheat the oven to 425°F (220°C) and move the oven rack to the top. Line a baking sheet with parchment paper, and line another baking sheet with cooling racks.

Punch down the dough and divide it into 12 equal portions. Shape each portion of dough into bagels by rolling it into an 8- or 10-inch (20 or 25 cm) rope, curving the rope around your hand to bring the ends together and rolling it back and forth a few times to seal the ends.

Working with three or four bagels at a time so as not to crowd the pot, boil the bagels for 90 seconds, flipping them halfway through. Remove the bagels from the pot, place on the cooling racks, and let cool until they can be handled.

As the bagels are cooling, place the sesame seeds and poppy seeds on separate plates. Coat both sides of the bagels in sesame and/or poppy seeds and place on the prepared baking sheet.

Bake the bagels for 20 minutes, rotating the baking sheet halfway through and flipping the bagels over. The bagels should bake on the top rack of the oven for the first 10 minutes and be moved to the bottom rack for the last 10 minutes. When they're finished, the bagels should be golden brown with a few dark brown spots.

Serve with cream cheese and/or Montreal Steak-Spiced Gravlax (page 36).

Grazing

STARTERS, APPETIZERS & SNACKS

SPICED YOGURT CHEESE BALLS

Valerie Lugonja is the Edmonton-based creator of the blog *A Canadian Foodie* and was one of *FEAST*'s first friends in Canadian food. Ever since we announced our project, she proclaimed herself to be our #1 fan and has been encouraging us ever since. Her enthusiasm is inspiring, and she's a woman with more energy than the two of us combined. This is a *labneh*-like recipe she makes from her own home-made yogurt, but store-bought yogurt works just as well. Though it's simple, it is useful to start this recipe a day ahead, so plan accordingly.

SERVES 6 TO 8

YOGURT CHEESE

1 package cheesecloth, or a reusable alternative such as a nut milk bag
One 650 g container plain yogurt, 6% or higher
1¼ cups (310 mL) extra virgin olive oil, divided

SPICE MIX

1 clove garlic, finely minced
1 tsp (5 mL) dried oregano
1 tsp (5 mL) dried basil
½ tsp (2 mL) fennel seeds
½ tsp (2 mL) caraway seeds
¼ tsp (1 mL) dried red pepper flakes
¼ tsp (1 mL) cumin seeds
1 tsp (5 mL) flaky sea salt
⅛ tsp freshly ground black pepper

FOR SERVING

Crackers or crostini

To make the yogurt cheese, lay multiple layers of the cheesecloth (or the reusable bag) in a strainer or a sieve set up over a bowl. Scoop the entire container of yogurt into the centre of the cheesecloth or bag, tie the edges together, and hang the cheesecloth or bag over the bowl. If you would rather have plain, unspiced yogurt cheese balls, mix 1 tsp (5 mL) of kosher salt into the yogurt before you drain it.

Let the yogurt drain at room temperature overnight for 12 to 14 hours, or until the yogurt has lost enough moisture that it pulls away easily from the edge of the cloth. If you make your own bread, you can reserve the whey (the drained liquid) and use it in your next loaf.

Next, make the yogurt cheese balls. Using a spoon, form the cheese into balls the size of cherry tomatoes, rolling them lightly between your palms to round them out (a little olive oil on your hands prevents them from sticking too much). Place them on a tray as they're rolled. Once finished, transfer all the balls, in layers, into a large bowl. Drizzle a small amount of the olive oil over each layer so they don't stick together.

If using the spice blend, mix all of the spices and salt together and sprinkle over the cheese. Using another large bowl, gently roll the balls from bowl to bowl, repeating until they are evenly coated with the spices. Skip this step if you're making plain yogurt cheese balls.

At this point, you can serve these right away with crackers or crostini, or you can transfer the cheese balls to mason jars and pour in enough olive oil to cover them. Tap the sides gently to release any trapped air and keep covered in the refrigerator for up to 2 weeks. Bring to room temperature before serving.

MONTREAL STEAK–SPICED GRAVLAX

Gravlax is a type of cured salmon that originated in Scandinavia but has since found a home within the Jewish food repertoire. Thinly sliced, it's exactly what you want to be eating on a Sunday morning, draped over bagels spread with a thick layer of cream cheese. This recipe is the second from the Wandering Chew (page 30) and uses Montreal steak spice to season the fish—we used a small bottle we picked up at the iconic Schwartz's Deli on the road trip. This dish is really impressive, yet so simple to make at home. You'll want to start it a few days before you're planning on eating it, though.

SERVES 12

2 skin-on salmon fillets, 1/2 pound (227 g) each
1 1/2 Tbsp (22 mL) salt
3/4 Tbsp (11 mL) white sugar
1 1/2 Tbsp (22 mL) Montreal steak spice
1 Tbsp (15 mL) whisky, divided

If the fishmonger hasn't already done so, remove the pin bones from the salmon fillets. To do this, run your fingers along the top of the fish, pinch the end of a bone with tweezers, push down on the flesh with your other hand, and pull the bone out. Repeat with all the bones.

In a small bowl, combine the salt, sugar, and steak spice. Place the fillets on a large piece of plastic wrap, skin side down. Sprinkle each fillet with an equal amount of the salt mixture and pour 1/2 Tbsp (7 mL) of whisky over each one.

Place the salmon fillets on top of each other so they're touching flesh to flesh with the skin facing outward. Wrap the fillets tightly in the plastic wrap and place them in a bowl or dish with high sides to contain any juices released during the curing process. Weigh the fillets down by placing cans of beans or a plate weighed down with a bag of flour on top of them.

Refrigerate the salmon for 2 to 3 days, making sure to flip the fish over every 12 hours. The gravlax is finished curing when the thickest part of the fillets feel firm to the touch.

Unwrap the fillets and wipe off the excess curing mixture. Using a sharp knife, cut the skin off the fillets. To do this, keep the knife at an angle pointed toward the skin and use a slow back-and-forth movement to cut the skin away.

Using a very sharp knife, cut the gravlax on the bias into thin slices. Eat with crackers, pumpernickel, or—our favourite way—on Montreal-Style Bagels (page 30)! Well wrapped, the gravlax will keep in the refrigerator for about 1 week.

PEMMICAN

WITH SASKATOONS OR BLUEBERRIES

Pemmican is a traditional First Nations and Métis food made of ground dried meat and berries mixed with fat; it's a high-density staple designed to help people survive long winters. Traditionally, its preparation involved hunting or fishing followed by sun- or fire-drying the meat, grinding it to a powder with stones, mixing it with fat in equal parts, and storing it in rawhide bags. This is a modern pemmican recipe contributed by Shane Chartrand, a Plains Cree Edmonton chef, and is a slightly sweet and very sustaining snack. Because it keeps so well, it's a perfect protein source for multi-day hikes.

SERVES 4 TO 6

1 pound (454 g) bison, salmon, Arctic char, or pickerel
1 cup (250 mL) fresh Saskatoon berries or blueberries
6 to 9 Tbsp (90 to 135 mL) rendered fat or bacon grease, room temperature, as needed
1/8 tsp salt (optional)

First, slice the meat as thinly and consistently as possible so the pieces dry evenly. If using bison or another lean game meat, remove any large pieces of fat, as these will not dry out consistently with the meat. If using any kind of skin-on fish, remove the skin and thinly slice the fish.

Preheat your oven (or a dehydrator, if you have one) to 145°F (63°C). If your oven doesn't go that low, preheat to its lowest setting and prop open the door 3 to 4 inches (8 to 10 cm) while the meat dries. An oven thermometer is really useful here.

Distribute the sliced meat evenly over metal racks (cooling racks work well) and place the berries on a parchment-lined baking pan. Place on opposite sides of the preheated oven and let dry for 20 to 24 hours. Alternatively, if using a dehydrator, lay the sliced meat and berries on opposite sides of the tray(s) and let dry for 24 hours.

Once dried, roughly chop the meat, transfer the meat and berries to a food processor and blend until very fine. There will likely be pieces that still need to be crushed with a mortar and pestle, or you can choose to leave those pieces whole and have pemmican with a slightly coarser texture.

Starting with 6 Tbsp (90 mL) of the room-temperature fat or bacon grease, mix with the ground meat and berries until incorporated. Add more fat, 1 Tbsp (15 mL) at a time, until your desired texture is reached, keeping in mind the mixture will firm up once refrigerated. Transfer the pemmican (you'll have about 1 cup at this point) to a piece of plastic food wrap. Shape into a 1-inch (2.5 cm) diameter log, roll tightly, and twist the ends to keep it together. Store in the refrigerator; when needed, cut off a piece and rewrap. Pemmican will keep for a very long time, especially when refrigerated, but it's best consumed within 2 to 3 months.

Yukon Territory

The Yukon is a wild, wild place. On our way from Whitehorse to Dawson City, we had to stop the car *in the middle of the highway* because two bald eagles were engaged in an epic battle; they were so intent on locking talons, they failed to notice our car barrelling toward them. We watched in disbelief, all the while exclaiming, "Where *are* we?! This place is CRAZY!"

Along with its intensely focused wildlife, the Yukon is also, very importantly, home to the largest cinnamon buns we've ever seen. Loaves of sourdough, a culinary vestige of the legendary Gold Rush, are also an easy find. At the Whitehorse farmers' market, we sampled fare like fireweed jelly and birch syrup; these foods, and many others, were born of the great boreal forest, a northern ecosystem that's spread above the 50th parallel. While driving, we passed through a remote area where the trees had been razed by a forest fire; one of the first plants to return was fireweed, which thickly carpeted the ground and made us feel as though we were driving through an ocean of purple.

We camped during the Dawson City Music Festival and each day explored the historic town, with its unpaved streets and tipsy old buildings. We took in as many shows as possible, ate southern-style barbeque with boreal ingredients at Klondike Kate's, and roamed for hours under the bright sky. Eventually we'd realize that midnight had come and gone and we should probably get to bed. In the summer, that far north, the sun barely sets.

Farmers in the Yukon are some of the most innovative and inviting people we've ever met. While it wasn't always easy to *get* to their farms (see The Farthest Farm, page 232), we learned so much with each visit and always left with a gift of freshly picked vegetables. We met a farmer named Brian who herds goats on his mountainous land, milks them by hand, and makes cheese almost every day. And he happens to be blind. If that doesn't express the hardy nature of the Yukon and its people, we don't know what does.

With cinnamon buns packed for the journey, we headed from our first territory toward the next . . .

WILD MUSHROOM TOASTS

WITH GOAT CHEESE & BLACK GARLIC VINAIGRETTE

This appetizer combines three of our favourite PEI experiences: the mushroom toasts we ate at Terre Rouge in Charlottetown, our visit to a permaculture farm called Island Forest Foods that grew mushrooms, and our time on Al Picketts's garlic farm. They feature tangy goat cheese, sweet black garlic, and, of course, meaty wild mushrooms.

SERVES 6 TO 8

MUSHROOMS

2 pounds (910 g) assorted wild mushrooms, such as chanterelles, morels, shiitakes, or oysters
2 Tbsp (30 mL) olive oil
3/4 tsp (3 mL) salt
1/4 tsp (1 mL) freshly ground black pepper
8 sprigs fresh thyme

GOAT CHEESE FILLING

3/4 cup (185 mL) firmly packed soft goat cheese
3 Tbsp (45 mL) whipping cream
1/2 tsp (2 mL) salt
1 Tbsp (15 mL) finely chopped flat-leaf parsley

BLACK GARLIC DRESSING

3 cloves black garlic or roasted garlic
3 Tbsp (45 mL) sherry vinegar
1/2 tsp (2 mL) salt
Freshly ground black pepper
1/2 cup (125 mL) extra virgin olive oil

FOR SERVING

Loaf of good-quality bread, such as sourdough or ciabatta
Flaky sea salt (optional)

Preheat the oven to 375°F (190°C).

Toss the mushrooms with the olive oil, salt, pepper, and thyme. Spread out on a baking sheet and bake in the preheated oven for 10 minutes. Drain the liquid from the mushrooms (you can reserve this for another purpose if you like—it's a great vegan seasoning) and return to the oven (again, spread out evenly) until the mushrooms are golden and the edges are starting to crisp, about 20 to 25 minutes.

While the mushrooms are roasting, make the goat cheese filling and the dressing. For the filling, add the goat cheese, cream, salt, and parsley to a small bowl and mix until combined. If needed, add a bit more cream until it reaches a smooth, spreadable texture.

For the dressing, add the black garlic, vinegar, salt, and pepper to a blender or food processor and blend well. Then, while the machine is running, slowly drizzle in the oil. Set aside until the mushrooms are done.

Cut eight even slices of bread and place on a baking sheet. Once the mushrooms are out of the oven, turn the oven to broil and toast the bread slices until they're golden brown, about 2 minutes on each side. Cut any especially large mushrooms in half, and toss them all in 1/4 to 1/2 cup (60 to 125 mL) of the dressing. Add more dressing according to your taste. Use up any leftovers on a future salad.

Spread the goat cheese mixture on the toasts, top with the dressed mushrooms, and finish with a sprinkling of flaky sea salt, if desired. Enjoy immediately.

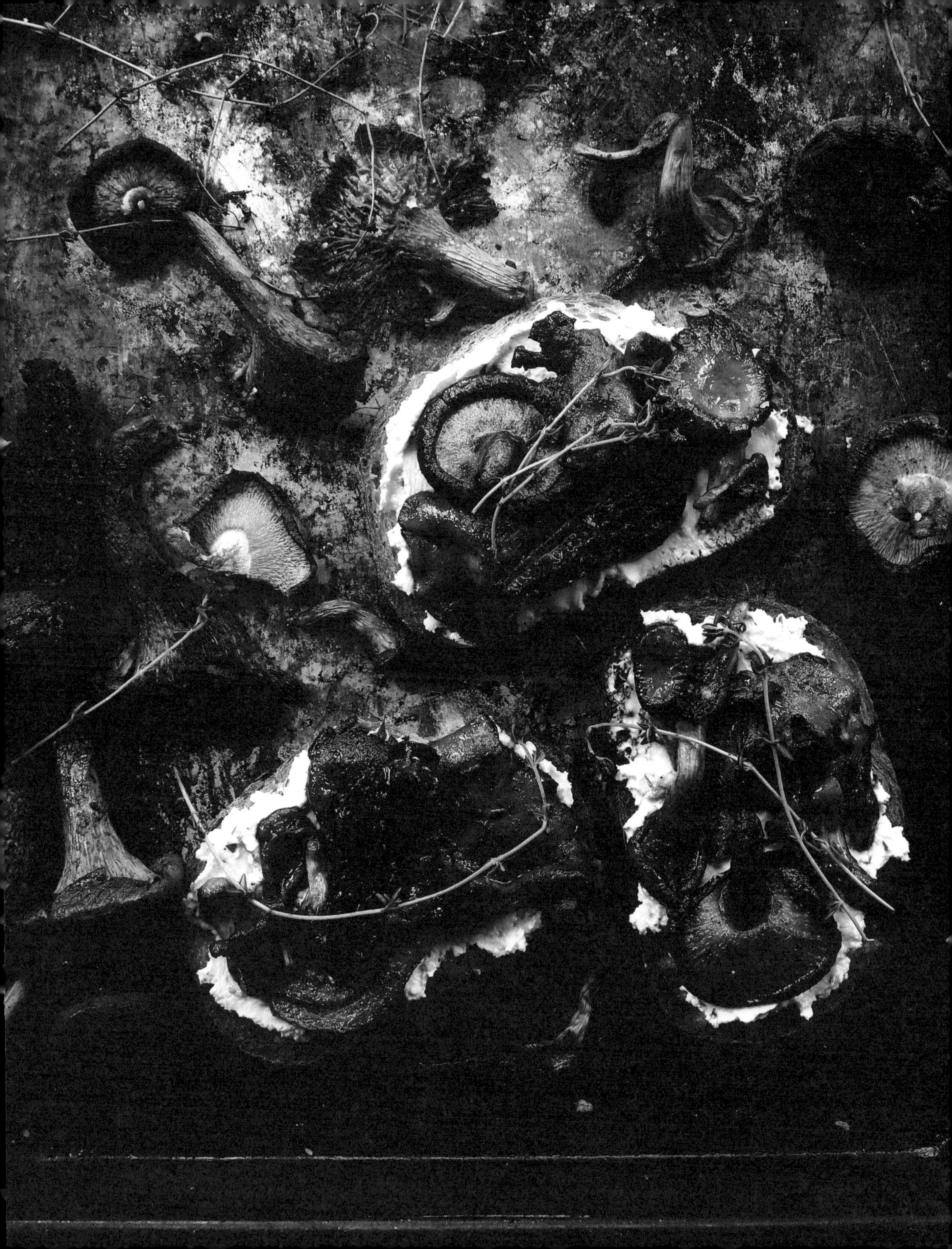

CRETON MAISON

Montreal is lucky enough to have four indoor public markets, providing a "butcher, baker, and candlestick maker" kind of shopping experience to thousands of people. Year-round, they're filled with stacks of seasonal produce, bottles of sparkling cider and maple syrup, prepared meals, baked goods, cheese, bread, and charcuterie. This recipe for Creton Maison, a simple, rillette-like potted meat dish, comes from Charcuterie de Tours at the Atwater Market. Though it can be eaten at any time of year, it's especially nice for Thanksgiving or Christmas.

SERVES 8 TO 10

2 pounds + 3 ounces (1 kg) ground pork or veal
1 medium yellow onion (160 g), very finely chopped
2 tsp (10 mL) salt
3/4 tsp (3 mL) freshly ground black pepper
Pinch nutmeg
1 to 1½ cups (250 to 375 mL) whole milk
¼ cup (60 mL) bread crumbs

FOR SERVING

- Dried or fresh bay leaves, for garnish
- Crackers or crostini
- Capers or gherkins

In a medium pot, mix the ground meat, chopped onion, salt, pepper, and nutmeg. Pour in enough milk to cover the top of the ingredients, but no higher.

Bring the mixture to a boil, then lower the heat. Gently simmer, uncovered, using a wooden spoon to regularly stir and break up the meat. After about 1 hour, the meat will be cooked and most of the liquid will have boiled off, though the mixture should still look moist. Stir in the bread crumbs and let cook 10 minutes more. Remove from the heat and let cool slightly.

Transfer the mixture to a food processor and blend until smooth—you should end up with about 3 to 4 cups (750 mL to 1 L). Spoon into glass jars or containers and press down. Top each jar with one bay leaf, and serve with crackers or crostini and gherkins or capers. Store any leftovers in the refrigerator and enjoy within 1 week.

SPOT PRAWN CEVICHE

Spot prawns, named for the two white spots on their carapace, are a sustainably harvested, quintessential BC food. The season to get these prawns is short—just six to eight weeks starting in the late spring/early summer—and beloved on the West Coast. This recipe comes from Eric Pateman of Edible Canada, a company that champions Canadian food on an unprecedented level. If you don't have access to spot prawns, seek out other sustainably sourced alternatives. If you are on the West Coast, you can head down to the docks mid-morning during spot prawn season and purchase them directly off the boats.

SERVES 6 TO 8

1 Japanese mini cucumber (60 g) or ½ English cucumber, peeled, seeds removed, and finely diced
1 tsp (5 mL) sesame oil
1 pound (454 g) live BC spot prawns
½ cup + 2 Tbsp (155 mL) freshly squeezed lime juice (about 5 limes)
¼ Vidalia or Walla Walla onion (about 90 g), finely diced
¼ cup (60 mL) finely chopped cilantro
1½ tsp (7 mL) hot sauce
1 tsp (5 mL) fish sauce
1 Tbsp (15 mL) coconut cream (optional)
Salt and freshly ground black pepper

FOR SERVING
Tortilla chips

Remove the heads and shells from the prawns (these can be reserved for making stock) and place the meat in a stainless steel, ceramic, or glass bowl. Add all the remaining ingredients except the salt and pepper and mix well. Cover with plastic wrap and refrigerate until the prawns start to turn from opaque to white, about 40 minutes.

After the prawns have been "cooked" by the acid, season to taste with salt and pepper, and serve with tortilla chips.

RASPBERRY POINT OYSTERS

WITH TWO MIGNONETTES

One bright, chilly afternoon on Prince Edward Island, we found ourselves standing on a Raspberry Point oyster boat. As it hummed across the bay, our guide, Rich, hauled baskets out of the icy water, scraped away the seaweed, and cracked them open for us to see. Inside, Raspberry Point oysters were growing, finely rippled bivalves famous for their briny taste and sweet, clean finish.

James Power, one of the company managers, shared two of his favourite mignonettes with us, one of which appropriately includes fresh raspberries. You can buy oysters from your local fishmonger (who'll even shuck them for you), and be sure to make the mignonettes a day ahead so the flavours have a chance to blend and soften.

EACH RECIPE SERVES 6 TO 8

RED WINE MIGNONETTE

3/4 cup (185 mL) red wine vinegar
1 small shallot (about 40 g), finely minced
1/2 tsp (2 mL) freshly ground black pepper

RASPBERRY MIGNONETTE

1/2 cup (125 mL) fresh raspberries
6 Tbsp (90 mL) raspberry vinegar
1 small shallot (about 40 g), finely minced
2 Tbsp (30 mL) water
1/2 tsp (2 mL) freshly ground black pepper
1 tsp (5 mL) white sugar

2 dozen freshly shucked oysters (see note)

FOR SERVING

Coarse sea salt or crushed ice

For the red wine mignonette, measure all the ingredients into a jar, secure the lid, and shake well to combine the ingredients. Let the mignonette sit for 24 hours in the refrigerator for best results.

For the raspberry mignonette, press the raspberries through a fine sieve to remove the seeds, and measure 3 Tbsp (45 mL) of the purée into a jar. Add the vinegar, shallots, water, pepper, and sugar and secure the lid. Shake well to combine and refrigerate for 24 hours before using.

When you're ready to eat the oysters, discard the top shells and line up the oysters (still in the bottom shell) on a bed of coarse sea salt or crushed ice. Spoon 1 to 2 tsp (5 to 10 mL) of either mignonette over the oysters, and enjoy!

Note: Oysters should be consumed the same day they're shucked. Once you or your fishmonger have shucked them, keep them on crushed ice in the refrigerator until you're ready to serve them. Be sure the ice can drain into a bowl below, as the oysters should not be submerged in the water that melts from the ice.

TRADITIONAL ARCTIC CHAR PIPSI

In Nunavut, we were invited to a Welcome Kablunaaq dinner (literally meaning "Welcome White Person") at one of the few restaurants in Rankin Inlet. During the meal, we were treated to several versions of pipsi, which is Arctic char that has been dried in chunks rather than slices, resulting in softer and chewier pieces of preserved fish. Arctic char is related to both salmon and lake trout and is the northernmost fish in the world; though char is traditional for pipsi, the process will work for almost any fillet of skin-on fish. This recipe was shared by Todd Johnson, whom we met at this dinner. He's the general manager of Kivalliq Arctic Foods, a food processing and distribution plant whose primary goals include supporting, increasing, and sustaining Nunavut communities' access to their traditional food.

SERVES 8 TO 10

2 fillets Arctic char, about 1 pound (454 g) each, deboned, skin on, and attached at the tail (if possible)
1 cup (150 g) salt
3 cups (750 mL) room-temperature water
Wire or twine (optional)

Cut a 1-inch (2.5 cm) squared checkerboard pattern into the meat of the fish, slicing all the way through the flesh but stopping once the knife hits the skin. Prepare a salt water solution by mixing the salt with the water (20% salt by weight) in a flat-bottom container large enough to fit both fillets. For best results, measure the salt with a scale, rather than a measuring cup. Stir to dissolve the salt, and once incorporated, submerge both fillets in the water. If you need slightly more water to cover, make sure to add the proportionate amount of salt to keep the solution at 20 percent. Soak the char in the brine for 20 to 30 minutes.

Remove the char from the salt solution and hang over a rack with the flesh facing out. If your fillets are not attached at the tail, use a bit of wire or twine to fasten the fillets in place—you may even need to pierce the skin and tie the fillets together. Have a constant high volume of air passing over the fillets for about 60 to 72 hours, maintaining a temperature of 63°F to 68°F (17°C to 20°C) throughout the process. You can use a medium-sized fan set to high speed to achieve this. The fish is done when the exterior of the cubes are firm and dry and the interior is soft.

To store, vacuum-seal (or seal as airtight as possible) the whole fish and place in the freezer. If vacuum-sealed and frozen, the fish will keep for at least 1 year. If frozen without a vacuum seal, the fish will stay good for about 3 weeks. If refrigerated, the fish will keep for 3 to 5 days. Cut off pieces as you use them, discard the skin, and consume all that you thaw within 1 to 2 days.

Note: Making pipsi is a simple process that takes several days. You can do it in almost any indoor space as long as you have a consistent temperature and air flow. The process is not nearly as aromatic as you might think!

Road Trip Snacks

Road tripping is worth it for the snacks alone, and we made a point of stopping when *anything* caught our eye. Here are three of our favourite side-of-the-road snacking experiences:

Bannock: While driving the lushly forested highway near Terrace, British Columbia, we spotted a small wooden shack advertising freshly made bannock. As we approached, a young woman pulled back a tea towel to reveal rounds of golden fried bread, which came with small containers of strawberry jam for dipping. She also had handmade cedar bark jewelry for sale. We were smitten.

Parking Lot Paillasson: On Quebec's Île d'Orléans we bought a package of curd-like Le Paillasson, one of the oldest styles of cheeses in North America. It has to be warmed in a skillet, so one night we stopped in a parking lot and got out our camp stove. On a small patch of grass, under the ambient glow of the McDonald's arches, we pan-fried the cheese until it had a golden-brown crust and ate it with fresh bread. Melty cheese > fries, any day.

Scones & Cream: Just outside of Gros Morne National Park in western Newfoundland, we came across a small shop selling locally knit sweaters, vegetables, and preserves. We bought a package of homemade scones, freshly churned cream, and bakeapple jam, then sat in the car and had a very decadent mid-afternoon meal. Why can't gas stations sell snacks like *that*?!

NANNA MARIA'S FIORI FRITTI

(FRIED ZUCCHINI FLOWERS)

One of our favourite road trip meals was in Mississauga with the Mancinis, the food-adoring Italian family of our friend Sophie. Both of her grandmothers, *Le Nonne*, came over, and together we made gnocchi with tomato sauce, fried veal, and braised rapini. Maria, Sophie's mom, battered and fried zucchini flowers for us to snack on as we cooked. She says, "This is the spring and summer treat that my mother would make us, and we would eat them by the dozens."

SERVES 6 TO 8

12 to 16 fresh zucchini, squash, or pumpkin flowers (see note)
1 cup (250 mL) all-purpose flour
1/2 tsp (2 mL) salt
1/4 cup (60 mL) Parmigiano-Reggiano or Grana Padano, grated then measured
1/8 tsp baking powder
1 egg
3/4 to 1 1/4 cups (185 to 310 mL) room-temperature water
1/4 cup (60 mL) finely chopped flat-leaf parsley

RICOTTA FILLING

1 cup (250 mL) ricotta cheese
1/2 clove garlic, finely minced
1/4 tsp (1 mL) salt
1 anchovy fillet, rinsed and finely chopped

Vegetable oil for frying
Zucchini, thinly sliced, for frying with any leftover batter (optional)

FOR SERVING

Grated Parmigiano-Reggiano or Grana Padano

Note: For a full batch, Maria likes to collect the flowers from her garden up to 3 days before she makes these. They're easy to grow yourself, or another good place to find them is at a farmers' market.

To prepare the flowers, pull out and discard the stamens. Gently wash the flowers and dry them well to make sure no little critters join you (don't worry if the flowers break, as it makes no difference in the end). It is important that the flowers are dry or they will wilt and rot. Once clean, roll them in paper towel and store in a tight-fitting container or a sealable plastic bag.

For the batter, mix the flour, salt, Parmigiano-Reggiano, and baking powder together in a bowl. Whisk in the egg, then slowly pour in 3/4 cup (185 mL) of water while stirring with a fork or whisk. Keep adding water in small increments until the batter looks like pancake mix or thick cream. You may need to thin it further once you start frying the flowers. Add the fresh parsley and mix again.

For the filling, in a small bowl mix the ricotta, garlic, salt, and anchovy thoroughly. Taste and add more salt if desired.

Now, the fun part—frying. Line up your flowers and batter and fill a large frying pan 1/4 inch (6 mm) full of oil and heat over medium. Drop 1 tsp (5 mL) of batter into the oil. When it starts to fry, the oil is hot enough. Place about 1 Tbsp (15 mL) of the ricotta filling into each flower and gently press the top together to seal it.

One at a time, dip the flowers in the batter, gently tap them on the side of the bowl to remove any excess, then place into the oil. You can fry two or three at a time, just be sure not to crowd them in the pan. Flip the flowers when golden on one side, let the other side brown, then remove and place in a strainer to let excess oil drain off before placing them on paper towels. If you have some zucchini slices, follow the same instructions to fry those as well. When all the flowers and zucchini slices are finished, sprinkle some Parmigiano-Reggiano over the top and *mangia*!

FRESH PICKLED BAY OF FUNDY HERRING

Chris Aerni is the owner and executive chef at the Rossmount Inn in St. Andrews by-the-Sea, New Brunswick. Our meal there was so good, Dana continues to reference it regularly. Whenever asked what she wants for lunch, her response is always the same, without fail: heirloom tomato bisque with goat cheese crostini. It's been *exhausting.*

For the book, Chris shared an entirely different (but just as memorable) recipe with us, one that features New Brunswick herring caught with traditional circular weirs. If you can't find fresh herring, you can use sardines instead.

SERVES 10 TO 12

1/4 to 1/2 cup (60 to 125 mL) coarse sea salt
1 pound (454 g) fresh herring or fresh sardine fillets
1 large red onion (about 220 g), thinly sliced
1 large carrot (70 g), peeled and thinly sliced
1 stalk celery (75 g), thinly sliced
2 cloves garlic, crushed
4 sprigs fresh thyme
10 whole cloves
4 bay leaves
20 whole black or white peppercorns
2 Tbsp (30 mL) white sugar
1 to 2 cups (250 to 500 mL) white wine vinegar or rice vinegar

FOR SERVING

Sour cream
Rye or pumpernickel bread

Sprinkle sea salt to cover the bottom of a medium-sized flat baking dish. Lay the herring side by side and sprinkle with more salt. Add another layer of fish and cover with more salt. Repeat until all the fish is used up. Keep the fish in the salt for 40 minutes, then remove the salt and rinse the fish under cold water. Pat the fish dry with a clean tea towel or paper towel.

To marinate, place the fish fillets side by side to cover the bottom of a flat baking dish that has at least a 2-inch (5 cm) rim. Mix the onion, carrot, celery, garlic, thyme, cloves, bay leaves, and peppercorns in a medium bowl and sprinkle over the single layer of fish. Add another layer of fish and sprinkle with more of the vegetable mixture. Continue this way until all the fish has been placed in the dish. Mix together the sugar and 1 cup (250 mL) of vinegar and pour evenly overtop. If needed, top up with more vinegar to ensure the top layer of fish is covered. Cover and let marinate in the refrigerator for 24 to 36 hours. If kept in the brine longer, the fish will continue to pickle and soften and will last 1 to 2 months. If removed from the brine, it is best consumed within about 1 week.

This herring is best served with sour cream and dark bread.

BISON SAUSAGE ROLLS

WITH ORANGE & FENNEL

"You two are insane."

This is what an Ontario cattle rancher told us after hearing about our visit to a bison ranch in Alberta. We prefer the term "adventurously ignorant." When we visited Gus Janke's Maple Hills Bison Farm, just south of Edmonton, he drove us right into the middle of his herd, which he raises for meat and sells to families in the area. While we were somewhat terrified, we were right to trust Gus; he sent us back on the road with limbs intact and some bison pepperoni to snack on—a good reminder that in addition to being enormous, bison are extraordinarily tasty. Many grocery stores now carry bison meat, but if you can't get your hands on any, you can use lean ground beef as a substitute. We've adapted this recipe from one made up by Lindsay's friends Suzie and Reena. It combines puff pastry with the brightness of orange zest and fresh fennel and has an easy-to-make tomato sauce for dipping.

SERVES 8 TO 10

ROLLS

- 1 Tbsp (15 mL) extra virgin olive oil
- 1/3 cup (80 mL) white onion, finely diced
- 2 garlic cloves, minced
- 1/2 cup (125 mL) fresh fennel, finely diced
- 2 tsp (10 mL) orange zest
- 14 ounces (400 g) ground bison or lean ground beef
- 3 ounces (85 g) ground pork
- 1/4 cup (60 mL) dried bread crumbs
- 1 tsp (5 mL) dried chili flakes
- 1 Tbsp (15 mL) finely chopped flat-leaf parsley
- 1 tsp (5 mL) salt
- 1/8 tsp freshly ground black pepper
- 1 egg
- 1/4 cup (60 mL) milk
- 2 sheets pre-made puff pastry, thawed (but kept cold in the refrigerator until needed)
- 2 Tbsp (30 mL) nigella seeds and/or sesame seeds

DIPPING SAUCE

- 1 Tbsp (15 mL) extra virgin olive oil
- 1/3 cup (80 mL) finely chopped white onion
- 1 garlic clove, finely chopped
- One 28-ounce (796 mL) can whole or diced tomatoes, with juice
- 1 tsp (5 mL) honey
- 1/2 tsp (2 mL) salt
- 1 tsp (5 mL) orange zest

See overleaf for preparation ▶

To make the sausage mixture, add the olive oil to a large pan and set over low heat. Sauté the onion and garlic until the onions have turned translucent, about 5 minutes. Add the chopped fennel and cook another 5 minutes. Lower the heat and add the zest. Cook a few more minutes, then remove from the heat and let cool.

In a large bowl, combine the bison, pork, bread crumbs, chili flakes, parsley, salt, and pepper. Add the cooled fennel mixture and gently combine with your hands. At this point, you may want to fry up a small patty of the meat mixture and taste it so you can be sure it's seasoned as you like. Divide the mixture into four equal parts.

In a small bowl, use a whisk or fork to beat the egg and milk together, then set aside. This egg wash will be used to seal and cover the sausage rolls.

Preheat the oven to 350°F (180°C). Cover a baking sheet in parchment paper.

Unfurl the puff pastry on a clean board or countertop. If you have two square-shaped sheets of pastry, cut each piece in half to create four long rectangular pieces. If you have two round sheets, cut each in half and reshape the ends to create rectangles.

With the first quarter of the bison mixture, use your hands to make a sausage-like shape the same length as the longest side of your pastry rectangle. Lay it along one long side of the pastry, about 1 inch (2.5 cm) from one edge. Using your fingers or a brush, apply the egg wash along the opposite edge of the pastry—this will work to seal the roll together. Starting with the side closest to the sausage mixture, gently roll the pastry over the meat and keep rolling until it meets the egg-washed edge. Adjust the roll so the seam is at the bottom. Repeat with the remaining three sheets of pastry.

Transfer the rolls to the prepared baking sheet. Brush the top of each roll with the egg wash, then score the tops with a sharp knife, making shallow cuts about 2 inches (5 cm) apart. Sprinkle the tops with nigella and/or sesame seeds.

Bake in the preheated oven for 30 to 40 minutes, or until the pastry is golden brown and the meat is cooked through (the internal temperature should be 160°F/71°C).

While the rolls are baking, make the sauce. In a medium pot, heat the olive oil over low to medium heat and sauté the onion and garlic until the onions become translucent, about 5 minutes. Add the tomatoes and bring to a boil, then lower the heat and simmer for about 20 to 30 minutes. Stir the sauce occasionally, breaking up the tomatoes with a wooden spoon or a fork. Once it has reduced to a nice thick sauce, add the honey, salt, and orange zest, then simmer a few more minutes. Taste the sauce to make sure the balance of salty and sweet is to your liking. This can be put in the blender if you prefer it smooth, but we love the chunky, more rustic version. Slice the sausage rolls into 2-inch (5 cm) pieces and serve warm with the dipping sauce.

SRI LANKAN CURRIED SHRIMP

Suresh Doss is a Toronto-based food writer, editor, and events producer whose family moved to Canada from Sri Lanka when he was 12 years old. In his words:

This curried shrimp dish was a quintessential pre-meal Sri Lankan snack growing up. When my parents would host guests, my mom would always whip up a few plates of snacks to accompany the cocktails and beers that were being passed around, and one of the crowd favourites was this easy-to-make, slightly messy shrimp dish. Served hot, it's great with beer. I remember guests reminiscing about life back home when they'd pop these spicy bites into their mouths.

Try to use fresh shrimp whenever possible, but if you're using previously frozen shrimp, make sure they're fully thawed and drained before cooking.

SERVES 4 TO 6

1½ Tbsp (22 mL) vegetable oil
1 medium red onion (about 160 g), thinly sliced
1 medium tomato (about 100 g), diced
1 Tbsp (15 mL) chili powder
1 tsp (5 mL) ground turmeric
1 pound (454 g) shelled shrimp
Salt and freshly ground black pepper

Place a large pot over medium heat. Drizzle in the vegetable oil and toss in the onions when the pot is hot. Stirring regularly, let them cook until they become dark brown and caramelized, about 12 to 14 minutes.

Toss in the tomatoes and cook until the mixture becomes soft, about 2 to 3 minutes. Add the chili powder and turmeric and stir for a few seconds, then add the shrimp, salt, and pepper.

Lower the heat and gently toss the mixture every few seconds. After 1 to 2 minutes, the shrimp will curl and become opaque. Remove from the heat and gently stir a few more times before transferring to a serving bowl. Serve immediately with cold glasses of beer and plenty of napkins!

From the Garden

Vegetarian Mains

SUNCHOKE BARLEY RISOTTO

We first met John Horne, executive chef at Toronto's renowned Canoe restaurant, when he sent us an email. He was putting together an all-Canadian menu and had come across our blog while doing his research. We were happy to recommend some of our favourite ingredients that we'd come across on the trip, and even happier when John enthusiastically agreed to contribute a recipe to the book. This risotto-style dish combines prairie barley with the sweet, subtle, and nutty flavour of sunchokes, also known as Jerusalem artichokes. They're best sourced in the fall, but stored ones are often available in the spring, too. Sunchokes are simple to prepare—the skins slip off easily with your trusty vegetable peeler. We love this dish with pickled or sautéed fiddleheads (if you have some in the freezer) and pan-fried mushrooms.

SERVES 6 TO 8

BARLEY

- 1/4 cup (60 mL) unsalted butter
- 1/2 large shallot (35 g), peeled and thinly sliced
- 1 cup (250 mL) pearl or hulled barley, rinsed
- 1/3 cup (80 mL) dry white wine (optional)
- 1 bay leaf
- 6 sprigs fresh thyme
- Small bunch flat-leaf parsley
- 10 whole black peppercorns
- Cooking sachet, or a small length of cheesecloth and string
- 8 cups (2 L) mushroom stock

SUNCHOKE PURÉE

- 1 1/2 tsp (7 mL) unsalted butter
- 1/2 large shallot (35 g), peeled and sliced
- 1/2 pound (227 g) sunchokes, peeled and quartered
- 1/4 tsp (1 mL) salt
- 1 Tbsp (15 mL) sherry
- 1 1/4 cups (310 mL) whipping cream

FOR SERVING

- Freshly ground black pepper
- Oka cheese or any other washed-rind or aged cheese
- Pan-fried wild or cultivated mushrooms
- Pickled or sautéed fiddleheads or roasted rapini

To prepare the barley, melt the butter in a medium pot over medium-high heat, then add the sliced shallots. Cook for about 10 minutes, until the shallots are translucent and beginning to brown. Add the barley and stir for 3 to 4 minutes. Deglaze the pot with the white wine, if using. Place the bay leaf, thyme, parsley, and peppercorns in the cooking sachet (or onto a piece of cheesecloth and tied into a bundle with string), and add it along with all of the mushroom stock to the pot. Cook until the barley is tender, about 25 to 35 minutes for pearl barley, and 15 to 20 minutes longer for hulled barley. If the stock is reducing below the barley, add some water. Once cooked, remove the sachet, strain off any liquid, return the barley to the pot, and set aside.

For the sunchoke purée (which can be made 1 to 2 days ahead of time), melt the butter in a medium pot, then add the shallots and sauté until translucent, about 10 minutes. Stir in the sunchokes and salt. Add the sherry and cook for 3 to 5 minutes, or until the raw alcohol smell is gone.

Starting with 1 cup (250 mL) of cream, pour it over the mixture, adding more as needed to cover the sunchokes by 1/2 inch (1 cm). Increase the heat and simmer until the sunchokes are fork-tender, about 15 minutes, then remove from the heat and let cool for 10 minutes. Pour into a blender and blend until smooth. Taste and add more salt if desired.

To make the risotto, add about three-quarters of the sunchoke purée into the pot with the barley and stir. Add more, depending on how loose you want the risotto. Taste and add freshly ground black pepper and/or more salt if desired.

Serve in bowls and top with slices of Oka cheese, pan-fried mushrooms, pickled or sautéed fiddleheads, and/or roasted rapini.

FAVA BEAN TART

WITH BLACK GARLIC & AGED CHEDDAR CRUST

This cheesy tart honours Prince Edward Island, where we ate plenty of clothbound Avonlea cheddar and black garlic made by farmer Al Picketts in Kensington. Black garlic is traditionally prevalent in some Asian cuisines, and it's made by slowly and consistently heating bulbs of garlic over several weeks. The cloves soften, turn black, and become slightly sweet, with a strong note of balsamic vinegar. Al makes his in an old refrigerator, which he's converted into an ultra slow cooker—he'll never share the magic temperature! As for fresh fava beans, while they are a bit of work to prepare, their nutty texture and flavour are totally worth the effort. If you can't find fava beans or black garlic, chopped roasted asparagus and roasted garlic make fine substitutes. This tart works well as a vegetarian main at dinner, lunch, or even brunch.

SERVES 4 TO 6

CRUST

- 1¾ cups (260 g) all-purpose flour (see note on page 6)
- ½ tsp (1.5 g) salt
- ½ cup (113 g) cold unsalted butter, cut into small pieces
- 1 cup (115 g) grated and loosely packed aged white cheddar
- 4 to 6 Tbsp (60 to 90 mL) ice water
- Extra flour for dusting

FILLING

- ½ cup (125 mL) shelled fresh fava beans
- 2 eggs, yolks and whites divided
- ½ tsp (2 mL) lemon zest
- ¼ tsp (1 mL) freshly ground black pepper
- 1 tsp (5 mL) salt
- ¼ cup (60 mL) finely chopped flat-leaf parsley
- 4 cloves black garlic, cut into small pieces
- 2 cups (500 mL) ricotta cheese
- ½ cup (125 mL) crumbled cow, goat, or sheep feta

To make the pastry, put the flour and salt in a food processor and pulse a few times to mix. Add the cold butter and cheese and pulse until the butter is broken into pea-sized pieces. Add the ice water 1 Tbsp (15 mL) at a time, pulsing the mixture until it just comes together but is not wet. Press the dough into a disc and wrap with plastic wrap. Chill in the refrigerator for about 30 minutes.

Preheat the oven to 400°F (200°C). On a well-floured surface, roll the dough out to a 6- × 15-inch (15 × 38 cm) rectangle (if using a 5- × 14-inch/12 × 35 cm rectangular tart pan), or a 10- or 11-inch (25 or 28 cm) diameter (if using a 9- or 10-inch/23 or 25 cm round tart pan or pie plate). Transfer the dough to the pan and press evenly along the bottom, sides, and edges, cutting off any excess. Lightly prick the bottom of the shell a few times with a fork and line with parchment and baking weights. Blind bake (page 6) for about 15 to 20 minutes, rotating once in the oven, until the crust is golden brown. Remove from the oven, remove the baking weights, and let cool for 15 to 20 minutes while you make the filling.

Lower the oven temperature to 350°F (180°C). While the crust is resting, prepare the fresh fava beans, first by removing them from their pods. Next, set a medium pot of water to boil, and fill a medium bowl with ice and water. Blanch the beans in boiling water for 30 seconds, then drain and place immediately in the ice bath for 10 minutes. Drain the water and peel off the waxy coating from each bean.

To make the filling, add the egg yolks to a large bowl and beat with a whisk. Mix in the zest, pepper, salt, peeled fava beans, parsley, and black garlic, followed by the ricotta and feta. In a medium bowl, whisk the egg whites until light and frothy. Gently fold them into the ricotta mixture. Spoon the filling into the cooled crust and smooth the top. Bake for 40 to 50 minutes, or until the filling (which will puff up slightly) is set in the middle and is a very pale, golden brown (it's okay if the surface is still shiny). Let cool for 10 minutes before slicing.

MOROCCAN CHICKPEA SOUP

We understand if the words "vegetarian" and "rural Newfoundland" don't seem like the most natural pairing. But that's what Two Whales Coffee Shop is all about, with their bustling café/restaurant in the quiet town of Port Rexton. They serve coffee, tea, baked goods, and healthy vegetarian comfort food, and they believe that restaurants can be about more than providing meals. They have an impressive commitment to using local, organic, and fairly sourced ingredients, paying livable wages to their employees, and educating their community about the connections between food and health. They have a garden on-site and even raise their own egg-laying birds! This well-spiced vegetarian stew is from the thoughtful Two Whales kitchen, a place we hope you get to visit.

SERVES 6 TO 8

1 Tbsp (15 mL) olive oil
2 medium yellow onions (about 320 g), diced
2 stalks celery (about 150 g), diced
1 tsp (5 mL) ground cinnamon
1 tsp (5 mL) ground cumin
1 tsp (5 mL) paprika (smoked or sweet)
1 tsp (5 mL) ground turmeric
2 medium carrots (about 100 g), peeled and diced
1 cup (250 mL) diced vegetables (any combination of peppers, zucchini, and eggplant)
½ cup (125 mL) puy or ⅔ cup (160 mL) brown lentils
4 cups (1 L) vegetable stock
One 28-ounce (796 mL) can chickpeas, drained and rinsed
1 cup (250 mL) chopped spinach or chard
One 14-ounce (398 mL) can diced tomatoes, with juice
1 Tbsp (15 mL) tomato paste
2 Tbsp (30 mL) freshly squeezed lemon juice
Salt and freshly ground black pepper

FOR SERVING

Yogurt, cilantro, raisins or currants, and chopped toasted almonds, for garnish

In a large pot, heat the olive oil over medium heat and gently fry the onions and celery until soft, about 5 minutes. Add the cinnamon, cumin, paprika, and turmeric and stir until the spices coat the vegetables. Cook for another 5 minutes, then add the carrots, diced vegetables, lentils, vegetable stock, and chickpeas. Bring to a boil, then lower the heat and simmer, covered, until the lentils are cooked, about 15 minutes for puy lentils and about 20 for brown lentils. Once the lentils are cooked, add the chopped greens, diced tomatoes, and tomato paste, and simmer for another 15 minutes.

Just before serving, stir in the lemon juice and season with salt and freshly ground black pepper to taste. Spoon into bowls and top with yogurt, cilantro, raisins or currants, and/or chopped almonds.

Northwest Territories

Our country's middle territory is immense, rugged, and, quite frankly, rather difficult to get to. Unless you trust logging roads (which, after one terrifying gravel road "shortcut," we decided we should avoid), it's nearly impossible to get from the Yukon to the Northwest Territories as the crow flies. Instead, we headed south into British Columbia, crossed over to Alberta, and turned north again toward the territorial border. It was a three-day, 31-hour haul from Dawson City, but much of the landscape was either mountainous or painted yellow by canola fields, so it was a pleasing one.

While many areas in the south tend to offer infinite views of cities and farmland, the trek from one territory to the next was mainly forest, occasionally interrupted by a small town. We suddenly became far more concerned about where and when to fuel the car, as well as keenly aware that snacks would be few and far between. Such isolation also meant that *unbelievably* epic sites like Alexandra Falls, which would be a crowded tourist attraction any farther south, were barely advertised. One bluebird afternoon, we sat just inches from the waterfall's powerful crest, the only two people around.

We camped in Hay River, which sits on the southern shore of Great Slave Lake. Once we arrived, Andrew Cassidy, the Executive Director of the Territorial Farmers Association and the town's mayor at the time, took us on a tour. We visited the local community garden and met Jackie Milne, a farmer who, according to Andrew, has "singlehandedly spearheaded every local food security initiative in the area."

We also visited Andrew's farm, which he runs with his wife, Helen. They sell weekly at the town's small but well-attended farmers' market on the lake, where we bought fresh vegetables, jars of crabapple jelly, and two fillets of whitefish right off the boat.

Another afternoon, we sat in the trailer of a woman named Franziska, just metres from the home she was constructing for herself. An artist who moved to Hay River from Germany many years ago, she now knows the land as if she'd been born there. We drank tea made with foraged herbs and weeds, tasted her homemade dandelion mustard, and listened to stories about the winter farmers' market and Hay River Community Kitchen, which she pioneered. The town of Hay River may be small, but it is active and engaged.

Being in the Northwest Territories, and seeing places like Alexandra Falls, made us feel like we'd stumbled upon a secret. This territory takes up over 1 million square kilometres (over 386,000 square miles), yet we knew so little about it. Feeling enlightened, and with a very full tank of gas, we began the 11-hour drive south toward Alberta's capital . . .

BEATON'S MAC & CHEESE

Years ago, during the first of two stints in Calgary, Lindsay worked as a cheesemonger at Janice Beaton Fine Cheese. Though she could stay for only six months, the friendships she made there have lasted, including with her boss, Janice, a creative and highly successful Calgary entrepreneur. We saw Janice and her fiancé, Bob, when we passed through on our trip. She asked when we'd be in Cape Breton, the place she grew up, and we told her it would be around Thanksgiving. "Great!" she replied. "You can come to our wedding!" So we did. And it was perfect.

This recipe is from Janice, and uses several of the mainstay cheeses from her shop. It's the ideal mix of creamy cheesiness and crunch with just a bit of heat. We love using Quebec cheddars for this dish—the older the better.

SERVES 6 TO 8

3 cups (500 g) dried macaroni,
 or 4½ cups (500 g) penne
⅓ cup (80 mL) unsalted butter
½ cup (125 mL) finely chopped yellow onion
2 cloves garlic, minced
½ cup (125 mL) all-purpose flour
6 cups (1.5 L) whole milk
¼ tsp (1 mL) cayenne
¼ cup (60 mL) grainy mustard
1½ tsp (7 mL) salt
¼ tsp (1 mL) freshly ground black pepper
2 cups (500 mL) grated Gruyère
2½ cups (625 mL) grated aged white cheddar
½ cup (125 mL) dried bread crumbs

Preheat the oven to 400°F (200°C).

Set a large pot of salted water to boil for the pasta. Grease a 9- × 13-inch (23 × 33 cm) baking dish or casserole dish or a large ovenproof skillet.

Once the pasta water is boiling, cook the pasta to al dente according to package instructions. Drain when ready.

Meanwhile, in another large pot, sauté the butter with the onion and garlic. Whisk in the flour and cook the roux for 10 minutes, whisking occasionally, over medium-low heat. In a small pot, heat the milk until just below boiling. Add the hot milk, along with the cayenne, mustard, salt, and pepper to the roux. Cook until the sauce is creamy and smooth, about 10 minutes. Add the cheeses and stir until melted. Taste and add more salt and pepper if desired.

Combine the sauce and pasta (don't worry if it seems like a lot of sauce—the pasta will absorb it in the oven) and transfer to the prepared baking dish. Top with bread crumbs and bake, covered, for 15 minutes. Uncover and bake until golden brown and bubbling, about 15 minutes longer. Serve immediately.

LENTIL, MUSHROOM & WILD RICE VEGGIE BURGERS

This recipe came to us from Katie Gorrie, a friend of ours who grew up in Regina. She's a poet and the editor of the *Filid Chapbook*, a mixed-medium print periodical featuring the work of a diverse range of authors and artists. Katie has been a vegetarian all her life and is a wizard in the kitchen, a master of making something from what seems like nothing. Over the course of our friendship, she's always fed us well, and when we passed through her home on the road trip, we gave her a bag of Saskatchewan wild rice. With it, she developed this unbelievable veggie burger recipe—the chewy wild rice, crunchy seeds, and smoky paprika make for a hearty meal that represents Katie's home province so well.

SERVES 6 TO 8

1/2 cup (125 mL) wild rice
2/3 cup (160 mL) brown lentils
1 bay leaf
2 Tbsp (30 mL) ground flax seeds, or 1 egg
1 Tbsp (15 mL) water (omit if using an egg)
1 Tbsp (15 mL) extra virgin olive oil
1/2 cup (125 mL) diced white onion
1/2 cup (125 mL) chopped button or portobello mushrooms
2 cloves garlic, minced
2 to 3 tsp (10 to 15 mL) salt
1 tsp (5 mL) smoked paprika (hot or sweet)
1/2 tsp (2 mL) freshly ground black pepper
2 Tbsp (30 mL) chopped flat-leaf parsley
2 tsp (10 mL) tahini
1 tsp (5 mL) extra virgin olive oil
1 tsp (5 mL) freshly squeezed lemon juice
1/2 cup (125 mL) grated zucchini (squeeze to remove excess water before measuring)
1/2 cup (125 mL) unsalted sunflower seeds, toasted
3 to 4 Tbsp (45 to 60 mL) whole wheat flour (optional)

FOR SERVING

Hummus, dill pickles, red onion, summer greens, sliced radishes, avocado, cheese, and sprouts
6 to 8 burger buns, toasted

Cook the wild rice according to package instructions. Add the lentils and bay leaf to another pot and mix with 2 cups (500 mL) of water. Bring to a boil, reduce the heat to a simmer, then cover and let cook until the lentils are tender, about 20 minutes. Discard the bay leaf and drain any excess water.

In a small bowl, combine the flax seeds and water, and set aside (omit this step if using an egg).

Heat 1 Tbsp (15 mL) of olive oil in a frying pan over medium heat. Add the onion and cook for 3 to 4 minutes, until browned. Add the mushrooms and cook until soft, about 2 minutes. Add the garlic and cook until fragrant, about 1 to 2 minutes. Remove from the heat.

Combine the cooked lentils, onion mixture, and flax mixture (or egg) in a food processor. Add the salt, paprika, pepper, parsley, tahini, 1 tsp (5 mL) of olive oil, and lemon juice. Pulse until the ingredients are thoroughly mixed but maintain a grainy texture.

Transfer the mixture to a medium bowl and add the zucchini, sunflower seeds, and rice. Mix to incorporate. If you find the mixture is too sticky to handle, add the whole wheat flour, 1 Tbsp (15 mL) at a time, until you're able to form patties.

Split the mixture into six or eight portions and shape into patties (approximately 5 oz each). Line a baking sheet with parchment paper, place the patties on it, and freeze for 20 to 30 minutes before cooking.

To cook, brush the patties generously with olive oil and heat a cast iron skillet on the barbeque over high heat. Place the patties in the skillet and cook until the first side is nice and crispy, about 2 to 3 minutes, then flip and grill the other side to the same crispness. If you don't have a skillet, you can cook these directly on the grill. They are delicate, so be sure to flip them only once. Alternatively, you can cook the patties in a large frying pan on the stove over medium-high heat.

Serve on toasted hamburger buns with desired toppings.

Music Festivals

While the focus of our journey was food, not music, we managed to discover plenty of the latter as we went.

We started with the **Dawson City Music Festival**, which, if you're starting in Vancouver, is totally worth the three- to four-day northern trek. After all, there are few places you can watch performances in a theatre founded in 1899, then dance the night away under a summer sun that shines into the wee hours of the morning.

Next up was the **Harvest Sun Music Festival** in Kelwood, Manitoba, where children ran in and out of decorated teepees and parents lounged all day in camp chairs. We ate at the Supper in the Field event, a celebration of Manitoban food, then lay on the grass and watched bands like Red Moon Road perform late into the evening.

On an island famous for its music—Cape Breton—we arrived just in time for the **Celtic Colours International Festival**. For nine days, it completely took over, with dozens of concerts and events and musicians from around the world playing in everything from old fire halls to the chapel at the Fortress of Louisbourg.

Our last dance party was in Rankin Inlet, Nunavut, which happened to have its yearly **Beer Dance** while we were there. We listened to the awesomely raucous music of Iqaluit's the Jerry Cans, who, coincidentally enough, had also played at the Dawson City Music Festival! Talk about full circle.

BEET BORSCHT

WITH ROASTED GARLIC

Borscht became a mainstay on the Canadian Prairies with the arrival of Russian and Eastern European immigrants, who could grow root vegetables—including beets—with great success in their new home. People have strong opinions about how to make a proper beet borscht, but the truth is, there are about a million versions! Ours includes the sweet richness of roasted garlic and is vegetarian, though it could easily be made vegan—just swap out the butter for olive oil and skip the sour cream.

SERVES 6 TO 8

2 heads (about 60 g) garlic
1 tsp (5 mL) extra virgin olive oil
3 Tbsp (45 mL) unsalted butter
1 medium yellow onion (about 160 g), diced
1 medium leek (about 150 g), thinly sliced into rings (only the white and pale green parts)
1 medium carrot (about 50 g), peeled and diced
1 stalk celery (about 75 g), chopped
4 medium beets (about 500 g), peeled, 2 diced and 2 grated
1 medium russet potato (about 150 g), peeled and diced
¼ tsp (1 mL) freshly ground black pepper
1 tsp (5 mL) salt
¼ medium green or red cabbage (about 227 g), shredded or thinly sliced
1 bay leaf
8 cups (2 L) vegetable stock
One 14-ounce (396 mL) can diced tomatoes, with juice
1 Tbsp (15 mL) apple cider vinegar
2 Tbsp (30 mL) chopped fresh dill, plus more for garnish

FOR SERVING

Sour cream

Preheat the oven to 375°F (190°C). Cut the tops off the garlic heads to expose the cloves, brush the tops with the olive oil, wrap in tinfoil, and place in the preheated oven. Roast until soft and fragrant, about 30 to 40 minutes. Let cool, then squeeze out the cloves. Roughly chop one head's worth of cloves to add to the soup, keeping the others whole for garnish.

Melt the butter in a large pot over medium-low heat. Add the onions and leeks and sauté until soft, about 10 minutes. Next add the carrot, celery, beets, potato, chopped roasted garlic, black pepper, and salt. Sauté, stirring frequently, for about another 10 minutes. Add the cabbage, grated beet, and bay leaf and stir to combine. Pour in the stock and diced tomatoes and bring to a boil. Reduce heat and simmer until the vegetables are tender, then add the apple cider vinegar and chopped fresh dill. Season with more salt and pepper if desired.

Serve with a garnish of sour cream, roasted garlic cloves, and more fresh dill.

SOUR CHERRY & RICOTTA PEROGIES

WITH FARMSTAND CREAM

We asked Renée Kohlman, the Saskatoon-based chef/blogger behind Sweetsugarbean, to develop a perogy recipe for the book, and she chose to highlight sour cherries, an incredible ingredient from the Prairies. It's a sweet recipe, but you could easily enjoy them for breakfast, brunch, lunch, or dinner. In the parts of Canada where they grow, the sour cherry season typically runs for several weeks in July or August, depending on the region. Be sure to stock up when they arrive at your local farmers' market—they're popular, and they go fast.

SERVES 4 TO 6

SOUR CHERRY COMPOTE

- 3 cups (750 mL) fresh or frozen sour cherries, pitted
- 3/4 to 1 cup (185 to 250 mL) cane sugar
- 3 Tbsp (45 mL) balsamic vinegar
- 1/8 tsp salt

PEROGY DOUGH

- 2 eggs
- 1/2 cup (125 mL) water
- 1/2 tsp (1.5 g) salt
- 2 to 3 cups (300 to 450 g) all-purpose flour (see note on page 6)

FARMSTAND CREAM

- 1 tsp (5 mL) white sugar
- 1/2 cup (125 mL) whipping cream
- 1/2 cup (125 mL) full-fat sour cream

1 cup (250 mL) ricotta cheese
2 Tbsp (30 mL) butter, for frying (optional)

For the compote, combine the fresh or frozen cherries, sugar, vinegar, and salt in a medium saucepan. Bring the mixture to a boil, then lower the heat and simmer until reduced and slightly thickened, about 25 to 30 minutes. It will firm up as it cools. Transfer to an airtight container and refrigerate for up to 1 week.

For the perogy dough, beat the eggs, water, and salt together in a large bowl. Add the flour 1 cup (150 g) at a time, and mix just until a firm, yet soft and workable, dough forms. The dough should be pliable enough to roll out, but not overworked.

Turn the dough out onto a lightly floured work surface and knead until smooth. Shape into a ball and allow the dough to rest under an overturned bowl for 20 minutes.

To make the farmstand cream, add the sugar to the whipping cream, and whip until soft peaks form. Fold in the sour cream and refrigerate until ready to use.

To make the perogies, roll the dough out to 1/16 inch (2 mm). Cut into circles using a 3-inch (8 cm) cookie cutter or the top of a glass. Re-roll any large scraps and repeat the cutting-out process. Discard any small scraps.

Add 1 heaping tsp (5 mL) of sour cherry compote and 1 heaping tsp (5 mL) of ricotta cheese to the centre of each circle. Using your fingers, lightly brush the edges of the dough with water and fold it over. Press the edges together with your fingers, or use a fork to seal them. Repeat the process until all the dough is gone—you should end up with about 25 to 30 perogies.

Bring a large pot of salted water to a boil. While the water is heating up, prepare a plate lined with a few paper towels.

Add about 10 perogies to the water at a time and boil for 2 to 3 minutes, or until they float to the surface. Remove the perogies with a slotted spoon and transfer to the plate with paper towels to drain. You can eat them like this, warm with farmstand cream, but they taste even better when pan-fried for a few minutes!

If pan-frying, add the butter to a large skillet over medium heat. Place the perogies directly into the hot butter. Fry in an even layer, about 2 minutes per side, until golden and crispy. Continue cooking this way until all the perogies are done. Serve warm with a generous dollop of farmstand cream.

Feathers & Tails

MEAT MAINS

PRIME RIB

WITH HORSERADISH CREAM

Though the term "Alberta beef" has become absolutely ubiquitous, one place in Calgary continues to redefine what Alberta beef means: CHARCUT Roast House, led by co-owners and chefs Connie DeSousa and John Jackson. To our great delight, they shared their much-lauded recipe for prime rib.

Dana first tried this recipe out on her family, who are known to voice their opinions loudly and repeatedly, particularly when it comes to meat. The response was overwhelmingly enthusiastic, especially when it came to the horseradish cream, of which they were initially skeptical. Tasting fresh horseradish completely changed their minds, however. CHARCUT cooks their prime rib over a rotisserie, and we've included instructions for oven roasting as well.

SERVES 8 TO 12

PRIME RIB

- 8- to 12-pound (3.5 to 5.5 kg) piece beef rib-eye, choice or prime grade, bone-in preferably
- Butcher's Twine, if using a rotisserie
- 3/4 cup (185 mL) grainy mustard
- 3 Tbsp (45 mL) salt
- 1½ Tbsp (22 mL) freshly ground black pepper
- 4 cloves garlic, minced
- 4 sprigs rosemary, chopped
- 4 sprigs fresh thyme, chopped

HORSERADISH CREAM

- 1 cup (250 mL) whipping cream
- 1 cup + 1 Tbsp (265 mL) fresh horseradish, peeled and finely grated
- 1 cup (250 mL) sour cream
- 1 Tbsp (15 mL) Dijon mustard
- 3/4 cup (185 mL) white wine vinegar
- 1¾ tsp (8 mL) salt

FOR SERVING

- Arugula, coarse or flaky sea salt, lemon wedges, and extra virgin olive oil

Mix the mustard, salt, pepper, garlic, rosemary, and thyme together and rub evenly over all sides of the rib-eye. Cover and let the meat marinate in the refrigerator for 45 minutes, or ideally overnight. Remove the meat from the refrigerator, uncover, and let sit at room temperature for 30 to 60 minutes before cooking.

If using the oven, preheat it to 250°F (120°C).

Place the rib-eye, bone side down, on a grill rack in a sturdy metal roasting pan on the bottom shelf of the oven. For a rare roast, cook for 4 to 5 hours, or until an instant-read thermometer inserted in the deepest part of the meat reads 122°F (50°C). Timing will vary based on the shape and size of the cut of meat, so it's best to use a thermometer here. If the meat still has bones, make sure the thermometer is measuring the meat, as the bones will read at a higher temperature. The internal temperature of a rib-eye roasted at low heat will not rise very much once taken out of the oven, so remove it when it has reached the temperature you desire.

While the rib-eye is cooking, make the horseradish cream. The cream is best when made at least 30 minutes ahead of time so the flavours have a chance to blend. In a large bowl, whip the cream to soft peaks with an electric mixer. In a separate medium bowl, mix the grated horseradish, sour cream, mustard, white wine vinegar, and salt until combined. Gently fold in the whipped cream.

Once the meat has reached 122°F (50°C) (or higher, if desired), remove it from the oven and crank the temperature to 500°F (260°C). Create a loose tinfoil tent to cover (without touching) the meat while it rests for at least 30 minutes or up to 90 minutes. Just before you're ready to slice and serve, remove the foil tent and place the rib-eye in the preheated oven. Roast until the outside has browned and crisped, about 10 minutes. Remove from the oven, carve out the bones, slice, and serve.

If using a rotisserie, tie the rib-eye with butcher string, looping every 3 inches (8 cm) until secure. Skewer the rib-eye on the rotisserie and cook over medium-high heat, until the internal temperature reads 122°F (50°C). Remove and let rest for 30 minutes with a loose, tinfoil tent covering (but not touching) the meat. Once it has rested, slice and serve.

Serve with fresh arugula, a side of sea salt, lemon wedges, olive oil, and plenty of horseradish cream. The Warm Autumn Salad (page 179) goes well with this dish, too.

BISON, BUTTERNUT SQUASH & CRANBERRY PIE

Jo-Ann Laverty and Jennifer Heagle are the ladies behind Ottawa's the Red Apron, a wildly successful business specializing in high-quality fresh or frozen meals made from scratch with ingredients sourced from local producers. They started out in a closet-sized kitchen, and after years of hard work have expanded into their current location, a large and comprehensive shop. This recipe represents their region perfectly; they purchase bison from Takwânaw Farm in Quebec and cranberries from Eastern Ontario's Upper Canada Cranberries. The flour is locally milled, and the lard is from their favourite pork producer in Stratford.

SERVES 6

FILLING

- 4 Tbsp (60 mL) canola or extra virgin olive oil
- 1½ pounds (680 g) bison stew meat, cut into ¾-inch (2 cm) cubes
- 1 small yellow onion (about 120 g), diced
- 2 cloves garlic, minced
- ⅓ cup (80 mL) unsalted butter
- ⅓ cup (80 mL) all-purpose flour
- ⅔ cup (160 mL) dry red wine
- 2 cups (500 mL) beef stock
- 1 tsp (5 mL) salt
- ½ tsp (2 mL) freshly ground black pepper
- 1 Tbsp (15 mL) chopped fresh rosemary
- 2 cups (500 mL) butternut squash or yam, cut into ¾-inch (2 cm) cubes
- ½ cup (125 mL) dried cranberries

PIE CRUST

- 1⅔ cups (250 g) all-purpose flour (see note on page 6)
- 1 tsp (3 g) salt
- ⅓ cup (75 g) unsalted butter, cut into cubes and chilled
- ⅓ cup (75 g) lard, cut into pieces and chilled
- 4 tsp (20 mL) freshly squeezed lemon juice, chilled
- 4 to 8 Tbsp (60 to 120 mL) cold water

1 egg, beaten

Preheat the oven to 300°F (150°C).

To make the filling, heat the oil over medium heat in a Dutch oven. Once hot, add the bison and brown on all sides. Remove the browned meat and transfer to a large bowl.

Turn the heat down to medium and sauté the onion and garlic until the onions soften, 2 to 3 minutes. Remove and add to the bowl with the meat.

Increase the heat to medium-high again and add the butter and flour to the Dutch oven, stirring constantly to make a roux. When the flour mixture begins to brown, add the red wine and stock, then whisk in the salt, black pepper, and rosemary. Bring the mixture to a boil, then remove from the heat. Add in the bison, onion, and garlic. Stir, cover, and place in the middle of the preheated oven. Cook for 90 minutes, stirring once or twice.

Remove from the oven and add the squash. Cover and return to the oven to continue cooking for another 30 minutes. Once cooked, remove from the oven and stir in the dried cranberries. Allow the mixture to cool completely.

Increase the oven temperature to 375°F (190°C).

To make the dough, use a pastry cutter to blend the flour and salt with the cold butter and lard until the latter are pea-sized. This can be done in a food processor, pulsing for a few seconds at a time, but be careful not to overmix.

Pour in the lemon juice, add the water 1 Tbsp (15 mL) at a time, and mix (or pulse) until a dough forms. Divide the pastry into two pieces, shape each into a disc, and wrap separately in plastic wrap. Let rest for 15 to 30 minutes in the refrigerator.

On a well-floured surface, roll out the first piece of dough (sprinkling more flour as needed to keep it from sticking) and transfer to a 9- or 10-inch (23 or 25 cm) pie plate. Trim the edges, then fill with all of the prepared bison filling. Roll out the second piece of dough, place evenly over the filling, and trim the edges. Tuck the edges of the top crust beneath the bottom crust, and crimp. Cut steam vents into the surface of the pie and brush with the beaten egg.

Bake for 30 to 40 minutes, or until the crust is a rich, golden brown. Remove from the oven, let cool for about 15 minutes, slice, and serve.

Alberta

We ate exceptionally well in Alberta, land of flat farms, towering mountains, and a cowboy culture that's celebrated annually. We drove into Edmonton from the Northwest Territories looking tired and unkempt, having spent the previous night hiding from a storm in a picnic shelter.

Once tidied up and caffeinated, we headed to the opulent Duchess Bake Shop and met Valerie Lugonja, a blogger and food advocate who was one of our biggest supporters throughout the trip. Over slices of sour cherry pie, we told her about our triumphs and difficulties so far, and she offered encouragement about those yet to come.

We also met Kevin Kossowan, one of Canada's great renaissance men when it comes to food and media. He's a successful urban farmer, hunter, forager, and filmmaker, and he kindly invited us over to his house for lunch. We ate an omelette made from his own chicken eggs, which he baked in an outdoor wood-burning oven he built himself; he also served cider made from apples harvested from the tree overhead. His business partner, Chad Moss, added his homemade Red Fife bread and charcuterie to the mix. *Come on.* It doesn't get any better than that.

Farther south, we drove into rural farmland to meet rancher Gus Janke, who took us to see the herd of bison he raises for meat. Considering that bison are essentially still wild and could easily leave if they're unhappy, Gus "manages" the herd more than he "raises" them. We stood within a stone's throw of animals that weigh up to 900 kilograms (2,000 pounds) and tried to pretend we weren't nervous (our near-hysterical laughter didn't hide it well). Later, we visited Rock Ridge Dairy and stood next to a herd of baby goats. Significantly less intimidating than the bison, they thought our fingers were milk bottles from which they could feed.

In Calgary, we dropped in on Sidewalk Citizen Bakery and tried to eat a year's worth of sourdough and pastries in an hour. We snacked on Grizzly Gouda at Janice Beaton Fine Cheese, recharged with cocktails at Model Milk, and got our Alberta beef fix at CHARCUT. Out in the countryside, we were fed cobbler by Tony and Penny Marshall at Highwood Crossing Farm. They sent us away with containers of ripe haskap berries, their organically grown steel cut oats, and buttered banana bread.

We felt like we'd been taken in by a big family of Albertans, passed from one caring group of relatives to the next. Feeling relaxed and very full, we headed east into the flatlands . . .

PORK & SHRIMP WONTONS

WITH SWEET & SPICY VINEGAR SAUCE

Stephanie Le is the culinary genius behind *i am a food blog*, a blog that combines the very best in food, photography, and design. Though she also lives in Vancouver, we met in Las Vegas at the *Saveur* Best Food Blog Awards, where her site was named Blog of the Year.

These wontons represent both the food she grew up eating and the plethora of Chinese dumplings available to Vancouverites. Wood ear mushrooms (also sold as "dried black fungus" or "cloud ear fungus") are sold in Asian grocery stores, but if you can't find them where you are, no problem. Just substitute half a cup of any type of cooked mushroom, as long as they're drained well to ensure they don't add excess water to the filling.

SERVES 4

SWEET AND SPICY VINEGAR SAUCE

- 3 to 4 cloves garlic, minced
- 2 Tbsp (30 mL) sweet soy sauce or tamari
- 1 Tbsp (15 mL) chili oil
- 2 tsp (10 mL) Chinese black vinegar or Worcestershire sauce
- 1⁄4 tsp (1 mL) ground Sichuan pepper
- 1 tsp (5 mL) sesame oil
- 1 Thai chili (about 2 g), seeds removed, minced (optional)

PORK AND SHRIMP WONTONS

- 1⁄2 pound (227 g) lean ground pork
- 1⁄4 pound (113 g) whole shrimp, shelled, deveined, and roughly chopped
- 1⁄2 small shallot (about 20 g), finely chopped
- 1⁄8 cup (30 mL) wood ear mushrooms, rehydrated in water, drained, and roughly chopped
- 2 Tbsp (30 mL) chopped fresh cilantro
- 2 Tbsp (30 mL) finely chopped green onions
- 1⁄4 tsp (1 mL) salt
- 1⁄4 tsp (1 mL) ground white pepper
- 20 to 24 square wonton wrappers

FOR SERVING

- 1 cup (250 mL) 1-inch (2.5 cm) pieces of asparagus
- 1 cup (250 mL) halved sugar snap peas

To make the sauce, mix together all the ingredients in a small bowl. Taste and adjust the seasonings as desired, then set aside.

To make the wontons, cover a baking sheet with parchment paper and set aside. In a bowl, combine the ground pork, shrimp, shallots, mushrooms, cilantro, green onions, salt, and white pepper. Have the wonton wrappers ready as well as a small bowl of water. Spoon 2 tsp (10 mL) of filling into the middle of the wonton wrapper, then dip your finger in the water and paint the edges of the wonton that are facing up. Gently bring two opposite corners of the square together and press to seal them. Try to avoid air pockets between the filling and the sealed wrapper. Again, dab water on the two opposite corners of the triangle and fold them in toward each other, envelope style, layering one slightly overtop the other. As they're made, lay the folded wontons on the prepared baking sheet—you should end up with about 20 to 24 wontons.

Bring a medium pot of water to a boil and prepare an ice water bath in a medium bowl. Blanch the asparagus and snap peas for 30 seconds, then remove from the boiling water with a slotted spoon and transfer to the ice bath. Once cooled, drain and spread out to dry on a clean tea towel.

Next, bring a large pot of salted water to a boil and add the wontons. They will sink at first, so stir gently to ensure they don't stick to the bottom of the pot. Once the wontons float to the top, add ½ cup (125 mL) of water and bring the pot back up to a boil. When the wontons float to the top again, about 3 to 5 minutes later, they're ready. To double-check, cut one open to see if it's cooked through.

Lift the wontons out with a slotted spoon, shaking off any excess water. Toss with half of the sauce to start, adding more if desired. Divide the asparagus and sugar snap peas between four shallow bowls. Top with the wontons and enjoy immediately.

REINDEER MEATLOAF

There are a handful of food trucks in Yellowknife, Northwest Territories, but the most popular one by far is Chef Robin Wasicuna's Wiseguy Foods. The seasonal truck opened in 2011, with long lines forming shortly thereafter, and in 2015, Robin began feeding people out of his brick-and-mortar location, the Twin Pine Diner. He's a creative chef with a talent for reworking old favourites with Northern ingredients, and this meatloaf is proof.

SERVES 6 TO 8

1 Tbsp (15 mL) extra virgin olive oil
½ cup (125 mL) yellow onion, diced to ¼-inch (6 mm) pieces before measuring
½ cup (125 mL) carrots, diced to ¼-inch (6 mm) pieces before measuring
½ cup (125 mL) celery, diced to ¼-inch (6 mm) pieces before measuring
Pinch salt and pepper
2 cloves garlic, minced
1 Tbsp (15 mL) smoked paprika (hot or sweet)
1 Tbsp (15 mL) sherry vinegar
½ cup (125 mL) bread crumbs
½ cup (125 mL) whole milk
1 pound + 2 ounces (500 g) ground reindeer/caribou, elk, bison, or lean beef
1 pound + 2 ounces (500 g) ground pork
3 eggs
2 Tbsp (30 mL) salt
¾ tsp (3 mL) freshly ground black pepper
2 Tbsp (30 mL) Worcestershire sauce
2 cups (500 mL) Clove-Spiced Lingonberry Sauce (page 260)

Preheat the oven to 350°F (180°C). Grease a large loaf pan or line it with parchment paper.

Heat the oil in a large skillet over medium-high heat. Add the onions, carrots, celery, and a pinch of salt and pepper. Cook until the onions are translucent, about 4 to 5 minutes. Add the garlic and paprika and cook until fragrant, about 2 more minutes. Deglaze the skillet with the sherry vinegar, remove from the heat, and set aside.

In a small bowl, combine the bread crumbs and milk and set aside.

In a medium bowl, mix the reindeer with the pork. Add the eggs, salt, pepper, Worcestershire, the bread crumb mixture, and the sautéed vegetable mixture, and mix until combined. Transfer the meat mixture to the prepared loaf pan.

Distribute at least ½ cup (125 mL) of the Clove-Spiced Lingonberry Sauce over the top of the meatloaf. Place the glazed meatloaf in a preheated oven and let cook for about 1 hour, until the loaf is firm to the touch, the juices run clear, and the internal temperature reads 160°F (71°C).

Remove the meatloaf from the oven. Let it rest for 20 minutes before removing from the pan and slicing. Serve with the remaining lingonberry sauce on the side.

TOURTIÈRE DE FLEUR-ANGE

Since neither of us grew up in Quebec, nor do we have a drop of Québécois blood in us, we didn't grow up with *tourtière*. We became familiar with this meaty French Canadian pie only in our 20s—a happy revelation—and found it in many forms across Quebec and the East Coast during the road trip. It is one of those dishes with an infinite number of recipes; everyone's mother or grandmother has a particular way of making it, so we were rather intimidated when it came to settling on one to include in the book. Luckily, Julian Armstrong, an expert in French Canadian cuisine, shared this recipe from one of her cookbooks, *Made in Quebec*. The recipe originally came from Ange Vanier Rochon, who was from one of the first families to settle in the Laurentians and was mother-in-law to Marcel Kretz, the first chef in our country to be named to the Order of Canada. Got that? It has a lot of history behind it, this *tourtière*.

SERVES 12 (MAKES TWO 9-INCH/23 CM PIES)

Note: The meat mixture may be made ahead and refrigerated. Unbaked pies may be refrigerated for 24 hours, or frozen. Thaw in the refrigerator before baking.

Pastry for 2 double-crust, 9- or 10-inch (23 or 25 cm) pies (The Pie Shoppe's Pastry, page 240, doubled)
2 pounds (910 g) lean ground pork
1 cup (250 mL) water
2 stalks celery (about 150 g), chopped
½ cup (125 mL) chopped celery leaves
2 large yellow onions (about 440 g), chopped
2 cloves garlic, chopped
½ cup (125 mL) chopped flat-leaf parsley
1 Tbsp (15 mL) chopped fresh savory, or 1 tsp (5 mL) dried
⅛ tsp ground cinnamon
⅛ tsp ground cloves
1 tsp (5 mL) salt
⅛ tsp freshly ground black pepper
1 egg yolk
1 Tbsp (15 mL) whole milk

FOR SERVING

Pickles, Green Tomato Chow Chow (page 252), and/or Peach & Apricot Chutney (page 244)

Prepare the pastry (page 240).

In a large, heavy saucepan over medium heat, combine the pork, water, celery and leaves, onions, garlic, parsley, savory, cinnamon, cloves, salt, and pepper. Break up the pork with a wooden spoon and cook, stirring occasionally, for 30 minutes. Add more water if necessary to prevent the mixture from drying out. Taste and add more salt and pepper if necessary. Let cool.

Preheat the oven to 400°F (200°C).

Line two 9- or 10-inch (23 or 25 cm) pie plates with pastry and fill with the meat mixture. Roll out the top crusts, cutting a generous vent in the centre of each; Madame Rochon always cut her vents in the shape of an evergreen tree. Cover each pie with the top crusts. To get a nice crimped edge, trim the bottom and top crusts to about ¼ inch (6 mm) beyond the edge of the pie plate. Pinch the top and bottom edges together slightly and fold them under. Then, while pinching the crust edge with your thumb and pointer finger from one hand, push with the thumb of your opposite hand in between the other two fingers, creating a big crimp. Repeat all the way around the edge of the pie. Cut additional small steam vents. Mix together the egg yolk and milk and brush it over the tops of the pies.

Bake the pies in the preheated oven for 35 to 40 minutes, or until the crusts are golden. Serve either hot or cold with pickles, Green Tomato Chow Chow (page 252), and/or Peach & Apricot Chutney (page 244).

MAPLE MOLASSES–BRAISED PORK BELLY

We first had this dish at the Roots, Rants, and Roars Festival in Elliston, an annual festival of food and music along the rugged coastline of eastern Newfoundland. It was prepared by Garry Gosse of Harbour Breeze Catering and was served during The Feast, the festival's final event. It was served with his Roasted Tomato & Fig Ketchup (page 264), and we were immediately smitten. In fact, we decided it was one of the most Canadian dishes we'd encountered.

We were thrilled when Garry generously agreed to share his recipes with us. It needs to cook twice, so it's easiest if prepared over the course of a few days, though it can be done in one day if started early enough.

SERVES 6 TO 8

2 pounds (910 g) fresh pork belly, skin off
1 cup (250 mL) maple syrup, divided
1 cup (250 mL) molasses, divided
1 cup (250 mL) fine maple sugar
6 slices (about 4.5 oz or 125 g) thick-cut, double-smoked bacon, chopped
1 large yellow onion (about 220 g), chopped
1 large carrot (about 70 g), chopped
3 cloves garlic, minced
2 cups (500 mL) vegetable stock
1 to 2 Tbsp (15 to 30 mL) sherry vinegar (optional)
½ tsp (2 mL) ground cinnamon
½ tsp (2 mL) Chinese five spice
¼ tsp (1 mL) ground cloves
1 tsp (5 mL) chopped fresh thyme

To prepare the belly, gently score the fat side in a crosshatch pattern and place fat side up in a casserole dish. Measure out 1 cup (250 mL) each of maple syrup and molasses. From the measured cups, take 1 Tbsp (15 mL) out of each and rub into the belly (reserving the rest for the braise). Next, rub in the maple sugar. Wrap the meat tightly with plastic food wrap, place in a casserole dish, and let marinate in the refrigerator for a couple of hours, or ideally overnight.

To make the braising liquid, add the bacon to a small pot on medium heat and let it cook for a few minutes. Add the onion and carrot, followed by the garlic. Once they've softened, add the stock and the rest of the molasses and maple syrup. If you're not serving the belly with the Roasted Tomato & Fig Ketchup, then add the sherry vinegar at this time as well. Add the cinnamon, Chinese five spice, cloves, and fresh thyme. Bring to a boil, then simmer and reduce until slightly thickened, about 20 minutes.

After the pork belly has marinated, preheat the oven to 350°F (180°C) and heat a large skillet over medium-high heat. Once the skillet is hot, unwrap the belly and place fat side down on the skillet. Sear until the belly moves easily along the skillet, about 2 minutes. Remove and place in a casserole dish, fat side up, and cover with the prepared braising liquid. Cover and let cook in the preheated oven for 3 to 3½ hours, or until fork-tender.

Once cooked, remove from the oven and let cool. Transfer the cooled belly to the refrigerator and let sit for 2 hours, or ideally overnight. Reserve the braising liquid and reduce again over medium heat until the mixture is thick and syrupy, about 20 to 30 minutes.

For the second round of cooking, preheat the oven to 275°F (140°C). Remove the belly from the refrigerator, slice into 1-inch (2.5 cm) slices crosswise (the same way you would cut it into bacon) and let it come to room temperature. Return it to the casserole dish and pour the reduced braising liquid over it. Cover and cook in the preheated oven for 2 hours.

Remove from the oven and serve with Roasted Tomato & Fig Ketchup (page 264).

MAGRET DE CANARD LAQUÉ AU MIEL ET PIMENT D'ESPELETTE

(DUCK BREAST WITH HONEY AND ESPELETTE PEPPER GLAZE)

While staying with friends in Mississauga, we mentioned at a party that we'd soon be heading to Quebec. Half the guests turned and exclaimed, "Charlevoix! You *must* go to Charlevoix!" We took the advice and understood their love of the place immediately. The cheese! L'Accalmie shipwreck! L'Isle-aux-Coudres! There was just so much there to be enamoured with.

Chef Gilles Bernard, formerly of Auberge des Peupliers in La Malbaie, contributed this sweet, spicy, and easy-to-make duck recipe. Espelette pepper is a type of mildly hot dried chili from the Basque region in France; if you can't find it, just substitute hot paprika.

SERVES 4

½ cup (125 mL) honey
½ cup (125 mL) white vinegar
1 tsp (5 mL) cornstarch
⅛ tsp Espelette pepper, or hot paprika
4 duck breasts, ½ pound (227 g) each
⅛ tsp salt
⅛ tsp freshly ground black pepper
10 to 12 new potatoes (about 400 g)

FOR SERVING

Seasonal vegetables, such as carrots and asparagus, cooked
Small bunch of chives, for garnish

Preheat the oven to 375°F (190°C).

In a small pot, bring the honey and vinegar to a boil, then remove from the heat. In a separate small bowl, mix the cornstarch with a splash of cold water, add to the honey mixture, and return the pot to the element. Bring to a boil, then remove from the heat and add the Espelette pepper. Set aside.

Bring a large pot of water to a boil and blanch the potatoes for about 4 minutes. Immediately transfer to an ice water bath to cool.

Season each duck breast on both sides with the salt and pepper. Add a pinch of salt to a large pan and bring to medium heat. Add the breasts, fat side down, and cook until well coloured, about 6 to 8 minutes. Drain off the excess fat and reserve for cooking the potatoes.

Place the breasts on a baking sheet, fat side down, and brush the flesh liberally with the honey sauce. Bake for 8 minutes, or until they reach 126°F (52°C) internally (for rare meat). Let the duck rest at least 5 minutes before slicing.

Cut the blanched potatoes in half and sauté in the duck fat over medium heat, until golden, about 10 to 15 minutes. Season with salt and pepper to taste.

Slice the duck breasts thinly and arrange on a serving platter with the potatoes, sprinkling with more Espelette pepper. Serve with vegetables and garnish with chives, if desired.

FRICOT AU POULET ACADIEN

(ACADIAN CHICKEN FRICOT)

In New Brunswick, we visited Kouchibouguac National Park, the name of which we cheerfully repeated many times while driving. Our interest in the park led us to Camilla, who worked for Parks Canada at the time. When she heard about our trip, she planned an afternoon cooking lesson at the home of a treasured local Acadian cook—her mother! It was an honour to cook with Claira Vautour, who taught us the fine art of making *poutines râpées*, a type of potato and salted pork dumpling. Claira shared Chicken Fricot for the book—another Acadian classic. A relative of the American South's chicken and dumplings, it's tried and true comfort food from the East Coast.

SERVES 4 TO 6

SOUP

- One 2½ to 3½ pound (1 to 1½ kg) whole chicken
- 1 Tbsp (15 mL) salt
- 1 tsp (5 mL) freshly ground black pepper
- 1 tsp (5 mL) chopped fresh summer savory, or ½ tsp (2 mL) dried
- 1 large carrot (about 70 g), peeled and diced
- 6 to 8 medium potatoes (720 to 960 g), diced
- 1 medium yellow onion (about 160 g), diced

DUMPLINGS

- 1 cup (250 mL) all-purpose flour
- ¼ tsp (1 mL) salt
- 1 tsp (5 mL) baking powder
- ½ cup (125 mL) cold water

FOR SERVING

- Fresh summer savory or chopped flat-leaf parsley, to garnish

Rinse the chicken, place it in a large pot, and cover with cold water. Add the salt, pepper, and savory, then cover and bring to a boil. Once boiling, lower the heat to a simmer and cook until the meat is falling off the bones, about 60 to 90 minutes.

When the chicken is cooked (the temperature in the thickest part of the thigh should read 180°F/82°C), remove from the pot and let cool. Reserve the broth, and when it has cooled, skim off the fat.

Pull all the meat off the chicken, discarding the bones and skin, and coarsely shred the meat using two forks. Bring the broth to a boil again and add the carrot, potatoes, and onion. When the vegetables are tender, add the chicken. Taste the broth at this point, and season with more salt and/or pepper if desired.

For the dumplings, mix the flour, salt, and baking powder together in a medium bowl. Pour in the water and mix just until the dough comes together; do not overmix or the dumplings will be tough! The dough should be a little firm and not too sticky—if it is, sprinkle in about 1 tsp (5 mL) more flour.

Drop the dough in tablespoonfuls into the boiling broth. Once all the dough is in, lower the heat, cover with a lid, and simmer for 10 to 15 minutes, until the dumplings are puffed and fluffy looking. Serve immediately, topping with fresh chopped summer savory or parsley.

BRAISED ARCTIC HARE

WITH CHANTERELLES & GREEN PEAS

We've had the good fortune of eating Chef Roger Andrews's food on many occasions, both during our road trip and after. He's a quiet, humble guy who *really* knows how to cook, especially with classic Newfoundland ingredients. This one features the bright white Arctic hare, which is found across Newfoundland, Labrador, and the territories. Rabbit is an easy substitute for this dish, which is just what you'll crave in the middle of winter.

SERVES 6 TO 8

2 Tbsp (30 mL) extra virgin olive oil
1¼ pounds (570 g) Arctic hare or rabbit, bones in
6 slices (4.5 oz or 125 g) smoked thick-cut bacon, chopped
1 small yellow onion (120 g), finely chopped
1 large carrot (70 g), finely chopped
2 cups (500 mL) fresh or rehydrated chanterelle mushrooms
3 cloves garlic, crushed
1 Tbsp (15 mL) tomato paste
⅔ cup (160 mL) dry red wine
2 cups (500 mL) chicken stock
One 500 g package of pappardelle pasta (or fresh pappardelle, page 6)
2 sprigs fresh thyme, leaves removed and chopped
1 Tbsp (15 mL) Dijon or grainy mustard
½ cup (125 mL) whipping cream
½ cup (125 mL) fresh or frozen green peas

FOR SERVING

Parmigiano-Reggiano or Grana Padano, shaved or grated

Heat the oil in a large pot or Dutch oven over medium heat. Pat the hare dry with paper towel. When the oil is hot, add the hare and brown on all sides, about 7 or 8 minutes on each side, then remove from the pan and set aside.

Add the bacon, onion, and carrot to the pot and cook for 10 minutes. Add the mushrooms, garlic, and tomato paste. Stir for 1 to 2 minutes, then pour in the wine and chicken stock. Return the hare to the pan, cover with a lid, and cook over low heat for 1 hour, or until the meat is very tender.

Remove the hare from the pan, transfer to a large bowl, and let cool. Increase the heat under the pot and boil the liquid until reduced by half, about 15 minutes. Once the hare is cool enough to handle, pull all the meat off the bones and shred it using two forks. Be careful to remove all small bones. Add the shredded meat back to the pot and turn the heat down to low.

Cook the pasta in a large pot of salted water following the package instructions (if using fresh, see page 6). Drain when ready, reserving a little pasta water to thin the sauce if necessary.

Meanwhile, add the thyme, mustard, cream, and peas to the sauce. Stir and let the sauce simmer over low heat until the pasta is ready.

Add the cooked pasta to a large serving dish and ladle a generous amount of sauce overtop, tossing everything until well coated. Add a little of the reserved pasta water only if necessary. Top with shaved or grated Parmigiano-Reggiano or Grana Padano and serve.

LAMB STEAKS

WITH SAGE BUTTER

Michele Genest has authored two incredible books about cooking in the boreal forest, the expanse of land that starts around the 50th parallel and covers much of Canada's north. We met up with Miche and her husband, Hector, during the Dawson City Music Festival, and the two of them ensured we had a proper education in Yukonian food and landscape. They even hosted us for dinner at their home in Whitehorse.

For these steaks, Miche uses steaks from Dall sheep, a species native to the mountain ranges of the Yukon, Northern British Columbia, and Alaska, but lamb is an excellent substitution. This recipe is from her stunning second book, *The Boreal Feast*.

SERVES 4 TO 6

STEAKS

1 tsp (5 mL) salt
1 tsp (5 mL) freshly ground black pepper
1 Tbsp (15 mL) finely chopped wild or cultivated sage
2 pounds (910 g) lamb leg steaks (about 4 to 6 steaks)

SAGE BUTTER

¼ cup (60 mL) salted butter, room temperature
1 tsp (5 mL) chopped spruce or fir tips (optional)
1 Tbsp (15 mL) finely chopped wild or cultivated sage
Grapeseed oil, for grilling

For the steaks, combine the salt, pepper, and sage and sprinkle evenly over each steak. Stack the steaks on top of each other and wrap tightly in plastic wrap. Refrigerate for at least 2 hours.

For the sage butter, combine the butter, spruce tips, and remaining 1 Tbsp (15 mL) of sage. Lay out a piece of plastic food wrap or waxed paper and transfer the soft butter mixture to its centre. Fold the wrap over one end and roll, shaping the butter into a log. Twist both ends. Refrigerate for at least 1 hour.

Once you're ready to eat, heat the barbeque to at least 500°F (260°C). Once hot, brush the grill with grapeseed oil and put the steaks on. Close the lid and cook for 90 seconds (if rare meat isn't your thing, cook it for another 60 seconds or longer). Flip the steaks and repeat. Remove from the grill and let rest at least 10 minutes.

Remove the herbed butter from the refrigerator and slice into rounds. Slice the meat against the grain, top with the herbed butter, and enjoy!

CAR CAMPING

Have you ever wondered, "Is it possible to pack two people and all their things into a small hatchback for five months and still maintain sanity?" The answer is a confident YES. We made our way across the country in Dana's small white car, staying in a combination of campsites, hotels, and friends' houses along the way. Camping-wise, we slept everywhere from an empty, hike-in beach site on Haida Gwaii to the top of a hill overlooking the Atlantic on Prince Edward Island. Our best bit of advice for a long-term road trip? Keep a big suitcase in a permanent place in the car and think of it as your "closet." Store the things you need for a day or two in a smaller backpack and haul *that* in and out each night as you set up camp. Nobody needs to be lugging their autumn sweaters out of the car in July. Nobody.

ELK BURGERS

WITH BLUE CHEESE & BALSAMIC ROASTED RED ONIONS

When we arrived at his ranch in Kanata, Ontario, Thom van Eeghen handed us a pair of helmets, loaded us into the trailer of an ATV, and drove us out to his herd of elk. We first visited the cows and calves in the field, then made our way over to the woods, where an impressively antlered bull was hanging out on his own. The photo below remains one of our favourites from the trip—what a goofball.

Elk meat is a great alternative to beef. It's lean, a good source of vitamin B, and ever-so-slightly sweet, rather than gamey. If you don't have any elk producers nearby, you can easily substitute beef or bison.

SERVES 4 TO 6

ROASTED ONIONS

- 1 large red onion (about 220 grams), sliced into ½-inch-thick (1 cm) rings
- 1 Tbsp (15 mL) balsamic vinegar
- 1 Tbsp (15 mL) extra virgin olive oil
- ⅛ tsp salt

BURGERS

- ½ medium red onion (about 80 g), finely chopped
- 1 egg, beaten
- ⅓ cup (80 mL) finely chopped flat-leaf parsley
- 1 Tbsp (15 mL) grainy or Dijon mustard
- 1 Tbsp (15 mL) Worcestershire sauce
- ¾ tsp (3 mL) salt
- ½ tsp (2 mL) freshly ground black pepper
- 1½ pounds (680 g) ground elk, bison, or lean beef
- ¾ cup (185 mL) crumbled blue cheese (see note)

FOR SERVING

- 4 to 6 buns, toasted
- Tomatoes, lettuce, mayo, and any other desired burger toppings

Note: You can use any blue cheese you prefer, as long as it's firm enough to hold its shape when you're mixing the burgers. Some great Canadian options include Ciel de Charlevoix, Bleu Bénédictin, and Dragon's Breath Blue.

Preheat the oven to 400°F (200°C).

For the roasted onions, add the sliced onion rings to a large bowl and toss with the balsamic vinegar, olive oil, and salt. Spread out evenly on a large baking sheet. Roast in the oven for 15 minutes, turn the slices over, and roast again until soft and caramelized, another 10 to 15 minutes.

Preheat the barbeque on medium-high (about 450°F/230°C).

To make the patties, mix the onion, egg, parsley, mustard, Worcestershire sauce, salt, and pepper. Add the ground meat and gently mix with your hands until just combined (overmixing will make the burgers tough). Add the crumbled cheese and mix again until just combined. Divide the meat mixture into six even portions (or four, if you'd prefer larger burgers) and shape each portion into a patty. Grill on the barbeque, flipping once, until their internal temperature reaches 160°F (71°C) or they're no longer pink inside, 8 to 10 minutes. Serve the burgers on buns with the roasted onions, lettuce, tomato, mayo, and any other toppings you like!

Saskatchewan

Our journey through Saskatchewan offered yellow and purple fields of canola and flax, colossal skies, and small towns in which it was impossible to find lunch on a Monday. Every chance we had, we wandered off-highway to explore the province's many old ghost towns. In one of them, we walked gingerly through an abandoned house, just across from the town's one still-lively institution—a post office. A woman named Gloria noticed our BC licence plate and approached the car. "My, aren't you girls far from home!" she exclaimed, then invited us to her farm for beer and perogies.

Within Saskatchewan's communities, we found the ingenuity of food producers to be astounding. With the province's harsh winters, could you ever imagine buying produce from a farmer in December? Floating Gardens has figured out a way to do just that, with their sustainably fuelled year-round greenhouses and custom-built hydroponic systems. Or how about coming across an abundant crimson orchard of sour cherries in Saskatoon? Despite Saskatchewan being named a dead zone for the production of sour cherries, they mysteriously thrive in the province during the summer months.

The endless crop fields we passed included rye, wheat, mustard seed, chickpeas, oats, flaxseed, and others—all reasons behind the province's reputation as the "bread basket of Canada." Much of this farmland was established by Russian and Eastern European immigrants in the late 19th and early 20th centuries; thus, perogies are an easy meal to find, and Mennonite and Doukhobor farmers sell their produce each week at outdoor markets.

Our time in Saskatchewan was often charmingly eclectic. We ate Greek food in a rural 1950s diner that also sold fireworks and seemed to be a museum for vintage cars; visited a small-town traditional Mennonite restaurant run by a Bangladeshi couple; had trout quesadillas at Leyda's in Saskatoon; drank beer and listened to ghost stories in Regina's famous Bushwakker Brewpub; and stopped in at Lucky Bastard, one of the province's craft distilleries.

Each day, Saskatchewan had a surprise for us, and we delighted in never knowing what to expect. With a long drive to Manitoba ahead of us, we couldn't accept Gloria's kind offer of beer and perogies, but oh how we wanted to! It's a standing invitation, however, and we can't wait to take her up on it . . .

SASKATCHEWAN
CRAIK

VENISON LOIN

WITH WINE, RED CURRANT & DARK CHOCOLATE REDUCTION

Though we didn't make it as far as Yellowknife in the Northwest Territories, we have since managed to connect with several cooks who have called it home. Mark Plouffe is a chef and former high school culinary instructor who moved to the territory several decades ago. He developed this recipe for venison or caribou, which pair splendidly with the red currants and dark chocolate.

SERVES 6

VENISON LOIN

1½-pound (680 g) piece of venison, caribou or beef tenderloin
Salt and freshly ground black pepper
1 Tbsp (15 mL) extra virgin olive oil
1 Tbsp (15 mL) unsalted butter
1 sprig fresh thyme, leaves removed

RED WINE SAUCE

½ small (about 20 g) shallot, minced
1 cup (250 mL) dry red wine
1 Tbsp (15 mL) red currant or crabapple jelly
1 ounce (28 g) dark chocolate
1 Tbsp (15 mL) cold unsalted butter, divided
Salt and freshly ground black pepper

Pat the venison loin dry with a paper towel. Season both sides with salt and pepper. Add the olive oil to a large skillet and heat over medium heat. Once the olive oil is hot, add the venison. Cook until nicely browned, about 4 minutes. Add the butter and thyme to the pan, flip the loin over, and cook for 4 minutes on the other side, basting occasionally with the melted butter. When cooked (it will be medium-rare), remove from the pan and let rest for 5 minutes.

Add the shallots to the hot pan and sauté about 2 minutes. Add the wine to deglaze, and reduce for another 2 minutes. Turn the heat to low and add the jelly and chocolate, whisking until they're melted. Add half of the butter and whisk to incorporate. Add the rest of the butter and whisk again until smooth. Taste and season with salt and pepper, if desired, and remove from the heat.

Slice the meat against the grain into medallions, pour the chocolate sauce overtop, and serve with any extra sauce on the side.

SLOW-COOKER MOOSE STROGANOFF

While not native to the province, moose have certainly made a comfortable home for themselves in Newfoundland, with a population that's blown up since their introduction at the turn of the 20th century. Because they're often on the roads at dusk, we were on constant lookout; any scenario involving Dana's small car and those beasts would have been a tricky one. While we didn't see any on the highway, we did encounter them many times on our plates, including in burgers, preserved in jars, and even cured into pastrami! Chef Roary MacPherson, a beloved chef in St. John's, likes to use moose in his stroganoff. If you can't get your hands on any, bison or beef work well, too.

SERVES 4 TO 6

1½ pounds (680 g) moose, bison, or lean beef, cut into ¾-inch (2 cm) cubes
2 Tbsp (30 mL) paprika (hot or sweet)
One 10-ounce (284 mL) can good-quality beef broth
1 small yellow onion (about 120 g), thinly sliced
1 cup (250 mL) sliced button mushrooms
¼ cup (60 mL) pickle juice
2 medium dill pickles (about 100 g), diced
¾ tsp (3 mL) salt
¼ tsp (1 mL) freshly ground black pepper
1 Tbsp (15 mL) chopped fresh dill, plus more for garnish
2 Tbsp (30 mL) cornstarch (optional)
2 Tbsp (30 mL) cold water (optional)
10 cups (400 g) egg noodles

FOR SERVING

Sour cream, chopped fresh dill, and paprika.

Toss the moose meat in the paprika until evenly coated. Add the meat, beef broth, onions, mushrooms, pickle juice, pickles, salt, and pepper to a slow cooker and simmer on low heat for about 8 hours.

Once cooked, mix in the fresh dill and more salt and pepper, if desired. If the sauce is runnier than you'd like, combine the cornstarch and the cold water and mix thoroughly. Transfer the stroganoff to a medium pot over medium heat and add the cornstarch mixture, stirring until bubbling and thickened.

Cook the egg noodles according to the package instructions, and drain. Serve the stroganoff over the egg noodles and top with sour cream and fresh dill.

CLASSIC CABBAGE ROLLS

This recipe comes from the kitchen of Rose Murray, the prolific Canadian food writer and author of nearly a dozen cookbooks. She's been travelling the country and documenting Canadian food culture for over 30 years! We were thrilled to get her recipe for classic cabbage rolls, a popular dish in Waterloo, Ontario, where she grew up. This is a big recipe from her *A-Z Vegetable Cookbook*, and we highly recommend making the full batch and freezing some for later.

SERVES 10 TO 12

1 large green cabbage or soured cabbage (1.5 kg) (see note)

FILLING

- 1 cup (250 mL) long grain white rice
- 2 pounds (910 g) lean ground beef
- One 10-ounce (284 mL) can condensed beef consommé, divided
- 1 small yellow onion (about 120 g), finely chopped
- 1 egg
- 2 cloves garlic, minced
- 1 tsp (5 mL) Worcestershire sauce
- 1/2 tsp (2 mL) salt
- 1/4 tsp (1 mL) freshly ground black pepper

BUTTER SAUCE

- 1/4 cup (60 mL) unsalted butter, divided
- 1/2 cup (125 mL) lightly packed brown sugar, divided

TOMATO SAUCE

- 2 Tbsp (30 mL) all-purpose flour
- 2 small yellow onions (about 240 g), thinly sliced
- One 28-ounce (796 mL) can whole tomatoes, with juice
- One 14-ounce (398 mL) can tomato sauce
- 3/4 cup (185 mL) apple cider vinegar
- 2 tsp (10 mL) Worcestershire sauce
- 1/4 tsp (1 mL) salt
- 1/4 tsp (1 mL) freshly ground black pepper

Note: If you're using soured cabbage, we recommend using slightly less vinegar (1/2 cup/125 mL, instead of 3/4 cup/185 mL) in the sauce, since the brined cabbage already has extra acidity.

In a medium pot, cook the rice according to package instructions. Set aside.

If you're using fresh cabbage, set a large pot of water to boil. Once the water is boiling, blanch the cabbage whole for about 2 minutes. Remove from the pot and reserve the hot water. For either fresh or soured cabbage, peel the leaves off until there are no more. If at any point it becomes difficult to peel the layers from the fresh cabbage, simply re-blanch it in the reserved hot water and start again. Place any torn pieces on the bottoms of two 9- × 9-inch (23 × 23 cm) baking dishes and reserve the whole ones for making into rolls. To make rolling easier, cut out the thick rib from the bottom of each leaf.

For the filling, combine the raw beef, ½ cup (125 mL) of undiluted consommé, onion, egg, garlic, Worcestershire sauce, salt, and pepper in a large bowl. Mix in the prepared rice once it has cooled.

Place about ⅓ cup (80 mL) filling in the centre of each cabbage leaf. Fold the sides overtop the filling and roll up from the stem end. Secure with toothpicks. You should end up with about 24 to 30 rolls.

Next, melt half the butter in a large skillet over medium heat. Stir in 2 Tbsp (30 mL) of the brown sugar and, working in batches, place the rolls in the pan for 4 to 5 minutes each, turning to coat evenly. First, cook with the seam side (the side secured with toothpicks) up; when ready to turn, remove the toothpicks and cook the roll seam side down. Adding more butter and sugar as needed, continue until all rolls are coated. Arrange the rolls closely together, seam sides down, over the cabbage leaves that are lining the baking dishes.

Preheat the oven to 325°F (160°C).

In a small bowl, whisk together the flour and remaining consommé until smooth. Stir into the skillet and add the onions, tomatoes, tomato sauce, vinegar, Worcestershire sauce, salt, pepper, and any butter and sugar that were not used to coat the rolls. Bring to a boil over medium-high heat. Once boiling, turn the heat down to medium-low and cook, stirring, until slightly thickened, 3 to 5 minutes.

Pour the sauce over the cabbage rolls and bake, covered, until the cabbage is tender, about 2½ hours.

CAULIFLOWER STEAKS

WITH ROASTED BONE MARROW BUTTER

This is another gem from our friends at Sidewalk Citizen Bakery in Calgary, Alberta (page 28), developed by their head chef, Colin Metcalfe. The recipe makes more butter than you'll likely need, so we'll just go ahead and say *you're welcome*. In addition to tasting great on fried or roasted brassica vegetables, it's also perfect for spreading on toasted bread, tossing with hot pasta, and even drizzling over popcorn!

Bone marrow can be easily sourced from your butcher—if the bones are whole, ask for them to be sliced lengthwise, for easier roasting. This dish is best served with Herb Salad with Pickled Shallots (page 174).

SERVES 4

BONE MARROW BUTTER

1 large beef bone, halved
1⁄3 cup (80 mL) unsalted butter, room temperature
1 clove garlic, finely minced
1 Tbsp (15 mL) finely chopped chives
1 Tbsp (15 mL) freshly squeezed lemon juice
1 tsp (5 mL) salt
1⁄8 tsp freshly ground black pepper

SOURDOUGH BREAD CRUMBS

4 big slices (about 200 g) day-old sourdough bread
2 Tbsp (30 mL) extra virgin olive oil
1⁄8 tsp salt
1⁄8 tsp freshly ground black pepper

ROASTED CAULIFLOWER STEAKS

1 large head (about 680 g) cauliflower
2 Tbsp (30 mL) grapeseed oil
Salt and freshly ground black pepper

FOR SERVING

Herb Salad with Pickled Shallots (page 174)

Preheat the oven to 350°F (180°C) and line a baking sheet with tinfoil. Place the bone halves, marrow side up, on the prepared sheet, and roast for about 15 to 20 minutes, until the marrow is soft and the bones are lightly browned. Cool slightly, scoop the marrow out—you should have about 2 ounces (56 grams)—and let cool to room temperature.

In a stand mixer, with electric beaters, or by hand, mix the cooled marrow, butter, garlic, chives, lemon juice, salt, and pepper until smooth. Season with salt and pepper to taste.

Lay a 12-inch-long (30 cm) sheet of plastic food wrap on the counter. Fold the wrap around the butter mixture, twisting both ends of the wrap. Gently shape into an even cylinder and refrigerate for 1 hour. Once set, slice into 1⁄4-inch (6 mm) rounds and return to the refrigerator until needed.

For the sourdough crumbs, tear the bread into bite-sized pieces. Warm a pan over medium-low heat. Once the pan is hot, add the oil and torn bread. Toss to combine and let this toast in the pan until light brown, about 4 to 5 minutes. Season with salt and pepper. Remove from the heat and let the bread cool to room temperature. Place in a food processor and pulse until the bread has turned into coarse crumbs. Set aside until needed. The bread crumbs can be made a few days ahead and stored in an airtight container.

For the steaks, cut the cauliflower from top to bottom into slices about 1 inch (2.5 cm) thick. Warm the oil in a large pan over medium heat (to cook all the steaks at once, you might want to get another pan going as well). Season the steaks on both sides with salt and pepper, then sear them on one side until nicely browned, about 3 to 5 minutes. Flip over and repeat. Remove from the pan and, while still hot, top with the bone marrow butter. Sprinkle liberally with the bread crumbs and serve with a small portion of Herb Salad with Pickled Shallots (page 174) on the side.

CHOCOLATE RAVIOLI

WITH CIDER-BRAISED OXTAIL

We met the EVOO restaurant team during Montréal en Lumière, the city's annual winter festival. They're all about using Canadian ingredients in creative ways, like the candy cap mushroom ice cream with candied cedar they served us for dessert.

For this ravioli, they braise the oxtail in their favourite Quebec apple cider—La Face Cachée de la Pomme—but you can use whatever is available in your area. A note: this rich, flavourful recipe is time consuming—a project for the more adventurous cook! We'd recommend making the filling the day before, and you'll want to have a pasta maker on hand for rolling out the dough. The sheets of earthy, cocoa-flavoured pasta look like strips of stained walnut, and they complement the flavour of the braised oxtail brilliantly.

SERVES 4 TO 6

FILLING

- 4 cups (1 L) chicken stock
- 3 Tbsp (45 mL) extra virgin olive oil, divided
- One 2-pound (910 g) oxtail, halved
- 1 medium yellow onion (about 160 g), coarsely chopped
- 4 cloves garlic, crushed
- 2 large carrots (about 140 g), sliced lengthwise in half
- 2 stalks celery (about 150 g), chopped
- 1 Tbsp (15 mL) tomato paste
- 1 Tbsp (15 mL) finely chopped fresh ginger
- 4 bay leaves
- 3 sprigs fresh thyme
- 1 cup (250 mL) good-quality apple cider (sparkling, if available), divided
- 1½ tsp (7 mL) salt
- ¼ tsp (1 mL) freshly ground black pepper
- ¼ cup (60 mL) unsalted butter
- 1 large shallot (about 70 g), finely chopped

RAVIOLI DOUGH

- 2¼ cups (337 g) all-purpose or Italian "00" flour (see note on page 6)
- ½ cup (40 g) cocoa powder
- 15 egg yolks
- 1 whole egg

FOR SERVING

- Grated Parmigiano-Reggiano

See overleaf for preparation ▶

Preheat the oven to 375°F (190°C).

Pour the chicken stock into a small pot and bring to a simmer. Remove from heat.

Heat 2 Tbsp (30 mL) olive oil in a large pot or Dutch oven over medium-high and sear the oxtail on all sides until golden brown, about 10 minutes. Remove the oxtail and add the onion, garlic, carrots, and celery. Cook until lightly coloured, about 5 minutes. Add the tomato paste, ginger, bay leaves, thyme, and 1/2 cup (125 mL) cider and cook for 2 minutes. Add the warm chicken stock.

Place the oxtail back in the pot, add the salt and pepper, and bring to a boil. Once boiling, cover and place in the preheated oven for 30 minutes, then lower the heat to 280°F (138°C). Braise for about 5 to 6 hours, or until the meat is falling off the bone. Remove the oxtail from the pot, let cool, and remove all the meat from the bones. Strain and reserve the braising liquid.

To make the ravioli filling, melt the butter in a large pot over medium-low heat. Add the shallot and cook slowly until tender, about 5 minutes. Add the reserved braising liquid and remaining 1/2 cup (125 mL) of cider and reduce by half, about 20 to 30 minutes. Cool slightly. Pour half of this cider mixture (reserving the other half) into a bowl with the oxtail meat, and combine. You'll want the mix to be flavourful and slightly moist. It should hold together in tablespoon-sized portions. Taste and season with extra salt if desired.

Make the pasta according to the instructions on page 6. Once it's all rolled out, cut the pieces into 4- × 10-inch (10 × 25 cm) strips. Working with two strips at a time (and keeping the others dusted with flour and covered with a barely damp tea towel), place 1 Tbsp (15 mL) portions of the oxtail filling on one strip, about 3/4 inch (2 cm) apart (about four per strip). With a pastry brush, lightly brush water along all four edges of the strip as well as in the spaces between the filling. Place a second strip of pasta on top and press down evenly over the filling. Try to avoid air pockets between the filling and sealed edges. Once sealed, use a ravioli cutter (or knife) to cut the ravioli apart and trim the edges. Dust with a little more flour and store on a baking sheet covered with a barely damp tea towel. You should end up with about 24 to 30 filled ravioli.

When ready to eat, bring a large pot of salted water to a boil and warm up the rest of the cider mixture in a large pan. Drop the ravioli, about 10 at a time, into the boiling water and stir gently, making sure they don't stick. Let cook about 3 to 5 minutes, then pull one out and cut off the corner. Check it for doneness—it should be al dente. Cook a few more minutes if needed. Scoop out the cooked ravioli with a slotted spoon and continue with the next batch. Add the cooked ravioli to a pan with a few spoonfuls of the remaining cider mixture. Gently toss together and cook for 1 or 2 minutes. Serve immediately, topped with grated Parmigiano-Reggiano.

Fishing in Newfoundland

Fishing was once *the* way of life in Newfoundland, but the 1992 cod moratorium changed the island forever. Now there are more Newfoundlanders working in Northern Alberta than on fishing boats in their native province, and rural towns have been forced to reinvent their economies or face relocation. While fishing used to sustain numerous small communities, Newfoundlanders at the time of our visit were allowed to catch a limited number of cod during just three, week-long "food fisheries" per year.

We had two opportunities to meet fishermen in Newfoundland—David in Twillingate and Bruce in New Bonaventure—and both times we headed out on open water. From these experiences, we learned several things:

- ★ Fishers in Newfoundland, at least the two we met, are genuine characters.
- ★ The Atlantic is very wobbly, and neither of us is destined to become a long-term sailor.
- ★ We love dressing up in 12 layers of oversized fishing gear. It is amusing *every* time.

On our trip with David in Twillingate, he first bundled us in the warmest clothes he could find. Out on the water, he convinced us to let him tie our GoPro to a fishing line and lower it 27 metres (90 feet) to the bottom. The footage revealed fascinating (and dizzying) shots of the Atlantic's "cod highway."

Our trip with Bruce in New Bonaventure coincided with one of the three fisheries, so we got to "jig" for fish using the traditional hand-pulled hook-and-line method. Each time, the hook rested no longer than 30 seconds on the bottom before snagging a cod, which came up fat and thrashing into the boat. Back on shore, Bruce taught us how to gut and fillet the fish and remove the highly prized tongues from the fish head, which are typically floured and pan-fried.

Communities like New Bonaventure, with their winsome old homes and stilted fish shacks, are fewer and farther between, but they are still vital to the province's character. Nestled in along Newfoundland's dramatic coast, they were some of the most welcoming communities we've ever encountered. We recommend visiting as many of them as you can.

JIGGS DINNER

Off the northeast coast of Newfoundland lies Fogo Island, a place which to us has a sort of mythical air about it. It's rugged, dense with history, and now home to the acclaimed Fogo Island Inn. While we couldn't make it to the island itself, we did get to meet the inn's executive chef, Murray McDonald, and taste his food at the Roots, Rants, and Roars Festival in Elliston. Here, Chef McDonald kindly shares his recipe for one of the most classic of Newfoundland dishes: Jiggs Dinner. When done right, it's comfort food at its best, with a broth so flavourful we would happily consume it all winter long. The salt (or corned) beef needs to be soaked overnight, so plan accordingly.

SERVES 4 TO 6

1½ pounds (680 g) salt or corned beef
½ cup (125 mL) dried yellow split peas
1 small cabbage (about 450 g), cut into 6 wedges
1 small yellow onion (about 120 g), peeled and left whole
1 turnip (about 150 g), peeled and cut into 6 wedges
3 large carrots (about 210 g), peeled and cut in half lengthwise
3 medium potatoes (about 360 g), peeled
3 large parsnips (about 210 g), peeled
1 Tbsp (15 mL) unsalted butter
⅛ tsp freshly ground black pepper

FOR SERVING

Mustard pickles, Pickled Northern Beets (page 248), and/or grainy mustard

Soak the salt beef in cold water for 8 to 10 hours (or overnight), then drain.

Put the split peas in a cloth pudding bag or tied in a few layers of cheesecloth, leaving room for expansion. Place the soaked beef in a large pot and add the bag with the peas, fastening the bag to the handle of the pot. Cover with water, bring to a boil, then lower the heat and let simmer for 2 hours.

After the beef and peas have simmered, add the cabbage and onion and let cook for 20 minutes. Add the turnip and carrots and simmer for 20 minutes more. Add the potatoes and parsnips and cook until tender.

Remove the split pea bag from the pot and turn the peas out into a small bowl. Mix with the butter and black pepper and cover with foil until it's time to eat. Remove the salt beef and vegetables (excluding the onion) from the pot.

Reduce the cooking liquid over high heat for 15 minutes, or until it has become a flavourful jus.

While the cooking liquid is reducing, slice the beef and arrange neatly with the vegetables on a platter. When ready to eat, serve the peas in a side dish and pour the reduced cooking liquid over the dinner like a pan jus. Serve with homemade mustard pickles, pickled beets, and/or some grainy mustard.

ROAST TURKEY

WITH SAUSAGE & APPLE STUFFING

For both of us, there are few meals more comforting than turkey and stuffing. Our friend Debbie Levy is a chef, cheese expert, and mother to three grown children. Each Thanksgiving and Christmas, she, her husband Andrew, and their kids convene to cook dinner together, and they enthusiastically agreed to share this beloved family recipe. One of their tricks is starting the turkey with the breast side down at a high temperature, which helps distribute the juices evenly and keeps the breast moist. Silicone gloves are key for flipping it! If you're concerned about leftover stuffing "availability," do as the Levys do and make a double or triple batch. Whatever doesn't fit in the turkey can be cooked in tinfoil separately. The stuffing can be made a day ahead and kept in the refrigerator.

SERVES 12 TO 14

FOR THE STUFFING (ONE BATCH)

- 20 large slices good-quality white bread, left out overnight to dry
- 3/4 pound (340 g) sweet Italian sausage
- 2 Tbsp (30 mL) unsalted butter
- 1 large yellow onion (about 220 g), diced
- 2 stalks celery (about 150 g), chopped
- 3/4 pound (340 g) mushrooms, chopped
- 1 medium tart apple (200 g), peeled, cored, and diced
- 1/3 cup (80 mL) chopped flat-leaf parsley
- 1 tsp (5 mL) dried sage
- 1 tsp (5 mL) dried thyme
- 2 tsp (10 mL) dried rosemary
- 1/2 cup (125 mL) chicken broth (only needed if doubling the batch)
- Salt and freshly ground black pepper

FOR THE TURKEY

- One 12- to 15-pound (5.5 to 7 kg) turkey
- 6 Tbsp (90 mL) unsalted butter, melted and divided
- 1 tsp (5 mL) dried thyme
- 1 tsp (5 mL) dried sage
- 1 tsp (5 mL) dried marjoram
- 1 tsp (5 mL) salt
- 1 tsp (5 mL) freshly ground black pepper

See overleaf for preparation ▶

Break the dried bread slices into bite-sized pieces.

Remove the sausage from its casing and cook in a frying pan over medium-high heat, breaking it into small pieces with a wooden spoon. Once cooked, remove from the pan and set aside, reserving the fat.

In a large pot, add the reserved sausage fat and melt the butter over medium heat, then sauté the onions until cooked. Add the celery and mushrooms and cook until slightly softened, about 4 to 5 minutes. Add the apple and cook for 3 more minutes. Remove from the heat and add the bread, sausage, parsley, sage, thyme, and rosemary. Stir well to combine, and season with salt and pepper to taste. Add more parsley and dried herbs if desired. If making the stuffing a day ahead, cover and refrigerate overnight.

When you're ready to cook the turkey, preheat the oven to 425°F (220°C). Rinse out the cavity and pat it dry. Fill the turkey with stuffing and truss the legs. If you're doubling the stuffing recipe, mix ¼ to ½ cup (60 to 125 mL) of chicken stock into the extra stuffing just before you bake it. It won't be baked inside the turkey and therefore needs the extra moisture. Transfer it to a casserole dish or wrap up in tinfoil.

Brush 4 Tbsp (60 mL) of the melted butter over the turkey. Sprinkle with the thyme, sage, marjoram, salt, and pepper. Also brush some extra melted butter on the rack so the turkey doesn't stick.

Place the turkey, breast side down, on the rack. Transfer to the oven and roast for 15 minutes. Take it out, brush with the remaining 2 Tbsp (30 mL) of melted butter, and return to the oven for another 15 minutes.

Turn the heat down to 325°F (160°C) and remove the turkey from the oven. Using silicone gloves (or something else that will allow you to handle it securely), flip the turkey over so it is breast side up and return to the oven. Basting about every 30 minutes, cook it for about 2½ hours for a 12-pound (5.5 kg) bird, or longer, depending on its size. When cooked, the internal temperature should register 165°F (74°C), though it will come up to 170°F (77°C) while resting. If the turkey is browning too quickly, simply cover it loosely with a tinfoil tent. Put the extra stuffing in the oven about 1 hour before you'd like to eat.

When done, remove the turkey from the pan and cover loosely with foil. Let it rest for at least 20 minutes before scooping out the stuffing and carving the meat. Don't forget to reserve the leftover drippings for gravy!

WILD BOAR & FIG MEATBALLS

This recipe comes from Chef Tim Davies of the Willow on Wascana, one of Regina's premier restaurants. It features wild boar, an animal so abundant in Saskatchewan that hunting them is actually encouraged. These meatballs are rich, with an earthy crunch, and should be served with plenty of bread for sopping up the sauce. Leftovers can (and should) be used to make meatball subs the next day!

SERVES 4 TO 5

SAUCE

3 Tbsp (45 mL) extra virgin olive oil
8 cloves garlic, thinly sliced
Two 28-ounce (796 mL) cans of whole tomatoes, with juice
2 tsp (10 mL) salt

MEATBALLS

2 whole cloves
1/2 tsp (2 mL) fennel seeds
1/4 tsp (1 mL) whole mustard seeds
3 cloves garlic, minced
1 Tbsp (15 mL) finely chopped fresh rosemary
5 to 6 dried figs (about 40 g), finely chopped
3 Tbsp (45 mL) finely chopped walnuts
1/4 cup (60 mL) Parmigiano-Reggiano or Grana Padano, grated then measured
1/2 cup (125 mL) dried bread crumbs
2 Tbsp (30 mL) Dijon mustard
2 Tbsp (30 mL) salt
1 1/2 tsp (7 mL) freshly ground black pepper
2 Tbsp (30 mL) ice water
2 eggs
1 pound (454 g) ground wild boar, or a 50/50 mixture of ground pork and lean ground beef

FOR SERVING

Fresh bread
Grated Parmigiano-Reggiano or Grana Padano

Preheat the oven to 350°F (180°C).

To make the sauce, heat the olive oil and garlic in a medium saucepan. Once fragrant, add the tomatoes and salt. Bring to a boil, lower the heat, and let simmer, occasionally stirring. Use a wooden spoon to break down the tomatoes. Let cook until thick and saucy, about 60 minutes.

To make the meatballs, first add the cloves, fennel seeds, and mustard seeds to a small baking tray. When the oven is hot, toast the spices for 5 minutes, until fragrant and slightly darker. Remove, let cool, and grind with a mortar and pestle or spice grinder.

Turn the oven down to 325°F (160°C).

In a medium bowl, mix together the toasted ground spices, garlic, rosemary, figs, walnuts, cheese, bread crumbs, mustard, salt, pepper, and water. In a small bowl, lightly beat the eggs with a fork. Add them to the mixture along with the ground wild boar. Gently mix until just combined.

Divide the mixture into 10 to 12 even portions and shape into balls. Place in an ovenproof dish (they should fit snugly) and cover with the prepared tomato sauce. Bake in the preheated oven until firm, about 35 to 40 minutes. Top with extra Parmigiano-Reggiano and serve with slices of toasted bread.

Fins & Scales

SEAFOOD MAINS

SPICY HADDOCK & SNOW CRAB CAKES

This recipe is from Bryan Picard, one of our favourite East Coast chefs. We met Bryan when he was running the kitchen at the Chanterelle Country Inn on Cape Breton Island and cooked us a Thanksgiving feast. He now runs his own 12-seat restaurant, the Bite House, in an old farmhouse just outside of Baddeck. Since we love Bryan's food and also ate so *many fish cakes* on the East Coast, it's fitting we can share his go-to version. If you can't get haddock in your area, just use another mild white fish. To keep it classic, serve with some Green Tomato Chow Chow (page 252) on the side.

SERVES 4

FISH CAKES

- 2 tsp (10 mL) extra virgin olive oil, plus more for frying the cakes
- 1/4 cup (60 mL) dry white wine
- 9 ounces (250 g) haddock, or any other mild white fish
- 1 pound (454 g) potatoes, peeled and coarsely chopped
- 1 1/2 cups (375 mL) cooked snow or Dungeness crab meat (optional; see note)
- 4 to 5 green onions (60 to 75 g), finely chopped
- 1/4 cup (60 mL) chopped flat-leaf parsley
- 2 Tbsp (30 mL) freshly squeezed lemon juice
- Generous dash hot sauce
- 1 tsp (5 mL) salt
- 1/4 tsp (1 mL) freshly ground black pepper
- 1 Tbsp (15 mL) all-purpose flour (optional)

AIOLI

- 1 egg yolk
- 1/2 tsp (2 mL) Dijon mustard
- 1 1/2 Tbsp (22 mL) freshly squeezed lemon juice, divided
- 1/8 tsp salt
- 1/2 cup (125 mL) extra virgin olive, sunflower, or canola oil
- 1 clove garlic, minced

FOR SERVING

- Lemon wedges

Note: If omitting the crab meat, double the amount of fish.

See overleaf for preparation ▶

Preheat the oven to 350°F (180°C).

Put the 2 tsp (10 mL) of oil and the wine in a baking dish. Add the haddock and sprinkle the fillets with a pinch of salt. Bake in the preheated oven for 15 to 20 minutes, or until the fish flakes apart easily. Remove from the oven and let cool.

While the fish is baking, add the potatoes to a medium pot and cover with cold water. Bring to a boil and cook until tender, about 20 minutes. Drain, coarsely mash, and set aside to cool.

In a medium bowl, mix the fish, crab, mashed potatoes, green onions, parsley, lemon juice, hot sauce, salt, and pepper. Adjust seasoning to taste. If the mixture does not form cakes easily, add the flour, 1 tsp (5 mL) at a time, until the mixture comes together. Season further with salt and pepper, if desired. Form 16 patties about 2 inches (5 cm) in diameter, and slightly flatten them. Set the patties aside in the refrigerator while you make the aioli.

You can make the aioli with a hand blender and a deep measuring cup or with a whisk and a large bowl. If you choose to whisk it by hand, be warned that it will be a bit of an arm workout, as you have to rapidly whisk with very few breaks. In either scenario, it's easiest with two people—one person blends or whisks while the other pours in the oil.

Blend (or whisk) the yolk, then mix in the mustard, half the lemon juice, and the salt. While blending/mixing constantly, add the oil in a steady stream. Once the oil has been incorporated, you'll have a nice, thick aioli. Stir in the rest of the lemon juice and garlic and season further, if desired. Keep in the refrigerator until needed. Fresh mayonnaise is good for 2 to 3 days if kept cool.

Heat some oil in a large pan. Once hot, cook the fish cakes a few at a time, being careful not to overcrowd the pan. Cook for 2 to 3 minutes on each side, until golden brown. Make sure to flip the cakes only once. Repeat until all the cakes are fried. Serve with the aioli, a squeeze of fresh lemon juice, and a cold beer.

KYUQUOT FIRE-ROASTED SOHA (SALMON)

On the northwest coast of Vancouver Island is the Kyuquot Checleset First Nation, with nearby Spring Island inhabited seasonally by West Coast Expeditions.

Lana Jules, a cook from Kyuquot, treks over to Spring Island about twice a week each summer to cook for the hungry guests and staff of WCE. It's a decades-long tradition she's carried on from her mother and now often does with her sister, Kathy. Lana prepares lavish feasts, with salmon caught locally and cooked the traditional way—over a fire. For you, Lana has generously shared her method for setting it all up! It's a fun project and a great way to cook outside. Lana uses cedar, but almost any wood will do just fine. She suggests serving this meal with potato salad and bannock (page 22), and while any species of salmon will work, it must be wild-caught!

SERVES 10 TO 12

One 3-foot-long (91 cm) cedar stick, about 2 to 3 inches (5 to 8 cm) in diameter
6 to 8 pieces of cedar kindling
6 to 9 feet (1.8 to 2.7 m) of hay wire, or another strong wire
Extra wood, to build the fire
1 whole fresh wild Pacific salmon, head removed, deboned, and filleted butterfly style (your fishmonger can do this for you)
1 Tbsp (15 mL) salt, or 2 to 3 Tbsp (30 to 45 mL) seasoning blend of your choice (try Spike seasoning)

Lana uses a cedar stick and kindling system to cook her butterflied fish, which spreads out the filleted salmon so it cooks evenly. Once you've found a sturdy cedar stick, use a hatchet to carefully split it in half lengthwise, stopping about 6 inches (15 cm) from the end. Secure this end tightly with hay wire to keep it from splitting all the way—essentially, it should look like a big clothespin, with one end open and one end secured.

Once your cooking tools are collected, the first thing you need to do is start a fire. This should be done at least 30 to 60 minutes before cooking the fish, as you'll need a bed of hot coals for it to cook. Once the coals are established, it's okay to add more logs to the fire and have flames, just as long as they aren't big enough to scorch the fish.

See overleaf for preparation ▶

Once the fire is established and burning down, season the flesh of the salmon with the seasoning blend and lay the split cedar on a flat surface. Lift up the top arm of the cedar stick and slide the butterflied salmon, skin side down, into the opening (it's like a large clothespin clamping down lengthwise on the fish). Next, slide in three or four pieces of kindling perpendicular to the main cedar stick, making sure they are evenly spaced across the flesh, about 5 to 6 inches (12 to 15 cm) apart. Carefully grip the two open ends of the cedar stick together and flip the whole thing over. Slide the remaining three or four kindling pieces over the skin into the grooves that the other kindling has created—you will now have half the kindling sticks pressed against the flesh side of the fish and half the kindling sticks pressed against the skin side. Secure the open end of the cedar stick with more wire. You should end up with a fully spread salmon fillet that's securely fastened within the cedar apparatus.

Once the fire and fish are ready, prop the fish up at about a 60-degree angle as close to the hot coals as possible but without letting it get hit directly by flames. On Spring Island they used a cinder block, but you can use a bench, a few extra pieces of wood, or large rocks. If you're on the beach, you can dig one end into the sand and prop it up that way. While these tools require a bit of prep, they can be reused for future salmon feasts.

Set the fish up so the skin is facing the fire first, and let it cook until the skin turns crispy and starts to brown, about 30 minutes. You'll know the fish is cooking once it starts dripping. Once crisp, flip the fish and cook the flesh side until the surface no longer looks raw and the fish flakes apart easily, about 10 to 15 minutes. Cooking times can vary depending on the size of the fish and the fire, so make sure to check on it every few minutes.

Remove the fish from the fire, slide it out of its cedar set-up, cut into pieces, and serve.

CRISPY TROUT RICE BOWLS

WITH WILTED SUMMER GREENS & KIMCHI SAUCE

Lindsay met Michael Soucy while working at Janice Beaton Fine Cheese in Calgary; the two of them talked a lot about cheese and found each other hilarious. A trained chef and avid gardener, Mike now owns Seed + Soil, a farm dedicated to growing uncommon produce on small pieces of land in and around Calgary. Mike is one of Lindsay's favourite cooks in the whole world, and since he has a particular knack for cooking with Asian ingredients, he agreed to develop a rice bowl recipe for us. This one is simple to prepare and shows off Mike's greatest culinary love: fresh summer vegetables.

SERVES 4

1½ cups (375 mL) white, brown, or red rice
4 trout or salmon fillets, ½ pound (227 g) each, deboned and skin on
¼ cup (60 mL) soy sauce, plus extra to finish
2 Tbsp (30 mL) rice wine vinegar
1 jalapeño pepper (about 14 g), sliced (plus more for garnish, if you like)
4 cloves garlic, minced and divided
3 Tbsp (45 mL) minced fresh ginger, divided
¾ cup (185 mL) kimchi
¾ cup (185 mL) mayonnaise
4 Tbsp (60 mL) sesame oil, extra virgin coconut oil, or vegetable oil, divided
8 cups (about 2L) roughly chopped summer greens (see note)

FOR SERVING

Sliced radishes, summer squash, herbs, trout roe, seaweed, fried shallots, fried eggs, chopped green onions, sprouts, pea shoots, black sesame seeds

Cook the rice and keep warm until ready to serve.

Lay the trout fillets skin side down in a small casserole dish. Combine the soy sauce, vinegar, sliced jalapeño, 2 cloves of garlic, and 2 Tbsp (30 mL) of ginger and pour over the fillets. Let sit for at least 20 minutes in the refrigerator, turning over a few times. Remove from the marinade, pat with paper towel, and leave on the paper towel to dry, skin side down.

To prepare the sauce, put the kimchi and mayonnaise in a blender or food processor and process until smooth.

Add 2 Tbsp (30 mL) of oil to a large frying pan and heat over medium-high. Add the fish to the pan, skin side down, shaking the pan right away to make sure the trout doesn't stick. Allow to cook for 2 to 3 minutes (or longer for thicker fillets), continuing to shake the pan occasionally. Flip the fish over and cook for another 30 seconds, flesh side down. Remove from the heat and put on a plate, skin side up.

In the same pan, over medium-high heat, add the remaining 2 Tbsp (30 mL) of oil as well as the remaining garlic and ginger. Cook for 20 seconds, then add the greens. Cook until barely wilted. Hit with a dash of soy sauce and remove from the heat.

Divide the rice between four bowls. Top with the wilted greens, a few dollops of kimchi sauce, the crispy trout, and any desired garnishes.

Note: Any combination of fresh summer greens works well for this. We especially love radish tops, chards, beet tops, mustard greens, and kale.

SEARED SCALLOPS

WITH BLACK CURRANT PEAR SALSA

We visited Prince Edward Island in the fall, a time when all the trees are gold, orange, and red and the island is nearly tourist-free. It's also a time, however, when many of the restaurants close for the season, so despite being told, "You MUST visit the Pearl Eatery! It's incredible!" we could not. Fortunately for us, although the PEI institution in North Rustico was done for the season, their team still agreed to contribute to the book. This recipe comes from Chef Trisha Gordon and is our new favourite way to eat scallops. It's okay if you finish them before you finish the salsa; it's so good, you'll want to eat it with a spoon.

SERVES 4

SALSA

¼ cup + 2 Tbsp (90 mL) fresh black currants, or ¼ cup (60 mL) dried currants
1 medium firm ripe pear (about 150 g), finely diced
1 small shallot (about 40 g), finely minced
½ small jalapeño (about 7 g), seeds and ribs removed, finely diced
1 green onion (about 15 g), finely chopped
¼ small red bell pepper (40 g), finely diced
2 Tbsp (30 mL) freshly squeezed lime juice
1 tsp (5 mL) fresh lime zest
½ Tbsp (7 mL) honey
⅛ tsp salt

SCALLOPS

1 pound (454 g) scallops or halibut cheeks
¼ tsp (1 mL) salt
2 Tbsp (30 mL) canola oil
2 tsp (10 mL) unsalted butter

If using dried currants, place them in a medium bowl and pour enough hot water overtop to submerge them. Let sit for 5 to 10 minutes or until they have plumped up, then drain the water.

For the salsa, combine the pear, currants, shallot, jalapeño, green onion, red pepper, lime juice, lime zest, and honey in a bowl and season with salt to taste. This can be made a day ahead and stored in the refrigerator, but it is best consumed within 2 days.

Using paper towel, pat the scallops dry and season both sides with salt. Heat a large skillet over medium-high until very hot, then add the oil and butter. When the pan begins to smoke, add the scallops and sear until golden brown on the bottom, with the top three-quarters of the scallops remaining translucent, about 2 minutes.

Remove from the heat and flip the scallops to finish cooking on the other side, another 30 seconds to 1 minute. The scallops should still be visibly translucent in the centre when ready (halibut cheeks should no longer be translucent when ready). Serve immediately with the black currant pear salsa.

Manitoba

While it wasn't our original plan, we ended up travelling through Manitoba by car, train, *and* plane over two seasons. We first visited in the summer, when the province is baking hot and everyone retreats to the lakes. We made our way through Riding Mountain National Park, then headed to Kelwood, a small community with one well-loved hockey rink ("Home of the Old Puckers"), a legion, a café, and a handful of tidy homes. At an event called Supper in the Field, we feasted on a dinner made by farmers and producers from the area, then drank coffee sweetened with birch syrup and hung out at the Harvest Sun Music Festival.

Farther south, the province's capital charmed us thoroughly, especially when it came to food. Who knew we'd become obsessed with vegan burgers in Winnipeg? Or that, in winter, local chefs launch a pop-up restaurant in a large tent set up directly on the frozen river? Manitobans can make a party *anywhere*.

Close to the end of our trip we visited again, just as the province's famously cold winter was approaching. This time we parked our car in Winnipeg, boarded a Via Rail train, and headed north. Though initially worried the 48-hour journey to Churchill would be boring, we soon became the world's biggest fans of Arctic-bound travel by rail. We read, drank tea, stared out at the snow-covered landscape, and were rocked to sleep each night in beds that descended from the ceiling of our 1960s-era cabin.

In Churchill, we spotted an Arctic fox on our very first morning, and we quickly found our way to Gypsy's, a restaurant famous for its golden apple fritters. Bundled in parkas and the warmest long underwear we could find, we joined a tour to see polar bears, which we found a long way out on the windy tundra. Seeing those bears in the wild was a privilege we couldn't believe then, never mind now. We spent our evenings warming up by fireplaces, our fingers wrapped around hot mugs and bellies filled with local specialties like muskox rouladen and wild rice burgers. Unlike four months earlier in the Yukon, where the sun stayed late into the night, we watched it begin its descent in Churchill every afternoon around 3 pm.

Manitoba was our gateway to Ontario and Nunavut, and both times we left feeling dumbfounded by what we'd seen. There aren't too many places in the world where you can get a sunburn in the summer and just a few months later go on an Arctic adventure . . .

COD & COLD WATER SHRIMP GRATIN

Todd Perrin is one of Newfoundland's (and Canada's) most beloved chefs. He's an easygoing guy who champions food from the Rock at his award-winning restaurant in Quidi Vidi, Mallard Cottage, and he has always made time for the two of us.

We asked him for a cod recipe for the book, not only because it gave us an excuse to say "the cod from Todd!" as often as we liked, but because we couldn't imagine a better person to handle this iconic Atlantic ingredient. The cod moratorium in Newfoundland has been lifted enough that the fish is back on people's plates regularly—in this case baked with cold water shrimp in a creamy sauce and topped with crispy bread crumbs. This is Todd's take on Newfoundland's classic cod au gratin.

SERVES 4

2 Tbsp (30 mL) unsalted butter
2 Tbsp (30 mL) all-purpose flour
1¼ cups (310 mL) whole milk
1 Tbsp (15 mL) Dijon mustard
½ tsp (2 mL) dried savory
½ tsp (2 mL) salt
⅛ tsp freshly ground black pepper
4 fresh cod fillets (Pacific or Atlantic), about ½ pound (227 g) each, or another mild white fish
½ cup (125 mL) shelled cold water shrimp, cooked and drained
¼ cup (60 mL) grated Gruyère
1 cup (250 mL) grated mild cheddar, divided
½ cup (125 mL) dried bread crumbs or fresh bread crumbs, toasted
2 tsp (10 mL) extra virgin olive oil

Preheat the oven to 350°F (180°C). Grease a 9- × 9-inch (23 × 23 cm) baking dish or four individual gratin dishes.

Melt the butter in a medium pot over medium heat, whisk in the flour, and cook together for 2 minutes. Slowly pour in the milk, whisking constantly, and continue to stir until the sauce thickens. Add the mustard, savory, salt, and pepper. Taste and add more salt and pepper if desired. Remove from the heat.

Arrange the fish and cooked shrimp on the bottom of the prepared baking dish, or divide them equally in the individual gratin dishes. Place the sauce back on medium heat and whisk in the Gruyère. As soon as it's combined, pour the sauce evenly over the fish. Top with ¾ cup (185 mL) of the cheddar.

Mix the bread crumbs with the olive oil (and an extra ½ tsp/2 mL of savory, if you'd like) and sprinkle evenly over the gratin. Top with the remaining ¼ cup (60 mL) of cheese. Bake for 45 to 50 minutes, or until the gratin is bubbling and the top has browned evenly. Individual gratin dishes should take about 25 to 30 minutes—just carefully check the centre with a paring knife to ensure the fish has fully cooked. Serve immediately.

HAIDA GWAII HALIBUT BAKE

WITH SEA ASPARAGUS

On Haida Gwaii, we had one of the most memorable seafood meals of our trip. Keenawii's Kitchen is a dinner event put on by Haida chef Roberta Olsen in Skidegate; diners visit her oceanside home and eat food she has collected from the forests, farmers' markets, and ocean shores of her community. We ate at least 15 different kinds of seafood with Roberta, from dried herring roe on kelp and seafood chowder to freshly smoked black cod. As we tucked into a plate of octopus, she pointed outside to where it had been wrangled from below a rock.

We based this halibut dish on one Roberta served us. Sea asparagus carpets the beaches of Haida Gwaii in the spring and summer, though elsewhere you're more likely to find it at farmers' markets and in some grocery stores.

SERVES 4

2 Tbsp (30 mL) unsalted butter
¼ cup (60 mL) all-purpose flour
1½ cups (375 mL) whole milk
½ cup (125 mL) buttermilk
1 tsp (5 mL) mustard powder
1 tsp (5 mL) salt
⅛ tsp freshly ground black pepper
1 medium yellow onion (about 160 g), thinly sliced
4 tsp (20 mL) extra virgin olive oil, divided (plus 1 tsp/5 mL if using capers)
4 halibut fillets, ⅓ pound (150 g) each, or another firm white fish
1 cup (250 mL) sea asparagus, or ¼ cup (60 mL) drained capers

FOR SERVING

Brown, white, or wild rice, cooked
1 Tbsp (15 mL) chopped fresh dill
1 lemon, quartered

Preheat the oven to 350°F (180°C).

Melt the butter in a medium saucepan over medium-low heat. Whisk in the flour until smooth and continue to whisk for 1 minute, or until it's bubbling. Mix in the milk in ¼-cup (60 mL) increments, whisking constantly. Cook for 3 to 4 minutes, until the mixture is bubbling and thickened. Remove from the heat and whisk in the buttermilk, mustard powder, salt, and pepper. Taste and season further if desired. You can prepare this sauce ahead of time, too (see note).

Sauté the onions with 2 tsp (10 mL) of olive oil on medium-low heat until golden and soft. Place the halibut fillets in a baking dish and cover with the onions and prepared sauce. Bake for 25 to 30 minutes or until the fish flakes apart easily.

Right before serving, heat the remaining 2 tsp (10 mL) of olive oil over medium heat. When hot, sauté the sea asparagus for about 1 minute, just until they've turned a more vibrant green. If you're using capers, heat 1 tsp (5 mL) of olive oil over medium heat and sauté until the capers are crispy, 5 to 7 minutes.

Serve the halibut over rice topped with the sea asparagus, dill, and a squeeze of fresh lemon juice.

Note: If you're making this sauce ahead, prepare it as directed, then cover and chill in an airtight container. When you're ready to finish the dish, simply reheat it over medium heat in a saucepan with 2 Tbsp (30 mL) of milk (or more, if needed), whisking constantly.

PICKEREL IN PARCHMENT

It was the height of summer when we reached Wasagaming, a popular destination for Manitobans. After a day at Clear Lake, we recharged with a meal at Foxtail Café, a local favourite. This recipe is from Tyler Kaktins, the café's owner and chef, and combines the tradition of baking *en papillote* (in parchment) with pickerel, a prized lake fish. The simplicity of this recipe means that fresh, seasonal vegetables, high-quality olive oil, and good wine will all make a huge difference.

SERVES 4

¾ pound (340 g) local or new potatoes
4 small carrots (about 100 g), sliced into ¼-inch (6 mm) rounds
1 zucchini (about 200 g), sliced into ¼-inch (6 mm) rounds
1 to 2 green onions (about 15 to 30 g), finely chopped
2 Tbsp (30 mL) chopped fresh dill
4 cloves garlic, thinly sliced
4 pickerel fillets, about ¼ pound (113 g) each, or any mild white fish
2 garlic scapes
¼ cup (60 mL) dry white wine
¼ cup (60 mL) extra virgin olive oil
1 tsp (5 mL) salt
¼ tsp (1 mL) freshly ground black pepper
Parchment paper, for baking

Preheat the oven to 350°F (180°C).

Add the potatoes to a medium pot and cover with cold water. Set on high heat and let the water come to a boil. Cook until a paring knife can pierce the skin but the core of the potato still resists, about 10 minutes. Let cool and slice into ¼-inch (6 mm) rounds.

Lay out one large rectangular piece of parchment on a rimmed baking sheet (in landscape orientation rather than portrait orientation). Make sure it's large enough to hold all four fish fillets side by side, with enough extra to fold the parchment over the fish and vegetables (see note). Starting from the centre, line the parchment with the potato rounds, leaving a 2- to 3-inch (5 to 8 cm) border of parchment paper on the top and bottom, and a 10- to 12-inch (25 to 30 cm) border of parchment paper on either side. Add the carrots, zucchini, green onions, dill, and garlic. Top with the pickerel fillets and the two whole garlic scapes.

Drizzle the white wine and olive oil over the fish and season with salt and pepper. Crease and fold the two longer sides of the paper so they meet in the centre, and roll the two ends down toward the fish to make an envelope. Tightly fold in the shorter sides, rolling them toward the top of the package.

Place in the preheated oven and cook for 15 to 20 minutes, or until the fish is firm to touch (you can check this through the paper). Remove from the oven, unwrap, and serve immediately.

Note: You can also choose to make individually wrapped portions or packages with two fillets in each. If you do this, simply divide the vegetables and seasonings and distribute evenly among the parchment parcels.

ARCTIC CHAR SUSHI & TEMPURA

In Nunavut, we visited Kelly Lindell, a busy mother and well-known cook in Rankin Inlet. Born and raised in the territory, she left in her late teens to pursue culinary school on Prince Edward Island and later returned to her community to start a family and open a small canteen and catering business. At her home, she served us big platters of homemade sushi and an elegant partridgeberry cake. After many pieces of sushi and two slices of cake each, we understood why she has the culinary reputation she does.

This is her recipe, which features the slightly sweet flavour of Arctic char. For the additional fillings, you can use all the ingredients listed below, choose just a few, or substitute any others you'd like.

SERVES 4 TO 6

SUSHI RICE AND FILLINGS

- 1½ cups (375 mL) sushi rice
- ¼ cup (60 mL) white sugar
- ¼ cup (60 mL) rice vinegar (plus 1 Tbsp/15 mL for rolling)
- 1 large carrot (about 70 g), sliced into ¼-inch-thick (6 mm) strips
- 1 Tbsp (15 mL) sesame oil
- 1 Tbsp (15 mL) mayonnaise
- 1 fillet (7 oz or 200 g) sushi-grade Arctic char or salmon, skinned, deboned, and cut into thin strips
- Salt and freshly ground black pepper, for seasoning
- 1 tsp (5 mL) vegetable oil
- 2 eggs
- 1 English cucumber (about 300 g), sliced into ¼-inch-thick (6 mm) strips
- 1 avocado (about 170 g), thinly sliced
- 8 to 12 nori wraps

Bamboo sheet (or thick tea towel) and plastic food wrap, for rolling

TEMPURA

- ⅔ cup (160 mL) all-purpose flour
- ⅔ cup (160 mL) cornstarch
- 1 tsp (5 mL) baking soda
- 1 tsp (5 mL) baking powder
- 1 tsp (5 mL) salt
- 1 tsp (5 mL) white sugar (optional)
- ¾ cup (185 mL) cold water, or more if needed
- Canola oil, for frying
- 1 large sweet potato (about 250 g), peeled and thinly sliced into ¼-inch-thick (6 mm) strips

FOR SERVING

- Soy sauce, pickled ginger, and wasabi

See overleaf for preparation ▶

Cook the sushi rice according to the package instructions. Mix the sugar and vinegar together in a small bowl and pour over the cooked rice. Let the rice cool, stirring occasionally. Once cool, cover with a damp cloth to keep it from drying out, and set aside.

While the rice is cooking, bring a medium pot of water to a boil and fill a medium bowl with water and ice. Blanch the carrot strips for 60 seconds and remove to an ice bath. Once cool, remove from the bath and let dry on a tea towel. Mix the sesame oil and mayonnaise together in a small bowl. Dip the strips of char into the mixture and lay out on a plate. Sprinkle with salt and pepper and keep in the refrigerator until you're ready to make the rolls.

Put 1 tsp (5 mL) of oil in a skillet and set over medium heat. Beat the eggs in a small bowl and pour into the hot skillet. Cook until crispy on one side, then flip and remove from the heat. Once cool, cut the eggs into thin strips that are approximately the length of the nori wraps.

Next, make the tempura. For the batter, combine the flour, cornstarch, baking soda, baking powder, salt, and sugar in a medium bowl. Add the water and whisk until it's the consistency of a thin pancake batter. Add more water if necessary.

Fill a shallow frying pan or a small pot with ¼ inch (6 mm) of canola oil and heat over high heat. Line a large plate with paper towel. Once the oil is hot, dip the sweet potato strips in the batter, shake off the excess, and transfer to the hot oil. Fry until golden brown, about 1 minute on each side. Remove with tongs and set on the prepared plate.

When you're ready to roll the sushi, collect all the elements: the sushi rice, marinated char, fried egg strips, blanched carrots, cucumber strips, avocado slices, and sweet potato tempura. Prepare a small bowl of warm water mixed with 1 Tbsp (15 mL) of rice vinegar. Lay down the bamboo roller and cover in a large piece of plastic wrap. Lay a piece of nori, rough side up, over the plastic wrap.

With your hands, pat down a thin layer of rice over the seaweed, leaving about ½ inch (1 cm) at the top edge clear of rice. Dip your hands in the bowl of water and vinegar before grabbing more rice—this will make it easier to handle. Once the rice is spread out, add one-eighth of the filling ingredients in an even line along the bottom third of the seaweed wrap.

Using the bamboo mat and beginning from the side closest to you, roll up the sushi roll as tightly as possible. Once rolled, cut into 8 to 10 pieces. Repeat with the remaining nori wraps and ingredients.

Serve immediately with soy sauce, pickled ginger, and wasabi.

Caribou, Country Food & Paqqut

In Rankin Inlet, Nunavut, we watched the Arctic sun set early in the afternoon from the warm living room of Monica and Michael Shouldice. Monica grew up in Nunavut, and we listened for hours to her stories about life there. She was born on the remote tundra in a sod house built by her pregnant mother on the not-yet-frozen autumn ground. On a caribou skin and by the light of a *qulliq* (page 263), this resilient woman gave birth to Monica, alone, in the early spring.

Monica also told us all about "country food," the term given to plants and animals harvested from the Arctic land and sea that make up the traditional Inuit diet. During the summers when Monica was older, her mother took her and her siblings to the river. There, they intercepted the migrating caribou herd and caught and dried Arctic char, thus securing their food sources for the coming year. Even with increased access to food from the south, Monica continues these traditions annually.

The caribou is one of the most important animals in Inuit culture. Hides keep people warm in sub-zero temperatures, and all other parts of the animal are used in some way, much of it for food. *Paqqut*, one of the most fascinating delicacies we learned about, uses the most nutritious part of the caribou—the stomach. It is where all the grazed vegetation accumulates, and eating it provides something akin to eating vegetables. To make *paqqut*, the stomach lining is filled with the caribou's bone marrow, tied up, hung in the shade, and left to age for about seven days. The "bag" is then taken down, sliced like butter, and eaten with pieces of dried caribou.

Because all parts of the caribou are used, even the marrow-less bones are reserved. They are boiled to release their oils, producing a snow-white fat called *punnirniq*, traditionally eaten with dried meat, which we sampled at Monica's that afternoon.

SALAD OF CLAMS, SEAWEED & NEW POTATOES

When we began working on this book, a restaurant called Wild Caraway was recommended to us by John Eaton of Thinkers Lodge (see facing page). The restaurant once catered a dinner in the Lobster Factory, a gorgeous wooden building that served as the lodge's dining hall from 1930 to 1954. Based in Advocate Harbour, Nova Scotia, Wild Caraway also has several guest rooms in their old oceanside house. Chef Andrew Aitken is all about using local ingredients in innovative ways; we think this salad looks wonderfully similar to the coast on which it was created.

While fresh seaweed may not be readily available to you, you can often find dried dulse, sea lettuce, and other varieties in specialty grocery or health food stores.

SERVES 4

8 cups (2 L) water (optional, if the clams have not been cleaned)
4½ Tbsp (67 mL) salt (optional, if the clams have not been cleaned)
60 clams
1⅓ cups (330 mL) dry white wine, to steam
1 bay leaf
5 whole black peppercorns
1 small white onion (about 120 g), finely sliced
Handful of Scotch lovage or celery leaves, divided
3 ounces (85 g) fresh dulse, or 2 ounces (56 g) dried
2 ounces (56 g) fresh sea lettuce, or 1 ounce (28 g) dried
24 small new potatoes (about 800 g)
12 slices prosciutto or bacon (8.5 to 10.5 oz or 240 to 300 g)
1 cup (about 250 mL) half-and-half

If your clams have not yet been cleaned, fill a large bowl with 8 cups (2 L) of water and stir in the salt. First tap any partially open clams on the counter. If they do not close within several minutes, discard them, along with any that have cracked or broken shells. Place the clams in the salt water and let sit about 20 minutes. During this time, they should discard any sand trapped within them. Carefully pick them up out of the water and give them a quick scrub.

Bring the white wine to a boil in a large pot, then pour in the clams. Let them steam for about 10 minutes or until they open. Remove the clams and set them aside. Strain the remaining clam liquor out of the pot and reserve it. Add 1 cup (250 mL) of this liquor to a saucepan (reserving the rest for reheating the potatoes and clams) and add the bay leaf, peppercorns, onion, and half the lovage leaves. Boil for a few minutes to make an infusion and then strain, reserving the liquid.

Clean the fresh dulse and sea lettuce in a big bowl of salted water, or, if dried, rehydrate them in fresh water. Strain and reserve on paper towel.

Preheat the oven to 350°F (180°C).

Put the potatoes in a large pot of salted water. Bring to a boil and cook until tender enough that a paring knife can easily pierce through, about 15 minutes. Strain and set aside.

Bake the prosciutto or bacon on a baking sheet in the preheated oven until crispy, about 10 to 15 minutes.

To serve, reheat the potatoes in the reserved clam liquor (not the infusion), and in a separate pan, reheat the clams in the same way. Dress four plates (or one big platter) with seaweed in bite-sized pieces. To make the sauce, combine the infusion with the cream and bring it to just below a boil—but not over, or it may split. Arrange the potatoes and clams on top of the seaweed. Foam the clam sauce with an immersion blender, then spoon the foam and a little liquid over the potatoes and clams. Garnish with the remaining lovage leaves, top with the pieces of crispy prosciutto or bacon, and serve immediately.

Thinkers Lodge

In 1955, Bertrand Russell and Albert Einstein issued a manifesto urging scientists to discuss the imminent threat of nuclear weapons. Two years later, philanthropist Cyrus Eaton offered to host such an event, and from both sides of the Iron Curtain, the world's leading scientific thinkers came to his hometown of Pugwash, Nova Scotia. They gathered at an oceanfront family house he had earlier renamed Thinkers Lodge; the conference created a space for dialogue about the realities of a potential nuclear war and the scientists' responsibility to work toward its prevention. For their accomplishments in this sleepy Maritime town, they won a Nobel Peace Prize.

Fifty-six years later, because Lindsay's friend Kate's dad is friends with Cyrus Eaton's grandson John (got that?), we had the honour of staying in Thinkers Lodge for almost a week. We slept in the cozy old beds, sat on chairs donated by universities like Harvard and Louisville, pondered life from the most ponderable front porch in history, and ate our dinner each night next to an actual Nobel Peace Prize. It was the first place we'd spent more than three days since the road trip started, and it was sunny and educational seaside *bliss*.

Ontario

Ontario is a land of immense lakes and epic thunderstorms; within just a few days of being there, we had experienced both in a serious way.

After boating on Lake of the Woods and filling up on Finnish pancakes in Thunder Bay, we headed around Lake Superior as the sky began to darken. Already in a campsite and with no plan B, we set up our tent and fell asleep. At 3 am, we woke to deafening thunder, crackling sheets of lightning, and rain. *So much rain*. After lying for a few hours in a big puddle (it is the land of lakes, after all), we shoved our things into garbage bags and hit the road, stopping a few times (hello Giant Wawa Goose and Big Sudbury Nickel!) before reaching Midland, where friends were waiting for us with hot tea and dry beds. It was a storm like no other we'd experienced, and despite the waterlogged highways, we can say that Northern Ontario is as gorgeous as it is fierce.

From Midland we drove down the southeastern shore of Lake Huron, past the many beaches of Dana's youth, and arrived in her hometown of Sarnia. We ate perch fried by her Pake (grandfather) and french fries by the Bluewater Bridge.

Toronto was a whirlwind of tacos at Grand Electric; beer at Bellwoods Brewery; picnics in the park; fried chicken at Bar Isabel; cooking lessons with our friend's big Italian family; curry in Little India; and shopping in the abundant St. Lawrence Market and Distillery District.

We later retreated, as all good Torontonians do, to Prince Edward County. We spent the day biking from one tasty snack to the next and consuming plenty of wood-oven-fired pizza and wine at Norman Hardie Winery.

In Ottawa, guided by our blogger friend Kelly Brisson, we surrounded ourselves with great people who make great food. There were market visits and farm visits, one with new piglets playing in the mud and another with intimidatingly large elk. Having successfully journeyed through Canada's most densely populated province, we made our way toward its largest: Quebec . . .

PAN-FRIED WHITEFISH

WITH FIREWEED JELLY BEET GREENS

One common question we get asked about our trip is "How are you *still* friends?" We take pride in our answer: we're excellent travel companions who got along great. Mostly. There was that one time when we were camping in the Northwest Territories and were ill-equipped for an incoming thunderstorm. Each with our own stubborn determination to be right, we argued about the best way to secure a ridiculously small tarp over an already leaky tent. We finally reached an agreement, which was to pack up our belongings and escape to a picnic shelter instead. Once inside, we set up our sleeping bags on the concrete floor and started cooking. Somewhere between the smell of butter and frying fish, we were able to blame the tarp (the worst tarp *ever*) instead of each other and got back to our usual routine of (what we believe to be) incredibly witty banter.

For our dinner that night, we used fireweed jelly from the Yukon, produce from Hay River, and fish caught that day from Great Slave Lake. It turned out so well, we kept the recipe. The tarp, however, got tossed.

SERVES 4

SAUTÉED GREENS

- 3 Tbsp (45 mL) extra virgin olive oil or unsalted butter
- 1 medium yellow onion (about 160 g), sliced
- Beet greens and stems from 2 bunches beets (about 70 g) or 2 bunches chard (about 70 g), chopped, greens and stems separated
- 1½ tsp (7 mL) salt
- ½ tsp (2 mL) ground cumin
- 2 Tbsp (30 mL) fireweed or crabapple jelly
- 2 Tbsp (30 mL) freshly squeezed lemon juice

PAN-FRIED FISH

- 2 Tbsp (30 mL) unsalted butter, divided
- 4 whitefish fillets, ⅓ pound (150 g) each, or a white fish of your preference
- Salt and freshly ground black pepper

FOR SERVING

- Lemon wedges

Add the olive oil or butter to a large skillet and heat over medium. Once hot, add the sliced onion and chopped beet stems. Let cook until the onions are very soft and the stems are tender, about 10 minutes. Add the beet greens, salt, cumin, and jelly and stir to combine. Let the greens cook until they are wilted, about 2 minutes. Remove from the heat and stir in the lemon juice. Taste and season further, if desired, and transfer to a bowl or plate.

For the fish, heat the same skillet over medium heat and add 1 Tbsp (15 mL) of butter. Season both sides of the fish with salt and pepper. Once the butter is hot, place the first two fillets into the pan and cook for 2 minutes. Flip the fillets and let them finish cooking off the heat. Remove the fish from the pan once it's golden and flakes apart easily, about 2 minutes. Repeat until all the fish fillets are cooked.

You can eat this meal while camping, but for best enjoyment, try to avoid eating it on a cold concrete floor during a thunderstorm.

EAST COAST SEAFOOD CHOWDER

Chowder is an iconic East Coast dish, and we were lucky enough to get a recipe for it from Kathy Jollimore, an iconic East Coast lady. Creator of the website Eat Halifax, this woman knows her city like no other, and she also knows how to cook. Once you have your ingredients assembled, this is a really quick and easy dish to put together. For a truly Atlantic-to-Pacific experience, serve it with West Coast Salad with Hollyhock Dressing (page 188).

SERVES 4 TO 6

4 slices (about 3 oz or 85 g) thick-cut bacon, chopped
1/4 cup (60 mL) dry white wine
1/4 cup (60 mL) unsalted butter
1 large yellow onion (about 220 g), diced
2 stalks celery (about 150 g), diced
4 yellow potatoes (about 400 g), diced
3 cups (750 mL) fish or chicken stock
2 bay leaves
1 pound (454 g) mussels, cleaned
3 cups (750 mL) whipping cream
1/2 pound (227 g) haddock or any firm white fish, cut into large chunks
1 pound (454 g) scallops, halved
1 pound (454 g) cooked lobster meat, roughly chopped
Salt and freshly ground black pepper
2 Tbsp (30 mL) chopped chives

FOR SERVING

Baguette

In a large saucepan, cook the bacon over medium heat until crisp. Remove from the pan and place in a small bowl, leaving the grease. Deglaze the pan with wine and cook until reduced, 2 to 3 minutes. Add the butter, onion, and celery and sauté until the onion is translucent, about 5 minutes. Add the potatoes, stock, and bay leaves and bring to a boil. Lower the heat and simmer until the potatoes are almost tender, about 15 minutes.

Add the mussels, cover, and cook another 5 minutes until they open. Add the cream, haddock, and scallops. Cover and bring back to a gentle simmer for 5 minutes, or until the fish flakes easily with a fork. Add the lobster and reserved bacon and simmer until heated through. Season to taste with salt and pepper and garnish with chives. Serve immediately with a fresh baguette.

BIRCH SYRUP MISO BLACK COD

Birch syrup is less sweet than maple, and therefore lends itself well to savoury dishes. We've used it here to sweeten our version of miso black cod, bringing together Japan's culinary influence on the West Coast and an underappreciated Northern ingredient. If you can't find birch syrup, go ahead and use (just a little less) maple. Miso paste can be found at many grocery stores, particularly those that specialize in international foods. We prefer white miso, but any kind will do. This dish is simple to prepare, but requires at least 24 hours to marinate.

SERVES 6

¼ cup (60 mL) white miso paste
3 Tbsp (45 mL) birch syrup, or 2 Tbsp (30 mL) maple syrup
2 Tbsp (30 mL) rice vinegar
1 tsp (5 mL) fresh ginger, finely grated
4 to 6 black cod fillets (also called sablefish), about ¼ pound (113 g) each, or halibut

FOR SERVING

Brown, red, or white rice, or quinoa, cooked
Pea shoots

In a saucepan over low heat, whisk the miso, syrup, vinegar, and ginger together until fully mixed. Remove from the heat and pour into a shallow dish that's large enough to hold all of the fish. Let cool.

Lay the fillets skin side up in the dish with the marinade. Ensure the marinade is covering as much of the fish as possible. Cover tightly with a lid or plastic food wrap and leave in the refrigerator to marinate for at least 24 hours or up to 72 hours. The longer it marinates, the richer the flavour will be.

When you're ready to cook the fish, move the oven rack to the middle and preheat the oven to 400°F (200°C). Once preheated, set the broiler on high and let it preheat again. Remove the fish from the marinade and lightly wipe off any excess marinade. Place the pieces of fish skin side up on a baking sheet and put under the broiler. Broil until the skin blackens and bubbles, about 3 to 4 minutes, rotating the baking sheet halfway through. Remove from the oven, carefully turn the pieces of fish over so the skin side is down, and return to the oven. Broil until the top of the fish caramelizes and the flesh is opaque and flakes easily, about 2 to 3 minutes, again rotating the pan halfway through. Keep an eye on the fish while broiling, as it can burn easily.

Remove from the oven and serve immediately with rice or quinoa and pea shoots.

TWO TASTES OF WHALE: AGLANNGUAQ & MISIRAQ

Whales—whether belugas, bowheads, or narwhals—are some of the most important animals in Inuit culture. For centuries, they've provided people with food, bones for tools, and oil to keep the *qulliq* (page 263) burning. Today, hunts are regulated, and captured whales are distributed amongst northern communities.

We sampled two versions of whale in Rankin Inlet. The first was *aglannguaq*, which is the skin and blubber of a narwhal, served raw. The skin looked like marble, while the blubber glistened, the colour of pink watermelon. It was cut into small squares with an ulu, and our host, Sarah, provided a popular condiment to eat it with—China Lily soy sauce.

The narwhal smelled faintly of raw sunflower seeds and had a mild, almost sweet flavour, though the chewy texture was its most memorable feature; the soft fat gave way easily, while the skin required some work to gnaw through. It was pleasant, and we both ate several pieces.

Our second taste of whale was a fermented version, which we later came to know by its proper name: *misiraq*. To make it, fat is put in a container with a few holes in the lid and left to sit in a cool area for about four days. As it ferments, the blubber softens and intensifies in flavour.

At the Rankin Inlet Healing Facility, we sampled a batch of *misiraq* made by Harry Niakrok Jr., the centre's Inuk cook. *Misiraq* can be made from all kinds of fat—seal, walrus, or whale—but the version we tasted used beluga. We each grabbed a cube of frozen raw caribou, dipped it in, and started chewing. It was *extremely strong*—all the funk of a stinky blue cheese but turned way, way up. It crept into our every last pore, and neither of us could quite manage to go back for a second piece. However, just as blue cheese once horrified us as kids and we now adore it, we understand how someone who grew up with *misiraq* would crave it.

Mildly sweet and vigorously pungent—these are the somewhat disorienting flavours of whale that we'll never forget.

GRILLED SARDINES

WITH WHITE BEAN STEW

Shaun Hussey and Michelle LeBlanc are two of the kindest East Coasters we met. He's from Newfoundland, she's from Cape Breton, and together they own Chinched Bistro, a nose-to-tail restaurant in St. John's. They were with us the night we got Screeched in (see the sidebar), and we've been buddies ever since.

This stew is hearty, warming, and simple to make, but you'll want to give yourself some time, since you need to soak the beans.

SERVES 4

WHITE BEAN STEW

- ½ cup (125 mL) dry cannellini beans
- 1 link (about 5.5 oz or 150 g) good-quality cured chorizo
- 1 medium yellow onion (about 160 g), finely diced
- 3 cloves garlic, minced
- ½ cup (125 mL) dry red wine
- One 28-ounce (796 mL) can whole tomatoes, with juice
- Salt and freshly ground black pepper

GRILLED SARDINES

- 8 fresh or marinated small sardines (about 21 oz or 600 g)
- Extra virgin olive oil
- Salt and freshly ground black pepper (optional)

FOR SERVING

- Grilled bread
- Flat-leaf parsley, chopped
- Extra virgin olive oil
- Lemon wedges

Soak the beans in about 4 cups (1 L) of water overnight, or for at least 8 hours. Drain.

To make the stew, add the chorizo to a large skillet over medium heat and render off the fat. Remove the chorizo from the skillet and reserve for another use, but leave the fat behind. Cook the onion and garlic until fragrant, about 2 minutes. Pour in the wine to deglaze the skillet, followed by the tomatoes and soaked white beans. Bring to a boil and simmer for about 1 hour, or until the beans are soft. Taste and season with salt and pepper as desired. Keep warm while the sardines grill.

Preheat the barbeque to high (450°F to 500°F/230°C to 260°C). Rinse the sardines under cold water and pat dry. Brush with olive oil and, if using fresh sardines, season with salt and pepper. Once the grill is hot, cook the sardines for 2 minutes on each side, with the lid of the barbeque closed.

Scoop the stew into four large bowls and drizzle with olive oil. Top each with two sardines, a sprinkle of parsley, and a lemon wedge. Serve with grilled bread.

KISSING THE COD

Getting "Screeched in" is an outrageously charming tradition in Newfoundland. After reciting a few lines and planting a big smooch on a cod fish, you're officially accepted as an honourary Newfoundlander. It's just that easy.

We were feeling burnt-out the night we decided to do this, and our plan was a lousy one: "We'll just quickly pop into a bar, kiss the cod, and go to bed." Of course, when we mentioned this sad little scheme to our dinner companions, we ended up with a *very* different evening.

Shaun Majumder, one of Newfoundland's most famous comedians and star of *This Hour Has 22 Minutes*, was part of the group at dinner, and he led the charge once we arrived at Christian's Bar on George Street. He disappeared into the back for a short time and re-emerged wearing an oversized fishing hat and holding an iPod cord, with a giant frozen cod tucked under his arm. The cord served a very important, impromptu purpose that we can't quite recall. Thus began our wacky—yet very official—Screeching-in ceremony in front of a bar full of onlookers. After many attempts at reciting the few, but difficult, lines ("Long may your big jib draw" is not easy after you've had a few), we took our shots of Screech and were presented with the cold fish to kiss. As freshly appointed Newfoundlanders, we finished the night with a 3 am moose charcuterie tasting with our new friends. THEN we went to bed.

THE GIANT LOBSTER ROLL

Though there are many lobster rolls to be had on the East Coast, we think we found the best one. It was at the Saint John Ale House in New Brunswick, a gastropub run by the hugely talented Chef Jesse Vergen. In his words:

The idea for this lobster roll started with a conversation over the tiny lobster rolls you get in tourist traps. Two common culprits are frozen lobster that is steamed, instead of boiled, in either seasoned or ocean water, and a lack of flavour is another. I wanted to see where I could take a lobster roll and create something that wouldn't leave you feeling like you should've ordered the fish and chips. Here's something that will hold a lot of tasty lobster and has a flavour you won't soon forget!

SERVES 4
(BUT REMEMBER, THEY'RE GIANT)

½ cup (125 mL) salt
4 live female Atlantic lobsters, 1–2 pounds (454 to 910 g) each

LOBSTER MAYO

4 egg yolks
1 Tbsp (15 mL) Dijon mustard
2 cups (500 mL) canola oil
Reserved tomalley and roe from lobsters
9 Tbsp (135 mL) freshly squeezed lemon juice
1 tsp (5 mL) salt
1 tsp (5 mL) Tabasco (optional)

1 large soft loaf of bread, preferably sourdough
½ cup (125 mL) unsalted butter, room temperature

FOR SERVING

4 romaine hearts
Potato chips

Fill a large pot with water, pour in the salt, and set to boil. The pot needs to be big enough to fit all the lobsters without crowding them, so you may want to prepare two pots and divide the lobsters between them.

Once the water is boiling, hold the bodies of the lobsters, cut the bands off the claws and place the lobsters head first into the pot. While cooking, they will turn a vibrant red, but this change in colour does not indicate they're ready. See the note below for cooking times.

Fill your sink or a large bowl with ice and water, and once the lobsters are cooked, transfer them to the ice bath to stop them from cooking further. Deconstruct the lobsters, and reserve the tomalley and roe as well as the meat.

To make the lobster mayo, whisk the egg yolks in a bowl with the mustard. Slowly drizzle the oil into the yolks, whisking constantly, until it's completely incorporated and thick. Add the tomalley and roe. Whisk to incorporate the lemon juice, salt, and Tabasco. Adjust the salt and spice amounts to your taste.

Slice the sourdough loaf into buns by first cutting off each end, cutting the loaf into four even slices, then cutting three-quarters of the way through each slice to make four large buns. Butter the outsides of the buns liberally and fry in a pan over medium heat—you're looking for the "grilled cheese" effect. Add more butter to the pan if needed.

Chop the romaine hearts and stuff into the warm buns, then spoon in a lobster's worth of meat into each bun. Drizzle the lobster mayo overtop. Alternatively, you can mix some of the mayo with the lobster meat before stuffing it into the bun. Use any leftover mayo as a dip for your side of potato chips!

Note: Cooking Times

★ 1–1½ pounds (454 to 680 g): 8–10 minutes
★ 1½–1¾ pounds (680 to 800 g): 11–13 minutes
★ 2 pounds (910 g): 15 minutes

We wouldn't recommend getting lobsters much bigger than 2 pounds, as the smaller ones are much easier to cook evenly.

BARBEQUED SALMON

WITH TREE TIP PESTO

What could be more Canadian than eating a tree? As we made our way across the country, spruce and fir tips kept popping up and flaunting their culinary uses. Foraging for them is easy . . . unless you're us. On our first attempt, we went too late in the season to a forest with no spruce trees, got caught in a rainstorm, and came home soaking wet with nothing but empty buckets. Though it may take one or two springtime hikes to get the timing right, you want to get the new, bright green buds at the ends of the branches. You can store any excess tips in the freezer for several months. An extra piece of advice: if you *just* missed the season, head to a higher elevation where the spring's new growth is slightly later.

We'd like to say thanks to our friend Joel, who happily endured the rainy first foraging trek with us, then later picked the fir tips we used for this recipe. Spruce or fir tips will work for this pesto—whatever your forest happens to provide!

SERVES 4 TO 6

PESTO

1 cup (250 mL) loosely packed fresh (or frozen and thawed) spruce or fir tips, or 2 cups (500 mL) chopped flat-leaf parsley
1/2 cup (125 mL) Parmigiano-Reggiano or Grana Padano, grated then measured
1/2 tsp (2 mL) salt
1/2 cup (125 mL) extra virgin olive oil
2 Tbsp (30 mL) coarsely chopped walnuts
1 Tbsp (15 mL) freshly squeezed lemon juice
1 garlic clove, minced (optional)

4 to 6 wild salmon or Arctic char fillets, about 1/2 pound (227 g) each, skin on, scaled and deboned
2 Tbsp (30 mL) extra virgin olive oil
Salt and freshly ground black pepper

FOR SERVING

Plain yogurt, 6% or higher

Put the spruce or fir tips, cheese, salt, olive oil, walnuts, lemon juice, and garlic into a blender or food processor and blend until smooth. Taste and add more salt if desired. Set aside in the refrigerator until needed.

Preheat the barbeque to medium-high (450°F to 500°F/230°C to 260°C). Brush both sides of each piece of salmon with the olive oil and sprinkle both sides with salt and pepper. Let the fish rest a few minutes.

When the barbeque is ready, place the pieces of fish skin side down on the barbeque and close the lid. Let cook for 3 minutes, until the skin is crispy and the edges of the fish are opaque. Carefully turn each piece over, close the lid, and let cook another 2 to 3 minutes. The fish will be opaque and flake easily when done.

Serve the salmon with several spoonfuls of the pesto over each piece, also adding a dollop of yogurt if desired. Serve with a green salad and/or spring vegetables like asparagus, artichokes, peas, or even fiddleheads if you're in the mood for more foraging!

Field Trip

Salads & Sides

GRILLED PEACHES

WITH SAGE

Dana Ewart and Cameron Smith are the superhuman duo behind Joy Road Catering, a company that makes the already stunning Okanagan even more extraordinary. While passing through the Okanagan, we attended one of their famous al fresco dinners at God's Mountain, an aptly named estate overlooking Skaha Lake. Joy Road is all about "Cuisine du Terroir," meaning cuisine particular to the area in which it is grown and eaten. These juicy, grilled peaches make an excellent side for summer meals, especially barbequed meats! While any firm, ripe peaches would work, the freestone peaches that are available later in the season (mid-June to mid-August) are ideal, as the pit releases from the fruit more easily. To season them, Dana and Cam use a Basque-style Espelette pepper grown in the Okanagan, but if you can't get that, use freshly ground black pepper or Korean chili flakes.

SERVES 8

¼ cup (60 mL) grapeseed oil
12 to 15 sage leaves (about 15 g), coarsely chopped
4 medium peaches (about 600 g), halved and pitted
Salt and Espelette pepper, freshly ground black pepper, or Korean chili flakes (*gochugaru*)

Add the grapeseed oil to a plate or container large enough to hold all eight peach halves. Put the cut sage leaves down, then place the peaches cut side down on top of them. Marinate for about 30 minutes, or as long as it takes you to grill whatever meat you're serving. While the meat is resting, you can grill the peaches.

Once the grill is free, clean the bars well and let it get hot, about 450°F to 500°F (230°C to 260°C). Season the cut peaches lightly with salt and pepper and place cut side down on the hot grill. Close the lid and grill on one side only until softened, but not mushy, about 6 to 7 minutes. If you'd like, you can rotate the peach halfway through to create crosshatched grill lines. Season further with salt and pepper, if desired, and serve immediately.

PANZAPRESE

(BREAD SALAD WITH MOZZARELLA)

Prince Edward County is an idyllic patch of Ontario located just a few hours east of Toronto. Friends told us we *had* to visit Norman Hardie Winery for wine (check), Slickers Ice Cream for their campfire flavour (check), and Vicki's Veggies for veggies (obviously, and check). Vicki Emlaw founded the small organic farm and sells her produce from a charming refurbished wooden garage. When we asked Vicki for a recipe, she shared this satisfying salad, which she and her family eat throughout the summer. It makes use of her heirloom tomatoes and herbs as well as other Prince Edward County goods, including cheese, honey, and mustard. Since it combines elements of two Italian salads—panzanella and caprese—we couldn't help but dub it the "Panzaprese."

SERVES 4 TO 6

CROUTONS

- ½ large baguette or ½ loaf ciabatta
- 2 Tbsp (30 mL) extra virgin olive oil
- 1½ Tbsp (22 mL) chopped fresh rosemary and/or thyme
- Salt and freshly ground black pepper

DRESSING

- 1½ Tbsp (22 mL) balsamic vinegar
- ¼ cup (60 mL) red wine vinegar
- 2 Tbsp (30 mL) Dijon or grainy mustard
- 2 Tbsp (30 mL) local honey
- 2 garlic cloves, finely diced
- 1 cup (250 mL) fresh basil
- ⅔ cup (160 mL) extra virgin olive oil
- Salt and freshly ground black pepper

SALAD

- 3 to 4 pounds (1.4 to 1.8 kg) various heirloom tomatoes, cut into ½-inch (1 cm) cubes
- 1 small red onion (about 120 g), thinly sliced
- ¼ to ½ pound (113 to 227 g) fresh or classic mozzarella, cut into ½-inch (1 cm) pieces
- 1 cup (250 mL) coarsely chopped fresh basil
- 12 pitted green or black olives (about 120 g), sliced

Preheat the oven to 425°F (220°C).

For the croutons, cut the bread into about 1-inch (2.5 cm) chunks and toss on a baking sheet with the olive oil, fresh herbs, salt, and pepper. Toast in the oven for 6 to 8 minutes, rotating occasionally and stirring the bread cubes until they're barely toasted on the outside and are still slightly chewy on the inside. Remove from the oven and let cool.

For the dressing, add the balsamic, red wine vinegar, mustard, honey, garlic, and basil to a food processor or blender and blend. Then, with the food processor running, pour in the olive oil in a steady stream. Season to taste with salt and pepper.

In a large bowl, toss the tomatoes, onion, cheese, basil, and olives together with the croutons and about one-third of the dressing to start, adding more if desired. Let sit a few minutes so the dressing can soak into the bread, and serve.

BARBEQUED CORN ON THE COB

WITH CHIVE & GARLIC SCAPE BUTTER

This is one of our favourite ways to eat corn: barbequed, with salty herbed butter melting over the sweet, smoky kernels. Making the butter is simple, and you can easily switch out the herbs for different ones that suit your taste.

SERVES 12

1 Tbsp (15 mL) finely chopped garlic scapes
1 Tbsp (15 mL) finely chopped chives
½ tsp (2 mL) salt
½ cup (125 mL) unsalted butter, room temperature
12 cobs of corn, still in husks
¼ cup (60 mL) extra virgin olive or grapeseed oil, for brushing
Flaky sea salt

To make the herbed butter, put the garlic scapes, chives, salt, and butter in a food processor or blender and pulse the mixture until it's combined but not perfectly smooth. Lay out a piece of plastic food wrap or waxed paper and transfer the soft butter mixture to the centre. Fold over one end and roll, shaping the butter into a log. Twist both ends in tightly. Let chill in the refrigerator for about 30 minutes, or until the corn is cooked.

Fill a large bowl or pot with cold water and submerge the cobs, still in their husks, for at least 15 minutes.

Preheat the barbeque to high (about 450°F to 500°F/ 230°C to 260°C).

Pull back the husks of the corn, but keep them attached. Remove the silk and brush each cob with about 1 tsp (5 mL) of oil. Wrap the corn back up, enclosing all the kernels in their husks once again.

Turn the barbeque down to medium and place the cobs on the grill. Remove the butter from the refrigerator and cut into 12 slices.

Cook the corn on the grill for about 15 minutes, turning occasionally so that all sides of the cob have a turn facing the grill. When they're done, the husks should be mostly charred and the corn inside will have turned bright yellow. Remove the corn from the grill and let it cool enough to handle. Husk the corn, top with slices of butter, sprinkle with flaky sea salt if desired, and serve immediately.

1640
AUBERGE DU TRÉS
HOTEL

Quebec

Quebec made our heads spin. The province is so large, so culturally dense, and so full of remarkable food, it was impossible not to feel overwhelmed by it.

We began in Montreal, a city that is way too cool to have such cheap rent. We hit up the obligatory classics, like the towering smoked meat sandwiches at Schwartz's and the Frite Alors! version of curd-laden poutine. At Au Pied de Cochon, we watched as a roasted pig's head was prepared for another table; the chef broke open the jaw and shoved a whole steamed lobster inside, then garnished it with a flourish of gold leaf. We both slammed our hands down on the bar incredulously.

We had beers with new food writer friends at Dieu du Ciel and rode our bikes to a half-dozen bakeries on our first-ever "Croissant Crawl." Any chance we had, we bought ourselves fresh bagels from St-Viateur and made exquisite sesame seed messes of our laps.

Next we travelled farther east to Quebec City, which, with its cobblestone streets, was like stumbling upon Europe. We walked around with our eyes up, admiring the lofty, centuries-old stone architecture. One day we crossed the bridge to Île d'Orléans, an idyllic island in the centre of the St. Lawrence River. It's flush with maple stands, farmers, and artisans, like Cassis Monna & Filles, the province's first producers of blackcurrant liqueur.

Farther north, Charlevoix was a region of quiet and calm. While cycling around the Isle-aux-Coudres, we met Noëlle-Ange, owner of Boulangerie Bouchard, a bakery famous for its sugar pies and pork turnovers. She showed us all the old equipment they still use, including a hefty hand-cranked mixer from the 1950s.

Quebec is proud of its culinary history, and justifiably so. Our entire five-month trip could have been spent there and we still wouldn't have come close to experiencing it all. We turned on our GPS to hear its terrible (and hilarious) attempts at directing us in French, and began our trek toward the Maritimes . . .

BRUSSELS SPROUTS

WITH HONEY & HAZELNUTS

We met Aimée Wimbush-Bourque, the award-winning blogger behind Simple Bites, in Montreal. After meeting up for beers, she invited us over to her house the next day, where she was hosting her annual jam swap. Not only did she give us jam (despite our being unable to swap any of our own), but she also fed us a sublime dinner and has been an encouraging friend and inspiration ever since. This recipe, which is great for Thanksgiving—or any time, really—is from her brilliant first cookbook, *Brown Eggs and Jam Jars*.

SERVES 4

¼ cup (60 mL) whole hazelnuts
4 tsp (20 mL) extra virgin olive oil, divided
2 Tbsp (30 mL) liquid honey, divided
Pinch salt
1 pound (454 g) Brussels sprouts
1 Tbsp (15 mL) unsalted butter
1 grapefruit, scrubbed
Salt and freshly ground black pepper

Preheat the oven to 350°F (180°C).

Toast the hazelnuts on a baking sheet in the oven for 8 minutes. Pour them into a clean tea towel and wrap them up. Vigorously rub the hazelnuts through the towel to remove the skins. Don't worry if they don't all come off. Discard the skins.

In a small pot, whisk together 1 tsp (5 mL) of the olive oil and 1 tsp (5 mL) of the honey. Warm over low heat and stir to combine. Add the nuts to the mixture and toss to coat. Sprinkle with a generous pinch of salt. Return the nuts to the baking sheet and toast in the oven for another 12 to 15 minutes or until they are light brown. Turn the pan of hot hazelnuts onto a cutting board and let them cool. Coarsely chop.

Trim the bottoms off the Brussels sprouts. Peel off the outer leaves and discard. Slice sprouts in half top to bottom.

In a large sauté pan over medium-high heat, melt the butter together with the remaining 3 tsp (15 mL) of olive oil. Add the sprouts and cook, stirring frequently, just until they turn a vibrant green, with brown bits, 6 to 8 minutes.

Reduce the heat to low and drizzle the sprouts with the remaining honey. Using a microplane, zest the grapefruit into the pan. Season the sprouts with salt and pepper and stir to combine thoroughly. Transfer to a serving bowl or platter. Sprinkle with the honey-roasted hazelnuts and serve hot.

HERB SALAD

WITH PICKLED SHALLOTS

This salad comes from Sidewalk Citizen Bakery and was created as a pairing for their Cauliflower Steaks with Roasted Bone Marrow Butter (page 108). The fresh herbs and tangy pickled shallots are perfect for cutting through the richness of the bone marrow and can do the same for many other meat entrees. The shallots should be prepared at least a few hours before you need them and can be made up to a week in advance.

SERVES 4 TO 6

PICKLED SHALLOTS

1 large shallot (about 50 g), thinly sliced into rings
2/3 cup (160 mL) white vinegar
1/3 cup (80 mL) water
1 Tbsp (15 mL) salt
1 Tbsp (15 mL) white sugar
1 clove garlic, cut in half
1 bay leaf

HERB SALAD

1/2 bunch (about 60 g) flat-leaf parsley, chopped
1/3 cup (80 mL) chopped chives
3 Tbsp (45 mL) chopped dill
1 bunch (200 g) watercress leaves, roughly chopped
Salt

For the pickled shallots, place the shallot rings in a 16-ounce (500 mL) glass jar with a screw-top lid. Place the vinegar, water, salt, sugar, garlic, and bay leaf in a small pot and bring to a boil on the stove for 2 to 3 minutes, swirling to dissolve the salt and sugar. Once dissolved, pour the liquid over the shallots in the jar and screw on the lid. Place this in the refrigerator to cool.

For the herb salad, place all the herbs and watercress in a large bowl. Drain off most of the pickling liquid from the shallots, leaving 1 to 2 Tbsp (15 to 30 mL) to act as a dressing. Remove and discard the bay leaf and garlic, then add the shallots to the salad bowl with the herbs just before serving. Lightly toss them together, season with salt if desired, and serve immediately.

ROASTED POTATOES

WITH DUCK FAT & MAPLE SYRUP

In the heart of Quebec City's old quarter, we found Le Chic Shack, a restaurant whose bright colours, young management, and trendy design stand out from the rest of the city's traditional dining scene. Alongside their inventive poutines, house-made sodas, and burgers, we were served a bowl of their chips. The crispy potatoes, seasoned with salt and pepper and drizzled with maple syrup, were the perfect salty/sweet snack. They're the inspiration behind these roasted potatoes, which go well with any kind of meat. Alternatively, you can just eat the whole pan on its own, like we often do. Ask your local butcher for duck fat, or render your own from a whole duck or breast.

SERVES 4 TO 6

1½ pounds (680 g) small or medium new potatoes
¼ cup (60 mL) duck fat
1½ tsp (7 mL) salt
2 Tbsp (30 mL) maple syrup, or more
Flaky sea salt and freshly ground black pepper

Preheat the oven to 425°F (220°C).

Add the potatoes to a medium pot and cover with cold water. Bring to a boil over high heat and cook until a paring knife easily pierces the skins but the cores of the potatoes still resist, about 10 minutes. Drain the potatoes and let cool until they can be handled. Cut in half and let dry on a paper towel.

Place the duck fat in a cast iron pan or on a baking sheet with raised edges. Heat it in the oven until the fat is bubbling, about 10 minutes. Remove from the oven, and be careful—it's hot!

Add the salt and potatoes to the hot fat and coat evenly using tongs. Return to the oven and let cook for about 30 minutes, tossing the potatoes about every 10 minutes to make sure they brown evenly.

Remove from the oven, drain the excess fat, and transfer to a serving dish. Drizzle generously with maple syrup and finish with flaky sea salt and pepper.

WARM AUTUMN SALAD

WITH SHALLOT VINAIGRETTE & GOAT CHEESE

Kent Van Dyk is a chef and high school teacher whom we met in Ottawa. He has owned his own restaurant, staged with some of the world's best chefs, and has now dedicated himself to building the coolest culinary arts program for youth we've ever heard of. We made overmixed muffins in our high school cooking classes, and his students are making dim sum! It's simply unfair.

Kent contributed this root vegetable salad, ideal for when the summer heat subsides. Though it requires some prep, it's all quite simple and can easily be done ahead of time. You can use all the vegetables listed or any combination of them.

SERVES 6

SHALLOT VINAIGRETTE

- 1 large shallot (about 70 g), finely minced
- 1/4 cup (60 mL) red wine vinegar or sherry vinegar
- 3/4 cup (185 mL) extra virgin olive oil
- 1 tsp (5 mL) salt

SALAD

- 6 small beets (about 300 g)
- 1 1/2 pounds (about 680 g) mini potatoes, a mix of purple, red, and white
- 5 Tbsp (75 mL) extra virgin olive oil, divided
- 1 large sweet potato or yam (about 250 g)
- 1 small rutabaga (about 150 g)
- 1 large handful (about 24) green and/or yellow beans (about 150 g)
- 8 Brussels sprouts (about 160 g), leaves removed
- Salt for cooking vegetables
- 6 Tbsp (90 mL) crumbled fresh goat cheese, divided

See overleaf for preparation ▶

For the dressing, soak the shallots in the vinegar for at least 30 minutes. Once soaked, add the olive oil and salt to the shallots and whisk to combine. While the shallots are soaking, prepare the vegetables.

Place the beets in a small pot and cover with water. Bring to a boil and season with 1 tsp (5 mL) of salt. Cook until the beets offer no resistance when pierced with a knife. Remove from the heat and cool under cold running water. Once cooled, rub the skins off the beets with your fingers, then cut the beets in quarters (wearing gloves here will prevent pink hands). Toss the beets with some of the vinaigrette and set aside.

At the same time as the beets are cooking, place the mini potatoes in a pot and cover with salted water. Bring to a boil and cook until fork-tender, about 15 minutes. Once cooked, drain the water, drizzle with 1 Tbsp (15 mL) of olive oil, and swirl the pot to coat the potatoes. Leave to cool. Once cool enough to handle, cut them in half and set aside.

Preheat the oven to 375°F (190°C) and line two baking sheets with parchment. Peel the sweet potato and rutabaga. Cut the sweet potato into 1-inch (2.5 cm) cubes, toss in a bowl with 1 Tbsp (15 mL) of olive oil and a pinch of salt, and place on the prepared baking sheet. Cut the rutabaga into 1-inch (2.5 cm) cubes and toss with 1 Tbsp (15 mL) of olive oil and a pinch of salt and place on the second baking sheet. Tossing occasionally, roast until both are fork-tender, about 15 minutes for the sweet potato and 20 minutes for the rutabaga. Transfer to a bowl and set aside.

While your potatoes, beets, sweet potato, and rutabaga are cooking, bring a medium pot full of salted water to a boil. Trim the ends of the beans and boil for 60 seconds, then immediately transfer to an ice bath. Set aside.

Using a small paring knife, cut the root end of the Brussels sprouts off and peel the leaves, stopping when you get to the core.

Heat a large ovenproof, non-stick frying pan over medium heat. Add the remaining 2 Tbsp (30 mL) of olive oil to the pan. Add the potato halves and season with a sprinkle of salt. Cook until the cut side is crispy, then add the other root vegetables. Toss and cook until heated through. Add the beans and Brussels sprout leaves and cook until the leaves begin to wilt slightly. Divide the beets between six plates and arrange the vegetables on top of them. Drizzle each salad with the vinaigrette and top with the goat cheese. Alternatively, mix everything together in one big serving bowl and top with the cheese.

FARMERS' MARKETS

After driving into any new place, one of the first things we did was look up the local farmers' markets. They're a great way to experience a community and get a sense of what people are growing and eating in each region. Plus, people are always in good moods at outdoor venues with vegetables for sale. That's just a fact.

Along with cheerful people, markets were an easy way to find good local food, both for cooking at night and snacking on in the car. A few of our best finds included edible flowers and salal berry jelly on Haida Gwaii; beets and whitefish in the Northwest Territories; butter tarts and whisky in Regina; sea buckthorn sorbet in Winnipeg; honey lavender chèvre ice cream in Ottawa; Honeycrisp apples and a wedge of Louis D'Or at the Atwater Market in Montreal; Dutch *boterkoek* (butter cake) and a savoury Tunisian flatbread in Moncton; crunchy oatcakes in Cape Breton; Lebanese *mezze* in Fredericton; and apple cider vinegar in Halifax. We bought vegetables too, we *swear*.

MOLASSES BAKED BEANS

Growing up, we both thought that "making baked beans" meant getting a can opener, opening a can, and unceremoniously dumping its saucy contents into a pot (usually during camping trips). They were ladled over toast or served alongside meat dishes, often an afterthought. In the Maritimes, however, baked beans are not only a weekly staple of many dinner tables, but are almost always made from scratch. Bridget Oland, a native New Brunswicker who now works for Crosby's Molasses, shared her family's recipe with us, which they always eat with oatmeal brown bread. If you're going to eat them as a side dish, use the full amount of sugar suggested; however, if they're the main show, be more conservative with the sugar.

While they're simple to make, the beans need to soak overnight and then slow-cook in the oven, so plan ahead.

TOUTONS

We love fried bread, and were happy with every version of bannock we discovered. However, we didn't encounter one of our favourite fried breads until after the seven-hour ferry trip from Nova Scotia to Newfoundland. At the Hotel Port aux Basques, we were treated to a classic island breakfast complete with eggs, baked beans, fish cakes, toast with jam, and toutons, which are briskly pronounced "tao-ins," not "two-tawns." In theory, toutons are just small pieces of bread dough fried in butter or pork fat, but in reality, they are so *much more*. They're a chewy and salty treat best served with a heavy-handed pour of dark, sweet molasses. They're their own perfect brand of carbohydrate, so we give you this advice: when in Newfoundland, for breakfast, lunch, or dinner, EAT TOUTONS!

SERVES 6 TO 8, OR 4 AS A MAIN DISH

2 cups (500 mL) dried navy or pea beans
1 small yellow onion (about 120 g), peeled
½ apple (about 50 g), cored and peeled (optional)
3 Tbsp to ⅓ cup (45 to 80 mL) lightly packed brown sugar
½ cup (125 mL) molasses
1 tsp (5 mL) salt
1½ tsp (7 mL) dry mustard
½ tsp (2 mL) freshly ground black pepper
1 slice bacon (about 1 oz or 25 g), chopped (see note)
Boiling water

Note: To make this dish vegetarian, simply swap 1 Tbsp (15 mL) unsalted butter for the bacon.

Soak the navy or pea beans in a large bowl of water overnight in the refrigerator.

The next day, drain the beans, transfer them to a medium pot, and cover with water. Bring to a boil and simmer for 30 minutes, or until the skins break when you blow on them.

Preheat the oven to 300°F (150°C) and set a full kettle of water to boil.

Drain the beans and put them in a large ovenproof pot or bean crock. Bury the onion (and apple, if using) in the middle of the beans.

Mix together the brown sugar, molasses, salt, dry mustard, and pepper and pour over the beans. Sprinkle the bacon pieces overtop, or dab with the butter. Pour over enough boiling water to just cover the beans. Cover the pot and cook in the preheated oven for 4 to 6 hours, stirring occasionally and adding water as needed so the beans do not dry out. Take the lid off for the last 30 minutes of cooking.

Serve with homemade bread, biscuits, toutons (see sidebar), or as a side dish.

New Brunswick

We entered New Brunswick on one of the province's quiet highways, which curve through large tracts of undeveloped land. The trees were dressed in the hues of a classic Maritime autumn, and we finally laid our eyes upon the Bay of Fundy's navy-blue waters. We'd made it to the other coast!

We were greeted in New Brunswick with the warmth and friendliness people have come to expect of the eastern provinces. For example, if you're walking on the sidewalk and look like you're even *considering* crossing the street, cars will very likely stop for you. The people are just that courteous.

We first met with an extremely affable group of men who are part of the team at Speerville Flour Mill. This food processing company, which still uses stone mills to turn wheat into flour, has always worked to support the food and agricultural economies of the Maritimes. They restocked our in-car pantry, a generous act which kept us fed for a very long time.

In Charlotte County, we strolled through the overgrown, historic apple orchard at Todd's Point, visited Canada's Chocolate Museum, and hiked along Passamaquoddy Bay with a few old friends. We ate soup made from foraged lobster mushrooms while overlooking the pristine Kingsbrae Garden, held actual lobsters at Spears' Fishing and Charter, and fell very hard for East Coast oatcakes.

When we entered New Brunswick, we entered a land rich with the history of Acadians, the descendants of 17th-century French colonists. We experienced Acadian culture first-hand with Claira and Camilla Vautour, who taught us how to make *poutines râpées*, a classic dish of salted pork potato dumplings.

After visiting La Boulangerie Française in Shediac, we packed an entirely local picnic of wild boar pâté, goat cheese, pastries, and ketchup chips, then headed to the pink sand at Plage de L'Aboiteau.

Cooled off by a salty breeze, we ate our lunch in the sun, then climbed back in the car and turned toward our country's smallest province . . .

WARM BELUGA LENTIL, CRABAPPLE & CHORIZO SALAD

Though he now lives in Calgary, Dan Clapson is a Saskatchewan boy, born and raised in Saskatoon. He's also a food writer, TV personality, co-founder of the website www.eatnorth.com, and an amazing friend to *FEAST*. Dan wanted to contribute a recipe that reflected his roots, and in his words:

This dish is an amalgamation of ingredients I love that are readily available in Saskatchewan. Yes, we do have terribly cold winters that stop us from having the diverse apple orchards you can find in places like BC, but we certainly have no shortage of crabapples. Their tartness adds a brightness to the lentils, mustard, and Three Farmers Camelina Oil, all of which are grown right outside of Saskatoon.

SERVES 4 TO 6

1½ cups (375 mL) dried beluga lentils
1 Tbsp (15 mL) camelina oil or extra virgin olive oil
1 link (about 5.5 oz or 150 g) good quality cured chorizo, diced
2 Tbsp (30 mL) dry white wine
1 Tbsp (15 mL) unsalted butter
1 tsp (5 mL) lemon zest
3 Tbsp (45 mL) freshly squeezed lemon juice
6 medium crabapples (about 60 g) or 1 Granny Smith apple (about 100 g), cored, quartered, and skin intact
¼ cup (60 mL) finely chopped flat-leaf parsley
1 Tbsp (15 mL) grainy Dijon mustard
1 tsp (5 mL) salt
½ tsp (2 mL) freshly ground black pepper

Cover the lentils with at least 4 cups (1 L) of water and set to boil for 15 to 20 minutes. Once tender, drain and set aside.

Heat the oil in a large pan over medium-high heat. Add the diced chorizo and sauté for 4 to 5 minutes, until the edges are slightly crispy. Deglaze the pan with the wine, followed shortly thereafter by the butter.

Once the butter is melted, add the zest, lemon juice, crabapples, cooked lentils, parsley, and mustard, and mix to combine. Lower the heat to medium and cook for 3 minutes to heat all the way through. Mix in the salt and pepper, and season further if desired. Transfer to a bowl or platter and serve warm.

THREE FARMERS CAMELINA OIL

In southeast Saskatchewan, there are, you guessed it, three farmers producing an oil that could very well replace olive oil in your kitchen. It comes from the northern-hardy *Camelina sativa*, an ancient seed that originated in Northern Europe and thrives in Saskatchewan. The Three Farmers company grows and cold-presses these seeds into a nutrient-dense oil with a high smoke point, making it great for cooking. The flavour is nutty, with grassy notes of asparagus and snow peas. It's now available across Canada, so you may soon be able to count one more Canadian-made staple in your pantry.

WEST COAST SALAD

WITH HOLLYHOCK DRESSING

This salad, with its blues and greens, both looks and tastes like the West Coast. It's tossed together with a dressing by Moreka Jolar and Linda Solomon from the kitchen at Hollyhock, a world-renowned retreat centre on Cortes Island. The dressing comes from the centre's popular book, *Hollyhock Cooks*, and packs the greatest umami punch imaginable. We consume it with near-manic dedication. It's also vegan!

SERVES 4 TO 6

HOLLYHOCK DRESSING

- ½ cup (125 mL) nutritional yeast (see note)
- ⅓ cup (80 mL) water
- ⅓ cup (80 mL) tamari or soy sauce
- ⅓ cup (80 mL) apple cider vinegar
- 2 cloves garlic, crushed
- 1½ cups (375 mL) sunflower or extra virgin olive oil

SALAD

- ¼ cup (60 mL) hazelnuts
- 8 cups (about 21 oz or 600 g) mixed greens, such as kale, lettuce, arugula, frisée, and/or pea shoots
- ¾ cup (185 mL) fresh basil leaves, torn
- ¾ cup (185 mL) fresh blueberries
- 1 avocado, peeled, pitted and sliced
- ½ English cucumber (about 225 g), diced
- 1 Tbsp (15 mL) hemp hearts
- ⅓ cup (80 mL) crumbled goat cheese or sheep's milk feta

Note: Look for nutritional yeast in the natural or organic foods section of your grocery store or at health food stores.

First, prepare the dressing. Place all of the ingredients but the oil into a blender or food processor and blend until smooth. Measure out the oil and, with the blender or food processor running, slowly pour the oil into the mixture in as thin a stream as possible. This will allow the dressing to emulsify properly. Once all the oil is incorporated, transfer the dressing to a sealed container and store in the refrigerator for up to 2 weeks.

Preheat the oven to 350°F (180°C). Toast the hazelnuts on a baking sheet in the oven for 8 to 10 minutes, or until golden brown. Pour them onto a clean tea towel and wrap them up. Vigorously rub the hazelnuts through the towel to remove the skins. Don't worry if they don't all come off. Discard the skins. Once the hazelnuts have cooled, roughly chop them.

For the salad, place all of the remaining ingredients in a large bowl. Just before serving, toss with about ¼ cup (60 mL) of the dressing. Add more dressing if desired, and reserve any extra for future use. Serve immediately.

GRILLED EGGPLANT & ROASTED TOMATO SALAD

WITH TAHINI DRESSING

We each knew Jess Weatherhead, the creator of this recipe, before we knew each other. Dana lived with her in a big old house in New Brunswick during university, and Lindsay cooked for her at a tree-planting camp in British Columbia. Along with her partner, Robin Turner, Jess now owns Roots and Shoots Farm, an organic vegetable farm serving the Ottawa area. We visited them at the height of summer and feasted on all kinds of farm food. Jess is a gifted cook who knows vegetables from seed to plate and generally doesn't measure a thing; we successfully wrangled this rare, *written* recipe out of her. It's simple, so use the freshest seasonal produce you can find!

SERVES 4 TO 6

SALAD

- 3 Tbsp (45 mL) pine nuts
- 6 to 8 Roma tomatoes (about 630 g), quartered
- 6 Tbsp (90 mL) extra virgin olive oil, divided
- 1 tsp (5 mL) salt, divided
- 2 medium eggplants (about 910 g), sliced into ¼-inch (6 mm) slabs lengthwise
- ½ cup (125 mL) chopped flat-leaf parsley

TAHINI SAUCE

- ½ banana pepper (about 35 g)
- 2 heads garlic (about 60 g)
- ¼ cup (60 mL) tahini
- 3 Tbsp (45 mL) freshly squeezed lemon juice
- 3 Tbsp (45 mL) extra virgin olive oil
- ½ tsp (2 mL) salt
- 2 Tbsp (30 mL) water

Place the pine nuts in a small pan over medium heat. Shaking the pan frequently, toast the nuts until golden brown, about 6 to 8 minutes. Remove from the pan and set aside.

Preheat the oven to 350°F (180°C).

In a large bowl, combine the tomatoes with 2 Tbsp (30 mL) of olive oil and ½ tsp (2 mL) of salt. Toss to combine and spread out on half of a baking sheet. To take advantage of the hot oven, you'll also roast two of the ingredients for the tahini sauce at this point; first, halve the banana pepper, brush with olive oil, and place next to the tomatoes on the baking sheet, skin sides up; then cut the tops off the garlic heads to expose the cloves, brush the tops with olive oil, wrap in tinfoil, and place next to the baking sheet on the oven rack.

Roast the pepper until the skin starts to blister and blacken. Remove from the baking sheet, but let the tomatoes keep cooking. Roast the tomatoes until they're soft and the edges start to blacken, about 45 minutes. Roast the garlic until soft, about 35 to 45 minutes; once cooled, squeeze out the cloves.

Preheat the barbeque to medium-high heat (450°F to 500°F/230°C to 260°C). While the vegetables are roasting in the oven, generously brush the eggplant slices with the remaining 4 Tbsp (60 mL) of olive oil (or more, if needed) and season with the remaining ½ tsp (2 mL) of salt. Once the grill is hot, place the eggplant slices on the grill and close the lid. Cook for 2 to 3 minutes, until the side facing the grill has nice grill marks and starts to blacken. Flip and repeat on the other side. Transfer the cooked eggplant to a dish. Continue this way until all the slices are grilled. You may want to let the grill heat up again between rounds. Cover the eggplant with foil and set aside.

To make the sauce, add the tahini, lemon juice, olive oil, roasted pepper, roasted garlic cloves, salt, and water to a blender or food processor and mix until combined. Taste and season with more salt if desired.

Gently toss the eggplant, tomatoes, and parsley together. Serve warm, drizzled with the tahini sauce and topped with the toasted pine nuts.

DISCOVERING NEW BERRIES

We were sure we'd discover foods that were new to us during the road trip, but we assumed it would happen in some far-flung corner of Quebec, not four days into our trip while still in the province we both call home. In Kyuquot, off the west coast of Vancouver Island, our kayaking guide Serena held out a palm full of salmonberries, which looked like a blushy cross between raspberries and blackberries. We were baffled. How had we not come across them before, and what other berries were out there that we hadn't yet tasted? Plenty, as it turns out. Over the course of the trip, we were introduced to haskaps, which tasted like merlot-flavoured blueberries; partridgeberries (also called lingonberries) on the tundra; dark salal berries, which we ate in jelly form on Haida Gwaii; and sea buckthorn berries across the Prairies, which tasted like unsweetened orange juice. Cloudberries, or bakeapples as they're known in Newfoundland, were perhaps the most interesting new flavour to us. They had an almost creamy texture, smelled surprisingly like an aged cheese, and tasted tart like a gooseberry. Also, they cannot be cultivated, so finding them in the wild feels like a true accomplishment.

Sweet Stuff

DESSERTS & BAKING

LUNAR RHUBARB CAKE

This cake, by Canadian food icon Elizabeth Baird, is ridiculously simple and tasty. Because she's the pro, here's Elizabeth's take on it:

Rhubarb is the universal Canadian fruit, growing as it does in Canada's north, south, east, and west. And yes, it is a vegetable, but in most Canadian kitchens, it's treated like a fruit. Many years ago I was working on an article for Canadian Living *magazine with home economist Sandy Hall. Wyn Hall, her mother-in-law, gave us her recipe for Rhubarb Cake to include in the article. It was a winner—a no-fail butter cake, with chopped rhubarb in the batter and a sugar-cinnamon crumble topping that baked into a crusty crater-like surface. As soon as Sandy and I took it out of the oven, its moonscape top inspired us to rename the cake "Lunar Rhubarb Cake."*

A number of these ingredients need to be at room temperature when you make the cake, so take them out of the refrigerator well before you start baking.

SERVES 12

CAKE

- 1/2 cup (113 g) unsalted butter, room temperature
- 1 1/2 cups (300 g) white sugar
- 1 egg, room temperature
- 1 tsp (5 mL) vanilla extract
- 2 cups (300 g) all-purpose flour (see note on page 6)
- 1 tsp (6 g) baking soda
- 1/2 tsp (1.5 g) salt
- 2 cups (500 mL) rhubarb, cut in 1/2-inch (1 cm) pieces (about 4 large stalks; see note)
- 1 cup (250 mL) buttermilk, room temperature

TOPPING

- 1 cup (213 g) lightly packed brown sugar
- 2 tsp (4 g) ground cinnamon
- 1/4 cup (57 g) unsalted butter, cubed and at room temperature

FOR SERVING

- Vanilla ice cream

Note: You can increase the rhubarb by another 1/2 cup (about 70 g) if you like. The cake will work with other fruits—apricots, plums, raspberries, and wild blueberries—but rhubarb is the best. If using frozen rhubarb, measure it while still frozen and let thaw completely. Drain in a colander, but do not press liquid out.

Line the bottom and sides of a 9- × 13-inch (23 × 33 cm) cake pan with parchment paper, or use soft butter to grease the pan; set aside. Preheat the oven to 350°F (180°C).

In a large bowl, beat together the butter and white sugar until smooth, light, and creamy, about 3 to 4 minutes. Scrape down the bowl once or twice during this process. Beat in the egg and vanilla and make sure all the ingredients are combined. In a separate bowl, whisk together the flour, baking soda, and salt. Scoop out 2 Tbsp of this mixture and toss with the rhubarb, then set the rhubarb aside.

Mix the dry ingredients into the butter mixture in three parts, alternating with the buttermilk in two parts. Sprinkle the rhubarb mixture over the batter and fold in. Scrape into the prepared pan and smooth the surface.

For the topping, add the brown sugar and cinnamon to a medium bowl and mash together using a fork. Add the butter and blend together until crumbly. Sprinkle evenly over the batter.

Bake in the centre of the oven until the fragrance from the oven overwhelms hangers-on in the kitchen and the surface is crusty and golden brown with pink lumps here and there. A toothpick inserted into the centre should come out clean. This takes about 45 minutes.

Let cool slightly. Enjoy warm with scoops of vanilla ice cream.

If making ahead, let cool completely. Double wrap in plastic food wrap and freeze for up to 2 weeks.

NANAIMO BARS

While in Nanaimo, British Columbia, we immersed ourselves in the most extensive Nanaimo bar experience possible. We went on a tour that specifically celebrates this classic Canadian treat, consuming everything from Nanaimo bar cheesecake and cocktails to a battered and deep-fried version. Our favourite of the day was eaten at a local café called Mon Petit Choux, whose popular bars take three days to make; very kindly, their pastry chef, Chelsea Tunnell, came up with a version for us that can be made in just one afternoon. They're rich and creamy, yet not as intensely sweet as the ones you'll get in the store. They also happen to be gluten free!

SERVES 16

BASE

- 1¼ cups (310 mL) rice cereal
- ½ cup (125 mL) unsweetened shredded coconut, toasted
- ⅓ cup (80 mL) chopped walnuts, toasted
- ⅓ cup (80 mL) chopped almonds, toasted
- ⅛ tsp ground cinnamon
- ½ cup (125 mL) unsalted butter
- ½ cup (125 mL) white sugar
- ¼ cup (60 mL) cocoa powder
- 1 egg
- 1 tsp (5 mL) vanilla extract

FILLING

- 2 Tbsp (30 mL) water
- ¼ cup (60 mL) white sugar
- ¾ Tbsp (11 mL) vanilla extract
- ½ cup (125 mL) unsalted butter, room temperature, divided
- ¼ cup + 2 Tbsp (90 mL) homemade or store-bought prepared vanilla custard, such as Bird's or Ambrosia Devon Custard
- ¾ cup + 2 Tbsp (215 mL) icing sugar, sifted

TOPPING

- ⅔ cup (160 mL) coarsely chopped semi-sweet chocolate (not chocolate chips)
- ⅓ cup (80 mL) whipping cream
- 1 Tbsp (15 mL) corn syrup
- Flaky sea salt (optional)

See overleaf for preparation ▶

Spray the bottom of an 8- × 8-inch (20 × 20 cm) pan with cooking spray and line it with a piece of parchment that hangs over the edges. Spray the parchment layer and lay another piece the opposite way, also leaving some overhang. Spray again. This will make it easier to remove the Nanaimo bars from the pan.

For the base, combine the rice cereal, toasted coconut, nuts, and cinnamon in a large bowl and set aside.

In a saucepan over medium heat, combine the butter, sugar, and cocoa powder. Stir until the butter is melted and the sugar and cocoa dissolve, about 2 to 3 minutes. In a separate bowl, whisk the egg and vanilla together. Slowly pour the cocoa mixture into the egg mixture, whisking to combine, and return to the saucepan. Heat over medium heat until it comes to a boil, about 3 to 4 minutes, then remove from the heat immediately.

Pour the cocoa mixture into the bowl containing the rice cereal mixture, and stir until well combined. Press the mixture evenly into the prepared pan and let it chill in the refrigerator while you prepare the filling.

For the filling, whisk the water and sugar in a medium pot until just combined, then cook over high heat for 6 to 7 minutes (not stirring), until it turns a deep amber colour (watch carefully so it doesn't burn). Remove from the heat and slowly pour in the vanilla—the mixture will bubble and spit, so stand back! Put back on low heat and stir to dissolve any caramel lumps. Add in one-third of the butter and stir until melted.

In a stand mixer fitted with the whisk attachment or using a hand mixer, transfer the caramel to a bowl and whisk on medium speed until it thickens slightly and begins to cool, about 6 to 8 minutes. While still mixing, add in the remaining butter, a little bit at a time, until the mixture is light and fluffy.

Add the custard and mix for 2 to 3 minutes on medium speed until fully combined, thoroughly scraping down the bowl as you go. Add the icing sugar and reduce the speed to low, mixing until the icing sugar is combined. Switch to high speed and beat 2 to 3 minutes more. Spread the filling evenly over the prepared base and return to the refrigerator for 1 hour to set.

For the topping, place the chopped chocolate in a bowl. In a saucepan, combine the whipping cream and corn syrup and heat until just simmering. Pour the cream mixture over the chocolate and let sit for 2 minutes. Stir slowly until no streaks of cream remain and the mixture has become thick and shiny.

Working quickly, pour the warm chocolate on top of the chilled filling. Quickly swirl the pan and spread to distribute the chocolate and create an even coating. Once the chocolate has cooled for a few minutes, you can sprinkle the top with some flaky sea salt, if desired. Place the bars in the refrigerator for at least 2 hours, or until set.

To remove from the pan, grab the overhanging parchment and lift until the bars come out of the pan—they should be quite firm and sturdy at this point. Fold down the parchment and cut into 16 squares while still cold. Leftovers should be kept in the refrigerator.

ARCTIC APPLE FRITTERS

There's something about going north and eating treats; as we headed toward Dawson City, we were told, "Get the big cinnamon buns!" and as we boarded the train toward Churchill, "Make sure to go to Gypsy's for an apple fritter!" If there's a deep-fried piece of dough to be had, especially in sub-zero Arctic temperatures, we are on it. We dutifully visited Gypsy's restaurant, an institution in Churchill, and purchased both apple *and* pineapple fritters. This recipe was developed in honour of those delectable doughnuts, consumed with snow on our boots and toques on our heads.

SERVES 12

DOUGH

- 1/2 cup (125 mL) warm water
- 2 Tbsp (25 g) white sugar
- 1 Tbsp (9 g) active dry yeast
- 3 cups (450 g) all-purpose flour, plus extra for rolling (see note on page 6)
- 1 Tbsp (12 g) baking powder
- 1/2 tsp (1 g) ground cinnamon
- 1 tsp (5 mL) salt
- 1/2 cup (125 mL) buttermilk, room temperature
- 3 Tbsp (43 g) unsalted butter, room temperature
- 1 egg, lightly beaten

APPLE FILLING

- 3 Tbsp (43 g) unsalted butter
- 3 tart apples (530 g whole) such as Granny Smith, peeled and finely diced
- 2 Tbsp (30 mL) maple syrup
- 1 1/2 tsp (3 g) ground cinnamon
- 1/8 tsp salt

GLAZE

- 1 1/2 cups (173 g) icing sugar
- 3 to 4 Tbsp (45 to 60 mL) half-and-half
- 1 tsp (5 mL) vanilla extract
- 1/8 tsp ground cinnamon

4 to 5 cups (1 to 1.25 L) canola oil, for frying

See overleaf for preparation ▶

For the dough, mix the warm water and sugar in a large bowl (or the bowl of a stand mixer). Sprinkle in the yeast, stir gently, and let sit 5 minutes.

In a separate bowl, mix the flour, baking powder, cinnamon, and salt. Once the yeast is foamy, stir in the buttermilk, butter, and egg. Mix in the flour, 1 cup (150 g) at a time, with a wooden spoon or dough hook if using a stand mixer. Mix thoroughly, adding extra flour a bit at a time if the dough is too sticky. Knead (by hand or with the mixer) until you have a soft, smooth, and gently elastic dough. Place in a greased bowl, cover with a damp tea towel, and let rise until doubled in size, about 45 minutes.

While the dough is rising, prepare the apple filling. Melt the 3 Tbsp (43 g) of butter in a large frying pan over medium-low heat, then add the apples, maple syrup, cinnamon, and salt. Stir frequently for 10 to 15 minutes, or until the apples have softened. Remove from the heat and let cool.

Once the dough has risen, press it down, then turn it out onto a floured surface. Sprinkling with flour to prevent it from sticking, roll out the dough into a 9- × 13-inch (23 × 33 cm) rectangle. With the longer edges of the rectangle at the top and bottom, spread two-thirds of the apple filling on one side of the rectangle. Fold the other half of the dough over it and seal the edges. Turn the dough so the longer sides are on the top and bottom again. Spread the remaining one-third of the apple mixture on one side, fold the dough over, and seal once again. Now you have a layered square of dough filled with chunks of apple.

Sprinkle a generous amount of flour over a baking sheet and set aside. Using a knife or bench cutter, cut the dough so you have about 48 small squares. Gather four squares at a time and press them together to form one fritter. Don't worry if they look a bit rough or the apples have to be pressed back in—you want a crater-like surface for these. Once all the fritters are formed, place them on the prepared baking sheet, cover very loosely with plastic wrap, and let rise.

While the fritters are rising, fill a large pot with about 4 inches (10 cm) of oil and heat to 360°F (182°C). In a bowl, whisk together the icing sugar, half-and-half, vanilla, and cinnamon for the glaze.

Lay out a baking sheet and place a cooling rack on top of it. When the oil is hot, gently drop the fritters in one or two at a time, depending on the size of the pot (they shouldn't crowd each other). Fry until golden brown on one side, then flip over and fry until golden brown on the other, 3 to 4 minutes in total. Remove with a slotted spoon and place on the cooling racks.

Once the fritters have cooled enough to handle, dip one side into the glaze, shake off the excess, and place it back on the rack, glazed side up. The glaze shouldn't coat the fritters too thickly; once you start dipping the warm doughnuts into it, you'll know if you need to add more cream to thin it out. Repeat until all the fritters are fried and glazed.

These are best consumed the day they're made!

DARK CHOCOLATE-DIPPED EAST COAST OATCAKES

The sad thing about living on the West Coast is its lack of oatcakes, which were our favourite snack in the Maritimes. Because they're made with oats, we easily convinced ourselves they're a healthy alternative to any meal. No time for breakfast/lunch/dinner? No problem! *Just have another oatcake.*

Oatcakes came over with the Scots and have since been adapted into various crave-worthy forms all across the East Coast. They sit somewhere between a cookie and a biscuit—not quite sweet, but not quite savoury, so you can top them with cheddar *or* chocolate. Our favourite ones were Honeybeans's in St. Andrews by-the-Sea, New Brunswick. Thanks to Matt and Angela Honey for agreeing to share their recipe.

MAKES 12 OATCAKES

1 cup (227 g) unsalted butter, room temperature
1/2 cup (107 g) lightly packed brown sugar
1 1/2 cups (225 g) all-purpose flour (see note on page 6)
1 1/2 cups (160 g) old-fashioned rolled oats (not quick oats)
1/2 tsp (1.5 g) salt
2 Tbsp (30 mL) water, if needed
1 cup (130 g) coarsely chopped dark chocolate (optional)
Fleur de sel or flaky sea salt (optional)

Preheat the oven to 350°F (180°C).

In a large bowl of a stand mixer (or using beaters or a wooden spoon), cream the butter with the sugar until light and fluffy, about 3 to 4 minutes, scraping down the sides of the bowl once or twice. In a separate bowl, mix the flour, oats, and salt together, then add to the butter mixture in three increments, beating as you add. If you've added all the oat mixture and the dough is still quite dry, add the water, 1 Tbsp (15 mL) at a time, until the dough comes together.

Between two large sheets of waxed paper or parchment paper, use a rolling pin to roll the dough out to about a 1/4-inch-thick (6 mm) slab. Pull the top layer of paper off and cut the dough into circles about 3 inches (8 cm) in diameter with a cookie cutter or the top of a glass. Transfer the oatcakes to an ungreased baking sheet—you should end up with about a dozen.

Bake the oatcakes for 15 to 20 minutes in the preheated oven, or until they begin browning very slightly around the edges. Remove from the oven, let cool for 2 to 3 minutes on the baking tray, then transfer to cooling racks.

To make these a little more decadent, melt the chopped dark chocolate over low heat in a saucepan or over medium heat in a double boiler. Once melted, remove from the heat and dip half of each oatcake in the chocolate, then lay on a cooling rack or piece of parchment to set. For the ultimate experience, sprinkle a little fleur de sel or flaky sea salt over the melted chocolate before it hardens. Whether sweet or savoury, these are always great with a dram of whisky.

FINANCIER À L'ÉRABLE

(MAPLE & BUCKWHEAT FINANCIER CAKES)

Tucked away in Montreal's St. Henri neighbourhood is Patrice Pâtissier, a bakery opened by the talented Patrice Demers. We visited during our second trip to Montreal amidst the freezing February temperatures of the annual Montréal en Lumière winter festival. We warmed up with so many rounds of pastries and desserts, they became our dinner for the evening. Before we left, Patrice kindly packed us these financiers, which smelled distinctly of maple, for our flight back to Vancouver the next morning. We think they're the perfect tribute to Quebec's most quintessential ingredient.

You can either bake these in financier pans or muffin tins—just remember to adjust the baking times as suggested below. Also, the batter needs to rest for 3 hours, so plan accordingly.

SERVES 10 TO 12

½ cup (113 g) unsalted butter
1½ cups (200 g) maple sugar
¾ cup (72 g) almond flour (see note on page 6)
½ cup (75 g) buckwheat flour
¼ tsp salt
6 egg whites
⅓ cup (80 mL) canola oil

Brown the butter by melting it in a deep pot (light-coloured or stainless steel is best) over medium heat. Let it cook for about 8 to 10 minutes, swirling often, until the butter is a dark golden brown and nutty smelling. Watch it carefully—it can go from brown to burnt quite quickly! Once it's dark brown, remove it from the heat immediately and transfer to a heatproof bowl. Let cool slightly.

Combine the sugar, almond flour, buckwheat flour, and salt in a large bowl. Pour the egg whites into the dry ingredients and whisk to incorporate. Add the brown butter and canola oil and whisk until smooth.

Cover with a lid or plastic wrap and let the mixture sit in the refrigerator for at least 3 hours.

Preheat the oven to 350°F (180°C) and butter some financier moulds or a muffin tin—you should end up with about 48 to 60 financiers or a dozen muffins. Pour the batter into the financier moulds and bake for 20 minutes (25 to 30 if using a muffin tin), or until golden brown and a toothpick inserted into the centre comes out clean. Remove from the oven and let cool before eating.

SPEERVILLE'S COUNTRY HARVEST BREAD

We hadn't expected to find a bunch of organic-loving, local agriculture-championing men in rural New Brunswick, but that's exactly whom we met at Speerville Flour Mill, one of the friendliest places we've ever visited. Founded in the 1970s, Speerville uses granite stones to grind all their flours and sells a huge variety of organic staples across the East Coast. They're continually working with farmers to create a supply and demand for Maritime products, like the Acadia wheat variety, as well as finding innovative ways to run their ethically minded business. This seedy bread recipe comes from their community and highlights the kinds of ingredients Speerville carries. It's perfect for sandwiches or toasted for breakfast.

SERVES 4 TO 6

1¼ cups (310 mL) warm water
2 Tbsp (30 mL) liquid honey
2 tsp (6 g) active dry yeast
2 Tbsp (30 mL) sunflower or canola oil
3 cups (450 g) organic stone-ground spelt or whole wheat flour, or a mix of both (see note on page 6)
1½ tsp (4.5 g) salt
¼ cup (40 g) whole flax seeds
2 Tbsp (18 g) sunflower seeds
1 Tbsp (9 g) organic sesame seeds

In a medium bowl, combine the warm water and honey until dissolved. Gently stir in the yeast, cover, and let sit for about 5 minutes. Once foamy, add the oil.

In a large bowl, combine the flour, salt, flax seeds, sunflower seeds, and sesame seeds. Add the yeast mixture to the dry ingredients and combine in a stand mixer or with a wooden spoon until a dough forms. Turn it out onto a floured surface or, alternatively, knead the dough with the hook attachment of your stand mixer.

Knead the dough until it's smooth and elastic, adding additional flour in small increments if the dough is very sticky. Keep in mind, the dough will still be slightly tacky, and will never look as perfectly smooth as a white flour dough does.

Place the kneaded dough in a large greased bowl, cover with a tea towel, and let rise in a warm place until doubled, about 1 hour.

Grease a loaf pan. Gently punch down the dough, knead it again briefly, and shape into a loaf. Transfer to the pan, cover again, and let rise until doubled, about 45 minutes.

Preheat the oven to 350°F (180°C). Once risen, bake in the preheated oven for 35 to 40 minutes, or until golden brown and hollow sounding when tapped.

Remove from the oven, and after about 5 minutes, turn the loaf out from the pan and let cool on a wire rack.

Prince Edward Island

Despite being Canada's smallest province, Prince Edward Island was the only one we managed to get truly lost in. While "Bay Street" sounded like an important, modern thoroughfare that might get us somewhere, it turned out to be a waterlogged, unpaved road through the woods, thus resulting in a very muddied car and a call to the tow truck driver!

While that mishap cost us a few bucks, it's indicative of the island; at least visually, not *that* much has changed since Lucy Maud Montgomery wrote about Anne of Green Gables. The iron-rich soil is still the colour of copper, the beaches remain pristine, and hand-painted signs still advertise lobster suppers in cozily named towns like Cardigan. It's hard not to feel nostalgic there, especially if you grew up watching *Road to Avonlea*.

We drove around most of Prince Edward Island, pulling over at sites like the elaborate Bottle Houses—constructed entirely out of glass bottles and concrete—and the Mont Carmel Church and graveyard, built in 1898. We visited several organic farms, hopped on a flat-top boat at Raspberry Point Oysters, and met Al, a beekeeper-turned-garlic-grower who makes the best black garlic.

One evening while camping by the ocean, we made grilled cheese sandwiches with everything we'd purchased that day: bread from our new baker friend John, Avonlea clothbound cheddar, butter from Cows Creamery, and Al's black garlic. In both context and in flavour, we agreed they were the finest grilled cheese we'd ever had.

PEI may be small, but it's mighty, an island of rolling hills and truly hospitable people. From it, we boarded a ferry bound for Nova Scotia . . .

CAPE BRETON BUTTERSCOTCH PIE

This recipe comes from Calgary food entrepreneur Janice Beaton, a native of Cape Breton. When we asked her for a great hometown recipe, she consulted her clan in Mabou and got back to us. She wrote:

My sisters, mom, and my good friend, Madonna, who works with me here (also a CB'er) all feel that Butterscotch Pie is a classic sweet recipe. As my mom said, we were all poor but there was always milk, butter, eggs and sugar available, as everyone had cows, chicken, etc.

After having made it, and each consuming two slices in a row, we both agreed that this pie is unbelievable. Those thrifty Cape Bretoners are geniuses!

SERVES 6

1 bottom pastry shell (The Pie Shoppe's Pastry, page 240, halved)

CUSTARD

- 1/3 cup + 1 Tbsp (90 g) unsalted butter
- 1/3 cup (50 g) all-purpose flour (see note on page 6)
- 2/3 cup (142 g) lightly packed dark brown sugar
- 1/2 tsp (1.5 g) salt
- 2 1/2 cups (625 mL) whole milk, divided
- 2 egg yolks (reserve the whites for the meringue)
- 1 tsp (5 mL) vanilla extract

MERINGUE

- 3 egg whites
- 1/4 cup (50 g) raw cane sugar

Prepare the pie pastry (page 240) and blind bake (page 6) until the crust is barely golden but not fully cooked, about 8 to 10 minutes. Let cool completely.

While the pastry is cooling, prepare the custard. In a small pan, brown the butter over medium heat, swirling regularly, for about 8 to 10 minutes until very dark. This is the trick to amazing butterscotch: the fine line between really dark brown and burnt. As soon as the butter is dark brown and smells nutty, remove from the heat and pour into a bowl to prevent it from browning further.

In a large pot (off the heat), mix the flour, sugar, and salt together. Stir in the browned butter. Add 1/2 cup (125 mL) of cold milk and stir until smooth.

In a small pot, scald the remaining 2 cups (500 mL) of milk by bringing it almost to a boil over medium heat. As soon as bubbles begin to appear below the surface, remove from heat. Let cool slightly. Add the scalded milk to the browned butter mixture and cook over medium heat, whisking regularly, until the mixture has thickened, about 10 minutes. Remove from the heat.

Reserving the egg whites for the meringue, beat the egg yolks lightly, then temper them by stirring 1/4 cup (60 mL) of the browned butter custard into the yolks. Add this mixture back into the custard, return to medium heat, and cook for another 10 minutes, whisking regularly. Remove from the heat and add the vanilla. Let cool 20 to 30 minutes before pouring into the cooled pastry shell and smoothing the surface.

Preheat the oven to 375°F (190°C).

In a stand mixer or with an electric beater, beat the egg whites until soft peaks form, about 3 to 4 minutes. Add the sugar 1 Tbsp (about 12 g) at a time and continue to beat until stiff peaks form, about 1 to 2 minutes more. Spread and swirl the meringue over the top of the custard. Bake the pie for 5 to 10 minutes (checking on it every 2 minutes) until the meringue has golden highlights.

Remove from the oven and allow the pie to set for at least 3 hours before serving.

GOAT YOGURT FUDGE

We met Susan Ross and Brian Lendrum at their goat farm, which sits at the edge of Lake Laberge in the Yukon. Brian showed us how he makes cheese after milking the goats each morning, and Susan took us on a tour of their large garden and barn.

In addition to the cheese, Susan turns the goat milk into yogurt and uses some of it to make fudge. She's adapted this recipe—based on her grandmother's recipe for pecan sour cream fudge—to the goat yogurt, the consistency of which varies according to the time of year it's made. If the goat yogurt you buy is quite runny, strain it in cheesecloth for about 2 to 3 hours, or use sour cream. You'll also need a candy thermometer for this one.

SERVES 10

Butter for greasing the pan and pot
2½ cups (625 mL) lightly packed brown sugar
1 cup (250 mL) full-fat goat yogurt or sour cream
⅛ tsp salt
¼ cup (60 mL) unsalted butter
1 tsp (5 mL) vanilla extract
20 pecan halves

Butter the bottom and sides of an 8- × 8-inch (20 × 20 cm) pan. Set aside.

Butter the sides of a medium heavy-bottom pot, then add the brown sugar, goat yogurt, and salt. Over medium heat, whisk constantly until the sugar completely dissolves and the mixture comes to a boil, about 5 to 6 minutes. Stop whisking as soon as it starts bubbling, insert the candy thermometer (without letting it touch the bottom), and let it heat up to 240°F (115°C), or "soft ball stage," without stirring it. This can take up to 20 to 25 minutes, but you should start checking 15 minutes after you stop stirring. To test, dip a spoon in and drop a small bit of the mixture into a glass filled with ice water. If the drop stays together but remains soft and malleable when you pick it up with your fingers, you have reached the desired stage and should stop cooking, or the fudge will be too hard. If it's not ready, test again every 5 minutes until the soft ball stage is achieved and/or the temperature has reached 240°F (115°C).

Once it's ready, remove the fudge from the heat and add the butter and vanilla, but don't stir. Let cool for 20 minutes.

Next, transfer the mixture to the bowl of a stand mixer and beat on medium for 10 minutes. It will thicken significantly as it is beaten and will slightly lose its sheen.

Pour it into the prepared pan, evenly place the pecans overtop, and press them in gently. Let cool completely before cutting into 20 to 25 squares. Store in an airtight container.

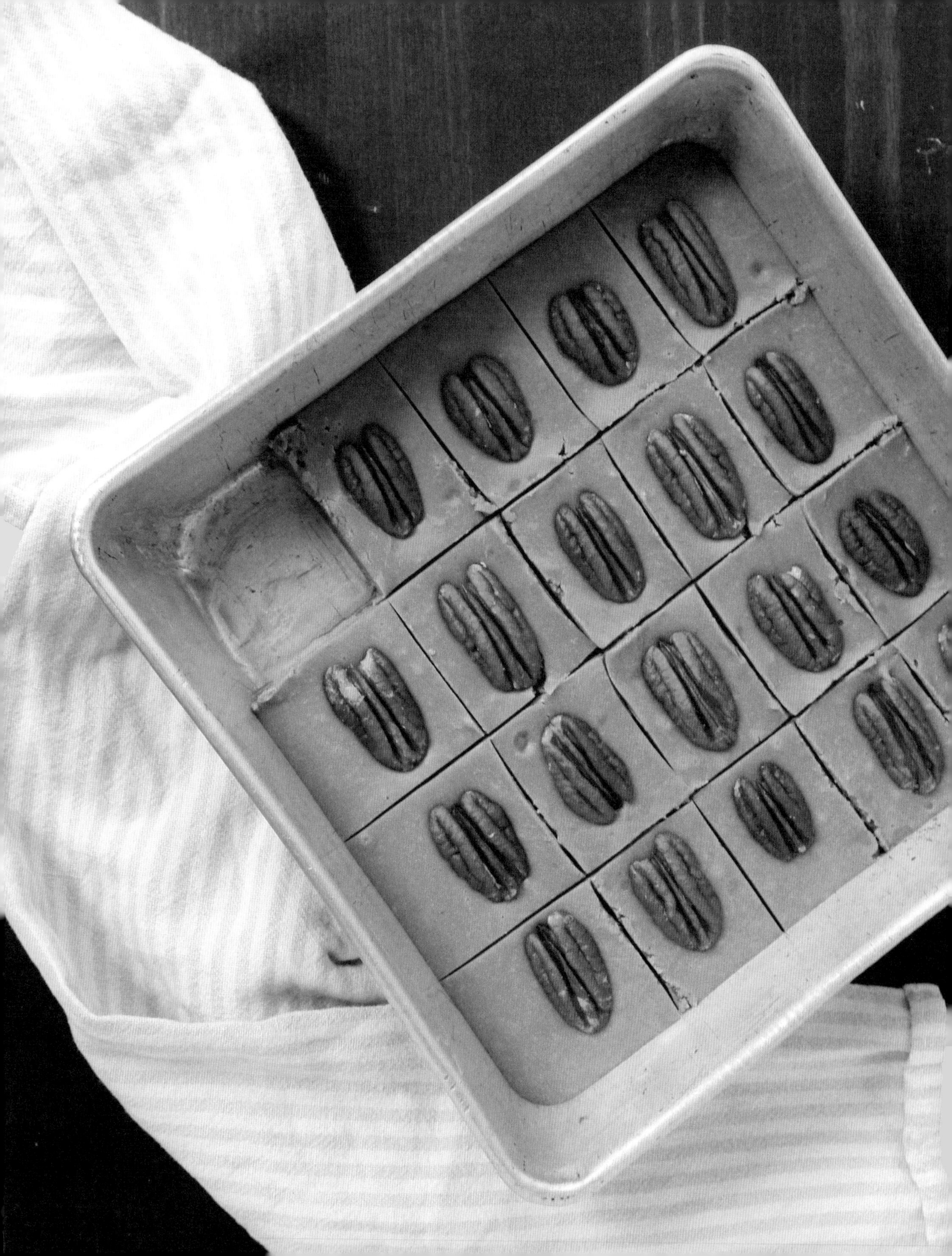

FIG TARTS

WITH *FROMAGE FRAIS*

Anytime we decide that we've been working extra hard and deserve a treat, we go to Beaucoup Bakery in Vancouver. Judging by the number of times we've treated ourselves there, we must be the hardest-working people in the world. We asked owner Jackie Kai Ellis if she could contribute a recipe that features figs, which can be seen ripening on trees all over the city in late summer. The recipe she gave us is lovely, just like every one of the dozens of pastries we've consumed there.

SERVES 6

6 pre-baked individual tart shells (store-bought, or homemade using the Pie Shoppe's Pastry on page 240, halved)

FIG COMPOTE

8 fresh figs (about 300 g), divided
¾ cup (185 mL) dried black mission figs, chopped into small pieces
¾ cup (185 mL) dry red wine
¾ cup (185 mL) water
2 vanilla beans, sliced open lengthwise and seeds scraped out
1 Tbsp (15 mL) orange peel, in strips
1½ tsp (7 mL) lemon peel, in strips
6 Tbsp (90 mL) lightly packed dark brown sugar
⅛ tsp nutmeg
¼ tsp (1 mL) ground cinnamon
⅛ tsp allspice

CHEESE FILLING

2 cups (500 mL) *fromage frais*, or quark cheese
7 Tbsp (105 mL) icing sugar, sifted
1 Tbsp (15 mL) orange zest
1½ vanilla beans, sliced open lengthwise and seeds scraped out
3 Tbsp (45 mL) whole milk, if needed
¼ cup (60 mL) apple jelly (optional)
1 Tbsp (15 mL) water (optional)

If making the pastry from scratch, preheat the oven to 350°F (180°C) and make a half batch of The Pie Shoppe's Pastry, page 240. Follow the instructions to make individual tart shells and blind bake (page 6) in the preheated oven for about 12 to 14 minutes.

For the compote, finely dice five of the fresh figs and add to a small pot along with the rest of the ingredients (include both the vanilla seeds and the scraped pods). Bring to a boil. Once boiling, lower the heat and let simmer, stirring constantly, until the mixture has reduced to about one-quarter to one-third of the original volume, about 20 minutes. Once simmered, remove and discard the vanilla pods. There will be enough compote for 10 to 12 tarts, but the leftovers are lovely eaten with yogurt or as a jam. It will keep in the refrigerator for up to 5 days.

For the cheese filling, mix the *fromage frais*, icing sugar, orange zest, and vanilla seeds in a medium bowl with a spatula until well incorporated. If the cheese is a bit stiff or dry, mix in some milk, 1 Tbsp (15 mL) at a time, until it softens to a somewhat spreadable consistency. This will keep in the refrigerator for up to 3 days.

To assemble, fill the tart shells half full with the cheese filling. Top the remainder of the tart with several spoonfuls of the fig compote.

Cut the remaining three figs in half lengthwise. Add the apple jelly and 1 Tbsp (15 mL) of water to a small pot and place over medium heat to thin out. Using a pastry brush, brush the cut side of the figs with the hot jelly to give them a nice shine and keep the figs fresh. Place the figs on the tarts.

The finished tarts can be made 3 hours in advance and kept in the refrigerator. Serve chilled.

S'MORE SCONES

Two If By Sea is a café and roastery (producing Anchored Coffee) with locations on either side of Halifax Harbour. These scones are from co-owner and baker Tara MacDonald, who believes that because baked goods aren't eaten often, they should be decadent. This version, a way to enjoy the nostalgic taste of s'mores any time of year, is a riff on her basic scone recipe, which she often mixes up with different flavours.

SERVES 12

4½ cups (675 g) all-purpose flour (see note on page 6)
¾ cup (150 g) white sugar
1½ Tbsp (18 g) baking powder
⅛ tsp salt
¼ cup + 1 Tbsp (71 g) cold salted butter, divided
1½ cups (75 g) mini marshmallows
1½ cups (200 g) milk chocolate chips
1¼ to 2 cups (310 to 500 mL) buttermilk
3 full-sized graham crackers
Dash of ground cinnamon

Preheat the oven to 350°F (180°C) and line a baking sheet with parchment paper.

In a large bowl, combine the flour, sugar, baking powder, and salt. Cut or grate ¼ cup (57 g) of cold butter, and use a pastry cutter to mix the butter into the flour mixture until it's pea-sized. Mix in the marshmallows and chocolate chips. In ¼-cup (60 mL) increments, pour in the buttermilk and mix with a wooden spoon until just incorporated each time. Stop adding buttermilk once the batter has come together and is not sticky. Do not overmix the dough or it will become tough.

Transfer the dough ball to a well-floured surface. Lightly press it into a 1-inch-thick (2.5 cm) disc and use a 2-inch (5 cm) round biscuit cutter to cut out the scones. Transfer them to the prepared baking sheet and keep in the refrigerator until ready to bake. You should end up with close to two dozen scones.

Melt the remaining 1 Tbsp (14 g) of butter in the microwave or in a small pot. Roughly crumble the graham crackers and mix them into the butter along with the cinnamon.

Remove the scones from the refrigerator and top them with the graham cracker crumble, pressing the mixture gently into the top of the scones. Bake in the preheated oven for 20 to 25 minutes, or until lightly browned. Remove from the oven and leave on the baking sheet for about 2 minutes before transferring to cooling racks. Enjoy the scones while they're still warm.

YUKON SOURDOUGH CINNAMON BUNS

While in the Yukon, there were two things we never had trouble finding: sourdough bread and cinnamon buns. While the former became popular during the Gold Rush days, we're still not sure when the territory's love affair with cinnamon buns began. On the day we drove from Whitehorse to Dawson City, we made sure to stop at the Braeburn Lodge for one of their famous plate-sized buns. They're baked up daily by the owner, who looks like Santa Claus dressed in biker gear. This recipe combines these two Northern favourites, and we're thrilled with the result. The sourdough starter is easy to prepare—just be sure to get it going about a week in advance!

SERVES 12

DOUGH

1 Tbsp (15 mL) honey
1/2 cup (125 mL) warm water
2 tsp (6 g) active dry yeast
3/4 cup (185 mL) freshly fed Yukon Sourdough Starter (see page 253)
1 egg
5 Tbsp (70 g) unsalted butter, melted
1 tsp (5 mL) salt
3 cups (450 g) all-purpose flour (see note on page 6)

FILLING

1/4 cup (57 g) unsalted butter, softened
2/3 cup (142 g) lightly packed brown sugar
1 Tbsp (7 g) ground cinnamon

GOO

1/2 cup (113 g) unsalted butter
1 tsp (2 g) ground cinnamon
1/2 cup (125 mL) maple syrup
1/8 tsp salt

See overleaf for preparation ▶

In the bowl of your stand mixer (or just a large bowl), stir the honey into the warm water. Sprinkle the yeast overtop, stir gently, and let sit for 5 minutes, until foamy.

Mix in the starter, egg, butter, and salt, then stir in the flour 1 cup (150 g) at a time with the stand mixer's dough hook, or a wooden spoon, until the dough comes together. At this point, either knead it in the stand mixer with the dough hook on low to medium speed, or turn the dough out onto a floured surface and knead by hand. Add more flour if the dough becomes sticky, but try to keep additional flour to a minimum. Knead for 5 to 6 minutes, or until the dough is smooth, soft, and elastic. Place in an oiled bowl, cover with a clean tea towel, and place in a draft-free (and preferably warm) spot. Let rise for about 1 hour, until doubled. While the dough is rising, make the filling and goo.

For the filling, mix the softened butter, brown sugar, and cinnamon until fully combined. Set aside.

For the goo, first grease a 9- × 13-inch (23 × 33 cm) baking dish. In a medium saucepan, melt the butter over low heat. Add the cinnamon, maple syrup, and salt, and heat until the mixture is bubbling, stirring often. Remove from the heat and pour into the prepared dish.

Once the dough has risen, press it down gently to remove the air, then turn out onto a floured surface. Roll the dough into a 12- × 18-inch (30 × 45 cm) rectangle, sprinkling the counter and rolling pin with flour when necessary to prevent the dough from sticking.

Next, spread the filling over the dough, all the way to the edges. Don't worry if it doesn't evenly cover every last bit.

Starting from the long side of the rectangle, roll the dough into a log, ending with the seam at the bottom to secure it. With a serrated knife or piece of thread, cut the log into 12 even pieces, and place the buns in the prepared baking dish. Cover with a clean tea towel and place in a draft-free spot to rise for 30 minutes.

Preheat the oven to 350°F (180°C).

Place the buns in the preheated oven and bake for 35 to 45 minutes, or until they're golden brown. Remove from the oven and let rest on a cooling rack for 15 to 20 minutes. When ready to invert the pan, first slide a knife around the edges to loosen the buns, then cover the pan with a baking sheet, preferably with raised edges. Wearing oven mitts and in one swift move, flip over so the baking pan is on top. Shake gently if the buns don't come out immediately, and slowly remove the pan from the top. Scrape out any remaining goo, and let the buns cool a few more minutes before tucking in.

PARTRIDGEBERRY STEAMED PUDDING

WITH WARM SCREECH BUTTER SAUCE

In Trinity, one of Newfoundland's most picturesque towns, we stayed in a quaint old house that's part of the Artisan Inn. Marieke Gow, one of the owners, gathered a few friends and had us over to her home for a classic East Coast kitchen party, complete with fried cod tongues, live music, and this satisfying dessert. It was an act of hospitality above and beyond, totally in the Newfoundland style. This recipe was created and kindly shared by Bob Arniel, the Artisan Inn's consulting chef. It makes us think of warm kitchens, new friends, and chilly winds off the Atlantic.

SERVES 9 TO 10

PARTRIDGEBERRY STEAMED PUDDING

- 1 loaf good-quality, slightly stale white bread
- 1/2 cup (113 g) unsalted butter, room temperature, plus extra for greasing the ramekins or pan
- 1 1/2 cups (320 g) lightly packed dark brown sugar
- 2 eggs
- 1/3 cup (50 g) all-purpose flour (see note on page 6)
- 1 Tbsp (12 g) baking powder
- 2 tsp (4 g) ground cinnamon
- 2 tsp (4 g) ground allspice
- 1/8 tsp salt
- 1 cup (130 g) dried bread crumbs
- 1 cup (250 mL) buttermilk
- 3/4 cup (185 mL) fresh or thawed frozen blueberries
- 3/4 cup (185 mL) fresh or thawed frozen partridgeberries or cranberries

SCREECH BUTTER SAUCE

- 1/2 cup (113 g) unsalted butter
- 1/2 cup (107 g) lightly packed dark brown sugar
- 3 Tbsp + 1 tsp (50 mL) Newfoundland Screech or another dark rum
- 1 cup (250 mL) whipping cream
- 1/8 tsp salt

See overleaf for preparation ▶

Slice the bread and break it into small pieces. In batches, place the bread pieces in a food processor—be careful not to put in too many pieces at once, or they'll clump together—and pulse until you have 2 cups (150 g) of coarse, fresh crumbs. Set aside.

Preheat the oven to 350°F (180°C). Generously butter the insides of 10 ramekins or an 8- × 8-inch (20 × 20 cm) baking pan.

In a medium bowl, beat the butter and sugar together until fluffy, about 2 to 3 minutes. Add the eggs and mix until smooth.

In another bowl, combine the flour, baking powder, cinnamon, allspice, salt, and the dried and fresh bread crumbs and mix until combined. Alternating between the dry ingredients and the buttermilk, add a little at a time to the butter and sugar mixture, stirring just until combined before adding more of each. Gently fold in the berries, then spoon into the ramekins or pour the entire mixture into the baking pan.

Place the ramekins or baking pan in a larger pan (a 9- × 13-inch/23 × 33 cm casserole dish is recommended). Boil a full kettle of water and pour the boiling water into the large oven pan, filling it a quarter of the way up the sides of the ramekins or baking pan and being careful not to splash any of the water into the pudding. Cover the ramekins or baking pan with parchment paper, then cover the larger oven dish tightly with tinfoil.

Bake in the preheated oven for 50 to 60 minutes if using the ramekins, or 60 to 70 minutes if using an 8- × 8-inch (20 × 20 cm) pan, or until a toothpick inserted into the centre comes out clean.

While the puddings are steaming, combine the butter and dark brown sugar in a small saucepan over medium heat. Stir constantly, and once the sugar is incorporated, add the Screech and stir to combine. Add the whipping cream and bring to a boil, stirring constantly. Let the sauce boil until thickened, about 3 to 4 minutes, then remove from the heat and set aside.

Serve the puddings while still warm, with a generous portion of the hot Screech butter sauce drizzled overtop.

It wasn't long before we would think of this dessert again. In Nunavut, Kelly Lindell (page 141) served a partridgeberry cake with hot butter sauce that transported us right back to that night. Partridgeberries (also called lingonberries) are a prominent ingredient in both Canada's extreme north and far east.

WILD RICE PUDDING

WITH BLUEBERRIES

We're both dedicated fans of rice pudding, though neither of us had ever eaten it with wild rice until we visited Neechi Commons in Winnipeg. The large not-for-profit grocery cooperative also runs Tansi, an eatery specializing in Aboriginal cuisine. Chef Talia Syrie, co-owner of Winnipeg's beloved restaurant, the Tallest Poppy, was running the café at the time, and she served us this pudding topped with big handfuls of wild Manitoba blueberries.

SERVES 4 TO 6

3/4 cup (185 mL) wild rice
1/2 cup (125 mL) white basmati rice
1 1/2 cups (375 mL) whole milk, divided
1 1/2 cups (375 mL) whipping cream, divided
1 tsp (5 mL) salt
2 eggs, beaten
1/3 to 1/2 cup (80 to 125 mL) white sugar
1/8 tsp cayenne
1/2 tsp (2 mL) ground cinnamon
1/2 cup (125 mL) golden raisins (optional)
1/4 cup (60 mL) unsalted butter
1 Tbsp (15 mL) vanilla extract
1 cup (250 mL) fresh blueberries

Add the wild rice to a medium pot and cook according to the package instructions. Add the basmati to another medium pot and cook according to package instructions. When both are finished cooking, fluff with a fork.

In a medium pot, measure out and combine 1 1/2 cups (375 mL) of the cooked wild rice and 1 cup (250 mL) of the cooked basmati, along with 1 cup (250 mL) of milk, 1 cup (250 mL) of cream, and the salt. Cook over medium heat, stirring frequently until thick and creamy, about 20 minutes.

Once thickened, remove from the heat and stir in the remaining 1/2 cup (125 mL) each of milk and cream. Ladle about 1/4 cup (60 mL) of the rice mixture into the beaten eggs to temper them. Whisk lightly and add the egg mixture to the pot, followed by the sugar, cayenne, cinnamon, and raisins (if using). Whisk well, then return to medium heat. Continue cooking until the eggs have set and the mixture has thickened again, about 5 to 10 minutes.

Once thickened, remove from the heat and stir in the butter and vanilla. Stir until the butter is completely incorporated.

Divide among four to six bowls and top generously with fresh blueberries. Serve warm or at room temperature.

BUTTER TARTS

This recipe for an iconic Canadian treat comes from Jillian Povarchook, our dear friend who assisted with much of the styling and photography for this book. When we first asked if she'd be willing to help, she said, "Yes! On one condition—that we put my nana's butter tarts in it." Of course, we *very* happily complied. When she gave us the recipe, Jill shared this story:

Mary Weissman, my nana, was born in 1934, in Princeton, BC, to Slovak immigrants. She only spoke Slovak when she started grade school, so when she wanted to invite a schoolmate over to play after school one day, she did the most logical thing, grabbed the little girl's arm and said, "Buchta, buchta!" Buchta *means bun or dumpling in Slovak, and it was her favourite snack. Bonding over food is something my nana continued to do for the rest of her life—most often over these butter tarts—and my family is thankful for it every day.*

For these tarts, you can prepare your own pastry shells using a full batch of The Pie Shoppe's Pastry (page 240), or use store-bought individual tart shells.

SERVES 12

1/3 cup (80 mL) unsalted butter, room temperature
1 cup (250 mL) lightly packed brown sugar
1 egg, beaten
2 Tbsp (30 mL) whole milk
1 tsp (5 mL) vanilla extract
1/2 cup (125 mL) dried currants
12 unbaked tart shells

Preheat the oven to 400°F (200°C).

Cream the butter with an electric mixer until pale, 2 to 3 minutes. Add the sugar and beat until well combined. Turn the mixer down to low and mix in the egg, milk, and vanilla. Mix in the currants.

Distribute the filling evenly among the prepared tart shells and place in the oven. Bake for 8 minutes, then lower the heat to 350°F (180°C) and bake for another 15 to 20 minutes, or until the filling is puffy and the pastry edges are a light golden brown.

Let cool before serving, as difficult as that may be.

CHOCOLATE RYE LOAF

WITH SASKATOON BERRIES

Saskatoons are *the* favourite berry of the Prairies, and we came across them in all kinds of baked goods at the farmers' markets we visited. One thing we didn't see, however, was a loaf featuring the berries with yet another classic Saskatchewan ingredient: rye flour. When paired with chocolate, the result is a not-too-sweet, finely textured loaf that our friend Heather's dad described as "comfortably chocolatey."

SERVES 6 TO 8

1 cup + 1 tsp (153 g) all-purpose flour, divided (see note on page 6)
2/3 cup (100 g) rye flour
3/4 cup (60 g) cocoa powder
1 1/2 tsp (6 g) baking powder
1/2 tsp (3 g) baking soda
1/2 tsp (1.5 g) salt
1 tsp (2 g) ground cinnamon
1/4 cup (57 g) unsalted butter, room temperature
2/3 cup (142 g) lightly packed brown sugar
3/4 cup (185 mL) buttermilk
1/2 cup (125 mL) plain yogurt, 6% fat or higher
1 egg + 1 egg white
3/4 cup (185 mL) fresh Saskatoon berries or blueberries (see note)
3/4 cup (100 g) chopped dark chocolate, plus a few extra squares for the top of the loaf

Preheat the oven to 350°F (180°C) and butter the inside of a loaf pan.

In a large bowl, combine 1 cup (150 g) all-purpose flour, the rye flour, cocoa powder, baking powder, baking soda, salt, and cinnamon.

In a separate bowl, cream the butter and sugar, then mix in the buttermilk and yogurt. In another bowl, lightly beat the egg and egg white, and mix into the wet ingredients. Pour the wet ingredients into the flour mixture and stir gently until just combined. Toss the berries in the remaining 1 tsp (5 mL) of flour. Fold the berries and chocolate into the batter, then pour into the prepared pan. Top with extra chocolate. Bake for 40 to 45 minutes, or until a toothpick inserted into the centre comes out clean.

Note: If using frozen berries, thaw and drain first.

OKANAGAN CHERRY BUTTERMILK CHESS PIE

WITH VANILLA BEAN CREAM

We are very fortunate to live close to the Pie Shoppe, a bakery run by sisters Andrea and Stephanie French in Vancouver's Chinatown. While writing this book, we often popped over for "pastry research," which involved asking one baking-related question and then ordering one (or more) slices of their unbelievable pie. While this recipe features Okanagan cherries, the custard is incredibly versatile, so you can swap out the cherries with whatever the season has to offer. Blueberries, strawberries, blackberries, raspberries, or peaches are all fine substitutes—just be sure to use fresh fruit. At the height of summer, this cherry buttermilk combination is one of our absolute favourites.

SERVES 6

1 pie crust (The Pie Shoppe's Pastry, page 240, halved)
1 cup (250 mL) fresh Bing, Rainier, or black cherries, halved and pitted (plus a few extra for serving)
1 Tbsp (15 mL) white sugar

BUTTERMILK CUSTARD

1 cup (250 mL) white sugar
3/4 tsp (3 mL) ground cinnamon
1 Tbsp (15 mL) all-purpose flour
1/2 tsp (2 mL) salt
1 tsp (5 mL) vanilla extract
1 tsp (5 mL) lemon zest
1/4 cup + 3 Tbsp (105 mL) butter, melted
3 eggs, plus 1 yolk
2/3 cup (160 mL) sour cream
1 1/3 cups (330 mL) buttermilk
1 tsp (5 mL) white vinegar
1 Tbsp (15 mL) fine cornmeal
1 Tbsp (15 mL) raw sugar for finishing (optional)

WHIPPED CREAM

1 cup (250 mL) whipping cream
1/2 vanilla bean, sliced open lengthwise and seeds scraped out, or 1 tsp (5 mL) vanilla extract
1 Tbsp (15 mL) maple syrup

Preheat the oven to 350°F (180°C).

Prepare the pie pastry (page 240) and blind bake (page 6) until the crust is barely golden but not fully cooked, about 8 minutes.

Place the cherries in a bowl and sprinkle with 1 Tbsp (15 mL) of sugar.

To make the custard filling, combine the sugar, cinnamon, flour, salt, vanilla, and lemon zest in a large bowl. Whisk in the melted butter, then beat in the eggs and the extra yolk one at a time. Incorporate the sour cream and buttermilk and finish by mixing in the vinegar. Mix in the prepared cherries.

Sprinkle the cornmeal over the slightly cooled crust and pour the custard and cherry mixture into the pie shell.

Bake the pie in the preheated oven for 35 to 40 minutes, or until the custard moves just a little when shaken and a light crust has formed on the surface. Let cool and sprinkle with raw sugar, if desired.

Whip the cream, the scraped seeds of the vanilla bean, and the maple syrup together until soft peaks form. Slice and serve the pie with whipped cream and more halved and pitted fresh cherries.

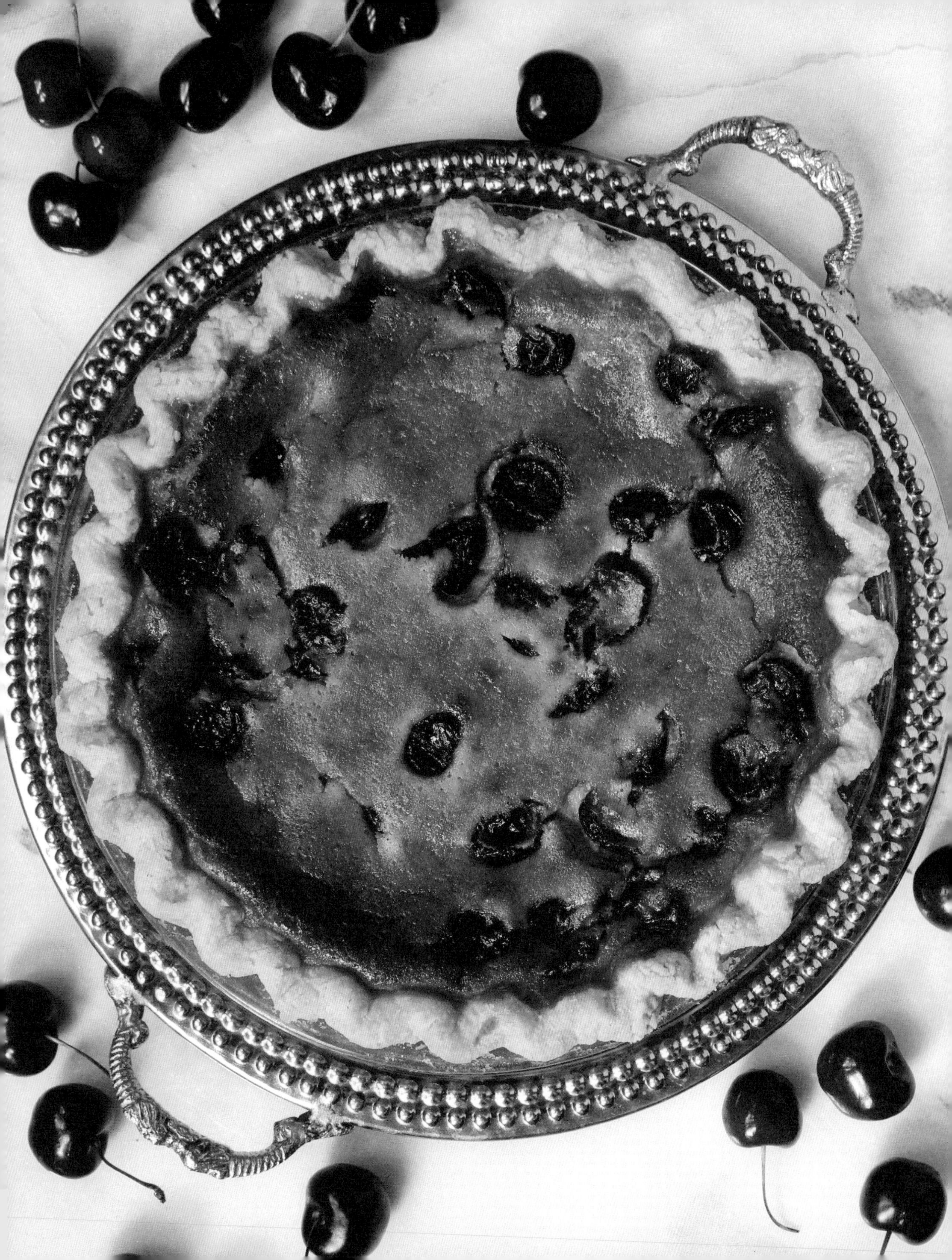

Nova Scotia

Historically, Nova Scotia has been an important gateway to Canada. During the 20th century, around 1 million immigrants entered the country through Pier 21 in Halifax, and nearly one-fifth of Canadians can trace their ancestry back to this port.

We boarded a ferry on Prince Edward Island and arrived in Pictou, Nova Scotia, an area settled by Scottish immigrants in the 1700s. Unsurprisingly, the area is praised for having the best shortbread in Canada, and we fuelled up with cookies and tea before leaving town.

In Halifax, we experienced the small but booming food scene. We brunched at Edna, sipped craft ales at many of the city's breweries, and found excellent coffee and baked goods at Two If By Sea Café. One day, we visited both locations of the Halifax Farmers' Market, established in 1750 and the oldest continuously running market in North America.

In the idyllic Annapolis Valley, we strolled through apple orchards and vineyards, sipped L'Acadie blanc—Nova Scotia's signature grape—and briefly considered staying forever. On our way to the historic town of Lunenburg, we came across an old wooden sauerkraut factory called Krispi Kraut, which had bins of freshly harvested cabbage outside and sold huge packages of kraut for *one dollar*! Another day, we were hosted by our friend Diane, who put on a big traditional lobster boil for us.

With its blazingly colourful forests, autumn was the perfect time to drive the Cabot Trail on Cape Breton Island, each bend in the road offering yet another brilliant view. We ate stew and soda bread at the famous Red Shoe Pub in Mabou and hauled out the best clothes we could find to attend the clifftop wedding of Lindsay's former boss, Janice. We even had a proper Thanksgiving dinner, prepared by the talented Chef Bryan Picard at the Chanterelle Country Inn. It was an ideal time to reflect on the many experiences we'd had and anticipate all that was to come.

After an amazing stint in Nova Scotia, we boarded yet another ship, and seven hours later, we arrived on the Rock . . .

BIRCH SYRUP & BLACK PEPPER COOKIES

While the Yukon wasn't the first place we tried birch syrup, it *is* where we fell in love with it. Birch syrup is the darker, lesser-known cousin of maple syrup, and it's a bit more expensive. That's because (fun fact!) it takes approximately twice as much sap to make syrup from a birch tree as it does from a maple.

There's a small but dedicated community of birch syrup producers across Canada, and one of our favourites is Lyndsey Larson, a.k.a. Uncle Berwyn, in the Yukon. His syrups have a complex, almost molasses-like character, yet are still light enough to use with breakfast. These perfectly spiced cookies come from the kitchen of Juliana Frisch, Lyndsey's mother-in-law, and are an ideal holiday cookie. If you can't find birch syrup, simply use an equal mixture of maple syrup and molasses to make 1/3 cup (80 mL).

MAKES 24 COOKIES

1 cup (227 g) unsalted butter, room temperature
1 cup (200 g) white sugar
1 egg
1/3 cup (80 mL) birch syrup
3 to 3 1/2 cups (450 to 525 g) all-purpose flour (see note on page 6)
2 tsp (8 g) baking powder
1/2 tsp (3 g) baking soda
1/2 tsp (1.5 g) salt
1/2 tsp (1 g) ground cloves
1/2 tsp (1 g) ground cardamom
1 1/2 tsp (3 g) ground cinnamon
1 1/2 tsp (6 g) freshly ground black pepper
1 tsp (3 g) ground ginger

Preheat the oven to 350°F (180°C).

Beat the butter and sugar until fluffy, then beat in the egg and birch syrup. Mix the flour, baking powder, baking soda, salt, and spices in a separate bowl. Gradually add the dry ingredients to the wet ingredients, mixing until just combined each time you add more. Let the dough rest in the refrigerator until firm, about 30 minutes. Shape into 24 balls and transfer to two ungreased baking sheets. Flatten slightly with the palm of your hand.

Bake in the preheated oven for 10 to 12 minutes. When they're ready, the cookies will have lost their sheen but will still be soft and quite pale. Remove from the oven and transfer to cooling racks immediately. Dust with cinnamon, if desired.

THE FARTHEST FARM

We had an opportunity to visit John Lenart's remarkable farm in the Yukon, and it was a piece of land that took some getting to. We first drove outside of Dawson City and met John down by the river. We canoed across, tied up the canoe, walked over the bank to another small river, and launched ourselves in a second canoe. We floated around a bend and deeper into the forest, until glimpses of a house and a farm appeared between the trees. Yes, we literally travelled over the river (twice!) and through the woods, which is the most fun way to get anywhere. John bought the property over 30 years ago as a young man, built himself a teepee, and set about clearing some land. Decades later, he and his wife, Sarah, now have a big wooden house, chickens, dogs, a huge vegetable garden, greenhouses, all kinds of apple trees and berries, and a spruce tree nursery. He even grows grapes! Working collaboratively with the University of Saskatchewan, John experiments with varieties of apples to determine which are best suited for surviving harsh winters. John is a genius in the North who forced us to completely rethink the possibilities of agriculture above the 64th parallel.

GOAT CHEESE BLANCMANGE

WITH RHUBARB & HONEY

Duchess Bake Shop, one of the country's most lavish bakeries, was one of our first stops in Edmonton. They turn out hundreds of gorgeous treats each day; here's the story of this particular dessert from the bakery's owner, Giselle Courteau:

When I was a little girl, my grand-mère often served us homemade blancmange, a cold, thickened dessert similar to pudding or custard. The basic ingredients of blancmange are usually cream and sugar. We've updated her version by using buttermilk and rhubarb and adding goat cheese and honey from our favourite local producer.

SERVES 8

Note: This dessert needs to set in the refrigerator for at least 4 hours.

BLANCMANGE

- 2 Tbsp (30 mL) ice water
- 1½ tsp (7 mL) powdered gelatin
- ½ cup (125 mL) whipping cream, divided
- ½ cup + 1 Tbsp (140 mL) white sugar
- ½ vanilla bean, sliced open lengthwise and seeds scraped out, or 1 tsp (5 mL) vanilla extract
- ¼ cup (60 mL) goat cheese, crumbled
- 2 cups (500 mL) buttermilk

STEWED RHUBARB

- 2 cups (500 mL) chopped fresh rhubarb (see note)
- ½ vanilla bean, sliced open lengthwise and seeds scraped out, or 1 tsp (5 mL) vanilla extract
- ¼ cup (60 mL) white sugar
- 2 Tbsp (30 mL) honey
- ¼ cup (60 mL) water

Note: If you're using previously frozen rhubarb, place it in a colander to drain the excess liquid as it thaws. Do not press out any extra liquid.

To make the blancmange, add the ice water to a small dish and sprinkle in the gelatin. Stir to dissolve and set aside until firmly set, about 1 to 2 minutes.

In a small saucepan, mix ¼ cup (60 mL) of whipping cream with the sugar and vanilla bean seeds. Bring the heat up to medium and whisk constantly until the sugar is dissolved, about 2 to 3 minutes.

Turn the heat down to low and whisk in the goat cheese until melted, then remove from the heat. Briefly melt the set gelatin in the microwave for a few seconds or by placing the container in another bowl of hot water—it will melt very quickly. Once melted, whisk it into the goat cheese mixture and allow it to cool for 5 minutes. Stir in the buttermilk and set aside.

Using a whisk or hand mixer, whip the remaining ¼ cup (60 mL) of cream until soft peaks form, about 3 to 4 minutes. Be careful not to over-whip the cream or the blancmange may turn out lumpy. Using a rubber spatula, gently fold the whipped cream into the goat cheese mixture.

Pour the mixture into eight ramekins, leaving a bit of space at the top for the stewed rhubarb. Refrigerate for 4 hours, or until set.

To make the stewed rhubarb, place all the ingredients in a bowl over a double boiler and cook over medium heat for about 30 minutes, or until the rhubarb is tender. Set aside to cool, then refrigerate.

Just before serving, spoon the stewed rhubarb over each blancmange.

Without the stewed rhubarb on top, the blancmange will keep in the refrigerator for up to 3 days.

TARTE AU SUCRE

(SUGAR PIE)

We stopped in at Pâtisserie Rhubarbe on our first Montreal Croissant Crawl, a self-planned, pastry-inspired bike trek throughout the city. It's a pretty little shop with cakes, tarts, pastries, and house-made popsicles sold from a window during the summer. They also do a big, pecan-rich version of Quebec's famous sugar pie, and owner Stéphanie Labelle happily shared the recipe.

SERVES 8 TO 10

PASTRY

- ½ cup + 3 Tbsp (155 g) unsalted butter, room temperature
- ¾ cup (85 g) icing sugar
- 1 egg
- 5 Tbsp (30 g) pecan powder, or ¼ cup (30 g) whole pecans ground in a food processor
- 1½ cups + 3 Tbsp (250 g) all-purpose flour (see note on page 6)
- ⅛ tsp salt

FILLING

- 8 egg yolks
- 2 eggs
- ¾ cup (185 mL) maple syrup
- 1¼ cups (266 g) lightly packed brown sugar
- ¾ cup + 2 Tbsp (198 g) unsalted butter
- ¾ cup + 1 Tbsp (200 mL) whipping cream
- 1 tsp (3 g) salt

TOPPING

- 3 Tbsp (45 mL) maple syrup
- 1 cup (about 125 g) whole pecans

To make the pastry, cream the butter and icing sugar for 2 to 3 minutes, until perfectly smooth. Add the egg and mix well, then add the pecan powder. In a separate bowl, combine the flour and salt, then add to the butter mixture in three additions, each time mixing until barely combined. Shape into a disc, wrap in plastic wrap, and refrigerate for 30 minutes.

Preheat the oven to 350°F (180°C). On a well-floured surface, roll out the dough to slightly less than ¼-inch (6 mm) thickness, and transfer to a 9-inch (23 cm) pie dish. Blind bake (page 6) for about 20 minutes, until golden. Let cool.

For the filling, first whisk all the yolks and whole eggs together in a medium bowl. In a large pot over medium heat, combine the maple syrup with the brown sugar, butter, cream, and salt. When boiling, ladle some of the sugar mixture into the eggs and whisk quickly to temper, then transfer the egg mixture back into the big pot, whisking constantly until thick, about 5 minutes. Strain through a sieve into a container and let cool (uncovered) in the refrigerator.

For the topping, line a baking sheet with parchment paper. Heat the maple syrup in a pot over low to medium heat, then add the pecans. Stirring constantly, let them cook until the sugar has caramelized and the nuts look sandy, about 2 to 3 minutes. Transfer to the prepared baking sheet and let cool.

When everything has cooled, pour the sugar custard into the pie crust and let set in the refrigerator for an hour. Garnish the top with the maple pecans and enjoy in small slices—it's lush!

APPLE BUTTER SORBET

We first met Pascale Berthiaume while sampling her ice cream at the Ottawa Farmers' Market, and we immediately became devoted fans. She invited us to her kitchen space, where we got to taste even more. Pascale is just the type of woman you want making your ice cream; her flavours are unique and inventive, she manages to get every combination spot-on, and she's just so, so friendly. This sorbet is a lovely fall treat—any variety of apple will do, but we love Gala or Honeycrisp. If your ice cream maker requires it, remember to put your churning bowl in the freezer at least 24 hours beforehand.

SERVES 12

2½ cups (625 mL) water
1¼ cups (310 mL) apple cider vinegar
5 pounds (2.25 kg) apples, peeled, cored, and diced
1 cup (250 mL) white sugar
1 tsp (5 mL) ground cinnamon
½ whole nutmeg (3 g), grated
¼ tsp (1 mL) salt
3 cups (750 mL) apple or pear cider
2½ Tbsp (38 mL) freshly squeezed lemon juice
3 Tbsp (45 mL) honey

To make the apple butter, add the water, apple cider vinegar, and apples to a large pot and set to boil. Once boiling, lower the heat and simmer until the apples are soft, about 30 minutes. Remove from the heat and press through a food mill, or blend the mixture and press it through a fine sieve to get a consistent texture. Transfer it back to a large pot over low heat and add the sugar, cinnamon, nutmeg, and salt. Stir regularly until the purée reduces by half, about 2 to 3 hours.

To make the sorbet, mix 5 cups (1.25 L) of the prepared apple butter (see note) with the apple or pear cider, lemon juice, and honey together in a pot. Heat on low and stir just until the honey is fully incorporated. Transfer to a container and let chill in the refrigerator for at least 2 hours.

Once chilled, it's time to churn the mixture into sorbet! Depending on the size of your ice cream maker, you may need to churn this in a couple of batches—follow the specific instructions provided for your machine. Churn until the mixture starts to look frozen and gains about 25 percent volume; this could be anywhere from 15 to 40 minutes, depending on your machine. You should end up with about 10 cups (2.5 L) of churned sorbet.

Once churned, transfer the sorbet to an airtight container and store in the freezer. To serve, let it sit at room temperature for 5 minutes before scooping. This is best consumed within 3 months.

Note: If you have leftover apple butter, use it as a topping for oatmeal or yogurt, as a condiment for roast meats, or spread it on toast or sandwiches.

THE PIE SHOPPE'S PASTRY

One thing we discovered while putting this book together is that CANADIANS LOVE PIE. This book has a lot of pie in it, but trust us, it could have had plenty more. Instead of providing half a dozen basic pastry recipes, we decided to give you just one, which is from Stephanie and Andrea French, the sisters who run the Pie Shoppe in Vancouver. They make hundreds of pies each month, and this is their go-to recipe. It's a great one.

MAKES ENOUGH FOR 1 DOUBLE-CRUSTED 9- OR 10-INCH (23 OR 25 CM) PIE (TOP AND BOTTOM)

1½ cups (225 g) all-purpose flour (see note on page 6)
¼ tsp salt
⅓ cup (75 g) cold unsalted butter, cut into ½-inch (1 cm) pieces
⅓ cup (61 g) cold shortening, cut into ½-inch (1 cm) pieces
¼ to ½ cup (60 to 125 mL) cold water

Sift the flour into a large bowl and mix in the salt. With a pastry cutter, incorporate the butter and shortening until they're in pea-sized pieces. Alternatively, you can do this in a food processor by pulsing the machine until the butter and shortening are the right size. Mix in the cold water bit by bit, stopping once a firm but pliable dough has formed. Be careful not to overmix the pastry or it will be tough. Once mixed, form the dough into a disc and wrap in plastic wrap. Let it rest in the refrigerator for 30 minutes.

Once chilled, divide the dough into two smaller balls and roll out on a well-floured surface, adding more flour as needed. If you need only the bottom crust, as with the Okanagan Cherry Buttermilk Chess Pie (page 228), simply wrap up the second ball of dough, or place it in an airtight container, and freeze for a later use.

A few tips:
For most pies, you want to roll the dough out to about ⅛-inch (3 mm) thickness. Always roll out from the centre toward the edges. To transfer the rolled dough from the counter to the pie plate, roll the dough over your rolling pin, then lift it and transfer it to the dish, letting it unroll from one edge to the other.

To get a nice crimped edge, trim the bottom and top crusts to about ¾-inch (2 cm) beyond the edge of the pie plate. For a double-crust pie, pinch the top and bottom edges together slightly and fold them under. Then, while pinching the crust edge with your thumb and pointer finger from one hand, push with the thumb of your opposite hand in between the other two fingers, creating a big crimp. Repeat all the way around the edge of the pie. For a single-crust pie, simply fold the edge under and crimp as instructed above.

To make individual tart shells, roll out the dough to ⅛-inch (3 mm) and cut out 4-inch (10 cm) circles (or 2- to 3-inch/5 to 8 cm circles if using mini muffin tins). Place the circles into the muffin tins and press them evenly into the bottom edges and along the sides. Alternatively, you can press them into fluted tart shells. You should be able to get about 12 tart shells from one full batch of pastry.

CRABAPPLE
BUTTER
L/S
CINN
CRABAPPLE
BUTTER
L/S
CRABAPPLE
BUTTER
L/S
CINN

For the Mason Jar

PRESERVES, PICKLES & SAUCES

PEACH & APRICOT CHUTNEY

This is another gem of a recipe from Elizabeth Baird. In her words:

This mildly spicy and gently piquant chutney pays homage to the abundance of summer fruit grown in Southern Ontario's Niagara Peninsula and along the shores of Lakes Ontario and Erie. Let this chutney mellow for a few weeks—then it's perfect with tourtière *(page 87); to snack on with cream cheese, chèvre, or Oka Classique; to layer on baked brie or pâté; or to serve with any chicken or pork, notably right off the barbeque. And don't forget how good it is on grilled old cheddar cheese and decent-bread sandwiches.*

All our friends who've sampled this chutney became instant fans. This is definitely a "make every year" type of preserve, a warmly spiced jar of summer you'll be glad to crack into mid-winter.

MAKES EIGHT HALF PINT (250 ML) JARS

4 cups (1 L) peeled, pitted, and sliced peaches (approximately 2 pounds/910 g whole)
4 cups (1 L) peeled, pitted, and sliced apricots (approximately 2 pounds/910 g whole)
2 medium yellow onions (about 320 g), diced
3 cups (750 mL) lightly packed brown sugar
2 cups (500 mL) golden raisins
1½ tsp (7 mL) brown or yellow mustard seeds
1½ tsp (7 mL) coarse sea salt
½ tsp (2 mL) ground cinnamon
½ tsp (2 mL) ground coriander
½ tsp (2 mL) ground cumin
½ tsp (2 mL) ground turmeric
½ tsp (2 mL) curry powder or ½ tsp (2 mL) curry paste
¼ tsp (1 mL) freshly crushed cardamom, or additional ground cinnamon
¼ tsp (1 mL) cayenne pepper
2 cups (500 mL) natural apple cider vinegar

Combine all of the ingredients in a large Dutch oven or heavy-bottomed pot. Bring to a boil over medium heat, stirring often. Lower the heat and simmer, uncovered, until the chutney becomes a rich golden colour and is no longer watery, about 1½ to 2 hours. Stir regularly, especially as the chutney thickens.

While the chutney simmers, fill your canner three-quarters full of water, set to boil, and lay out a clean tea towel. Sterilize your jars, fresh lids, and rings (see Canning Basics, page 7).

When it's ready, pour the chutney into the hot jars, filling to ½ inch (1 cm) below the top rim. Wipe any spilled chutney off the rims with a clean towel, top with the lids, and lightly twist on the canning rings. Submerge in the boiling water bath for 10 minutes. Remove the jars and let cool overnight on the clean tea towel.

Once cool, store in a cool, dark, dry place for up to 1 year. Once opened, store in the refrigerator and consume within 3 weeks.

PICKLED PUMPKIN

In Manitoba, the place where the Red River meets the Assiniboine has been a historic gathering place for centuries, an area where the fur traders, Métis, and First Nations people met to trade. Today, a market and shopping district now occupies this historic area, and it is full of remarkable shops, bakeries, and restaurants. Tall Grass Prairie Bread Company is one such business, a bakery that buys directly from farmers and uses ingredients with significance to the area. In addition to milling their own flour on-site daily for their huge baked goods selection, they have a shop with groceries, house-made meals, and an extensive line of preserves. They shared their recipe for a vegetable that isn't often pickled, but should be: pumpkin! This is a quick pickle to make and is great paired with cheese, or in a salad.

MAKES SIX PINT (500 ML) JARS

2 cups (500 mL) white vinegar
2 cups (500 mL) water
4½ cups (1.125 L) white sugar
1 cinnamon stick
8 whole cloves
8 whole allspice berries
Cooking sachet or cheesecloth bag
One 6-pound (2.75 kg) sugar pumpkin, peeled, seeded, and cut into ½-inch (1 cm) chunks (see note)

Note: Sugar pumpkins are also known as pie pumpkins and are an easy find at farmers' markets in the fall. Butternut squash could also be used.

Fill your canner three-quarters full of water, set to boil, and lay out a clean tea towel. Sterilize your jars, fresh lids, and rings (see Canning Basics, page 7).

Add the vinegar, water, and sugar to a large pot. Tie the spices in a cooking sachet and add to the pot. Bring the mixture to a boil. Turn the heat down to simmer and add the pumpkin. Simmer, covered, until the pumpkin chunks become slightly soft but still hold their shape, about 15 minutes. Remove the cooking sachet.

Using a canning funnel, fill the prepared jars with the pumpkin and top up with the spiced brine. The pumpkin should be at least 1 inch (2.5 cm) below the top of the jar, while the brine should be at least ½ inch (1 cm) below the top. Wipe any spillage from the rim with a clean, damp towel. Top with the lids and lightly twist the rings on.

Place in the water bath and process under a rolling boil for 20 minutes. Remove from the water to the clean tea towel and let cool overnight. The pickles are best if left at least 2 weeks before opening. Once unsealed, the pumpkin should be stored in the refrigerator and is best consumed within 3 to 4 weeks.

PICKLED NORTHERN BEETS

Crossing the territorial boundaries made us realize our ignorance when it came to farming north of the 60th parallel. While we'd (wrongly) assumed that farms would be few and far between, we met plenty of people in Hay River, Northwest Territories, who were growing phenomenal produce. We learned the harvests can be just as plentiful as in the south, and because of the extra daylight and shorter growing season, the harvest tends to move at an even faster pace. This means food preservation is important! Lone Sorensen, the woman responsible for this recipe, is a passionate advocate for Northern food. She moved from Denmark to Yellowknife in 1988, and she has been cultivating the local food economy ever since through her company, Northern Roots. As she says, "The north of 60 home-grown beets have an incredibly sweet taste—they are outstanding just as they are, no spices required." In case your beets need an extra boost, we've included the option of adding 1 or 2 whole cloves to each jar.

MAKES EIGHT PINT (500 ML) JARS

9 pounds (4 kg) golden, red, or chioggia beets
2 Tbsp (30 mL) salt
5 cups (1.25 L) white sugar
8 cups (2 L) white vinegar
8 to 16 whole cloves (optional)

Fill your canning pot three-quarters full of water and set to boil. Lay a clean tea towel on your countertop. Sterilize your jars, fresh lids, and rings (see Canning Basics, page 7).

Scrub the beets, place them in a large pot, and fill it with water until the beets are covered. Add the salt to the water and set to boil. Let the beets boil until they are just tender, about 20 to 30 minutes, depending on their size. When they are ready, a paring knife should pierce through without resistance. Drain the beets and let them sit until they are cool enough to handle.

Combine the sugar and vinegar in a medium pot. Simmer over medium heat until the sugar is fully dissolved.

Once the beets have cooled, peel off the softened skin and cut them into 1/4- to 1/2-inch (6 mm to 1 cm) slices. If your beets are small enough, you may even want to pickle them whole, though you'll likely need a few more jars if you do this. Fill the prepared jars with the beet slices and pour enough hot pickling liquid in each jar to fully submerge the beets, leaving 1/2 inch (1 cm) of headspace. Add one or two whole cloves to each jar, if desired.

Using a clean tea towel, wipe any spillage from the jar rims, top with the lids, and lightly twist on the rings. Submerge the jars in the boiling water bath for 30 minutes, then remove them to the clean tea towel. Let cool overnight. The beets should sit for at least 2 weeks before being enjoyed and can be stored for up to 1 year in a cool, dark place. Any jars that don't seal should be kept in the refrigerator and consumed within 2 months.

NEWFOUNDLAND

Icebergs, whales, puffins, cod, Viking settlements, and big-hearted folks: Newfoundland is one damn fine place.

One of our first stops in the province was to see our friend April in Corner Brook, who shuffled us into her car and drove us straight to a mountain trail. After hiking through the forest, we were met with a stunning view of a waterfall, and she hauled out a picnic she'd packed with some Newfoundland classics: Screech-spiked coffee and scones with jam and cream. The experience was an incredible gift, and it pained her that we were heading out so soon and she couldn't do more. "The things I could *show* you!" she yelled into the waterfall.

This was something we came across often—Newfoundlanders who fiercely love their province and were eager to share its very best. Whether that meant walking us to a patch of partridgeberries ripe for picking, organizing a kitchen party in our honour, or feeding us moose salami at 3 am after "Screeching us in," we were always well cared for.

Many people in the province live rurally, and it was in remote places that we had some of our most interesting experiences. We wandered through Gros Morne's Tablelands, ate Fogo pogos in Twillingate, authentic Cajun jambalaya cooked by a Louisiana native in Grates Cove, and fire-roasted breads and pizza at the Bonavista Social Club. Elliston, the root cellar capital of the world, fed us well over a three-day food festival called Roots, Rants, and Roars, during which we ambled through a landscape that looked straight out of Middle Earth.

At one point we stood at Cape Spear, the easternmost point in Canada, overwhelmed that we'd successfully travelled from coast to coast. We were truly grateful for all we'd done and seen, but the trip wasn't over yet. It was time to find some warmer clothes and head north again . . .

GREEN TOMATO CHOW CHOW

This recipe comes from our friend Karen Anderson, the owner of Alberta Food Tours. Though she's now Alberta-based, she grew up on the East Coast, the unofficial land of chow chow! Growing up, she watched her mother, Gerri, cut the green tomatoes and her father, Reg, slice the onions for the large batches they'd make to use up green tomatoes before the coming frost. This sweet, tangy relish is a well-loved preserve on the East Coast, and while road tripping, we tried many different versions, often with fish cakes. Any brand of pickling spice will work; just make sure it's a coarse blend that includes mustard, coriander, bay leaves, dill seed, fenugreek, cinnamon, allspice, black pepper, and cloves.

Enjoy this sauce as Karen's family does, with a dab of Greek yogurt on roasted potatoes, or with *tourtière* and meats of all kinds, including a Thanksgiving turkey.

MAKES EIGHT TO TEN HALF PINT (250 ML) JARS

4 pounds (1.8 kg) green tomatoes, sliced into 1/4-inch (6 mm) rings
2 1/2 pounds (1.1 kg) yellow onions, sliced into 1/4-inch (6 mm) rings
1/4 cup (60 mL) salt
5 cups (1.25 L) lightly packed brown sugar
4 cups (1 L) white vinegar
1/2 cup (125 mL) pickling spice mix
Cooking sachet or spice bag

Layer the tomato and onion rings in a large non-reactive bowl, sprinkling each layer lightly with the salt. Leave overnight or for about 8 hours.

Next, drain the liquid at the bottom of the bowl, then rinse the mixture with cold water and drain again.

Transfer the mixture to a large pot and add the sugar and vinegar. Put the pickling mix in a cooking sachet and add it to the pot. Bring to a boil, then turn down the heat and let simmer until the juices reduce and become a rich brown colour, about 2 hours.

While this is simmering, fill your canner three-quarters full of water and set to boil, then lay a clean tea towel on the countertop. Sterilize your canning jars, fresh lids, and rings (see Canning Basics, page 7).

Once the chow chow is reduced, fill the canning jars to 1/2 inch (1 cm) from the top rim. Wipe any spillage from the rims with a clean tea towel, top the jars with lids, and lightly twist on the rings. Process in the boiling water bath for 20 minutes. Remove the jars from the water bath to the clean tea towel. Let them rest on the countertop overnight. Once cooled, remove the rings and store for up to 1 year in a cool, dark place. Transfer any jars that don't seal to the refrigerator and enjoy within 3 weeks.

YUKON SOURDOUGH STARTER

Making a sourdough starter is actually very easy—it just requires a bit of time and care. This starter is similar to what gold miners in the Yukon would have carried with them to make bread at camp.

It works like this: Initially, you mix together flour and water, activating the wild yeast that's already present in the wheat. It then ferments, feeding on the flour's natural sugars and producing bubbles of carbon dioxide. The starter needs a continuous source of food, so you "feed" it more flour once every day. When used in bread, it's this sugar-turned-carbon-dioxide that acts as a leavening agent, eliminating the need for dried baker's yeast and adding rich flavour to the finished product. Since it takes a while to grow a strong starter that's capable of leavening all on its own, recipes like Yukon Sourdough Cinnamon Buns (page 219) are supported by this starter but don't rely on it fully.

To get started, all you need is a bag of organic white flour.

THE INITIAL MIX

¼ cup (60 mL) organic, unbleached all-purpose flour
¼ cup (60 mL) lukewarm water

In a medium glass or ceramic bowl, thoroughly whisk the flour and water together, then scrape down the sides of the bowl. Cover very loosely with plastic wrap (the mixture still needs access to air) and leave in a place that is at room temperature and out of the direct sunlight. Check on it after a day, but you may need to wait several days before tiny bubbles appear and it begins to smell sour.

When the bubbles appear (1 to 3 days later), thoroughly mix in:

½ cup (125 mL) organic, unbleached all-purpose flour
½ cup (125 mL) lukewarm water

Every 24 hours after that, for the next 4 days, discard half the starter and add:

½ cup (125 mL) organic, unbleached all-purpose flour
⅓ cup (80 mL) lukewarm water

As the days go by, the starter should become more and more bubbly and sour smelling. You'll need to keep discarding some of the starter (necessary to prevent your kitchen from being taken over by it) and feeding it new food. The longer this fermentation goes on, the stronger the starter becomes, and as long as it's good and active, you should be ready to use it in recipes after about 1 week. It may take longer before you can use it as the *only* leavener in sourdough bread recipes, however.

Don't worry if your starter isn't a carbon dioxide–producing beast from day one. Sometimes it takes a little while for them to get going. If after 1 week your starter doesn't look very "alive," just discard it and try again. You could try a different brand of organic flour the second time and see if it works better.

While it should smell funky and sour, if your starter develops mould or turns orange, toss it! If a slight crust has developed, that's okay. Just peel it off and keep going.

If you find your starter is separating and has a layer of liquid on top, that's also okay. Just try adding a little less water when you feed it. Once it's active, you can experiment with how much flour and water you feed it.

Unless you're regularly using your discarded starter in a recipe (for bread, pancakes, etc.) you may not want to feed your starter every day. Once it's active, you can move it to the refrigerator, but cover it loosely so it can still breathe. Remove from the refrigerator once a week, letting it come to room temperature before you feed it.

PICKLED ASPARAGUS

WITH LOVAGE & TARRAGON

This is another outstanding recipe from Dana and Cam of Joy Road Catering in the Okanagan. These asparagus pickles, which they sell countless jars of at farmers' markets each summer, are the Okanagan's favourite Caesar garnish, and once you've tried them, you'll know why. They're savoury, with a great crunch and a mildly sweet tarragon flavour. When you're ready to crack a jar, mix up a batch of Caesars (page 274)!

MAKES THREE QUART (1 L) WIDE-MOUTH JARS

6 bunches (about 6½ pounds/3 kg) asparagus
4 cups (1 L) water
2¼ cups (560 mL) white wine vinegar or white vinegar
¼ cup (60 mL) coarse sea salt
3 sprigs fresh lovage, or a few celery leaves
3 sprigs fresh tarragon
6 cloves garlic, sliced in half

Fill your canner three-quarters full of water, set to boil, and lay a clean tea towel on the countertop. Sterilize your canning jars, fresh lids, and rings (see Canning Basics, page 7).

Snap off the woody ends of the asparagus and discard. Cut the stalks so they'll stand about 1 inch (2.5 cm) from the top of the jars you are using. Reserve any trimmed asparagus pieces for another use.

Add the water and vinegar to a medium pot and set to boil. Once it has reached a simmer, stir in the salt until it dissolves. Once boiling, remove from the heat and set aside to cool slightly.

For each 1 L wide-mouth mason jar, place one sprig of lovage and tarragon and stuff the jars as full of asparagus as you can without squishing any of the spears. Add two cloves of garlic to each jar. Using a canning funnel, pour the warm brine over the asparagus and fill the jar until the tips are under brine and there is ½ inch (1 cm) of headspace from the top of the jar.

Once all the jars are full, wipe any spillage from the rings with a clean, damp tea towel. Top with lids, lightly twist on the rings, and process in the boiling water for 15 minutes. Remove, place on the clean tea towel, and let the jars cool overnight. Store in a cool, dark place and let them sit for at least 1 month before opening them. These are best consumed within 1 year. Once opened, keep in the refrigerator and consume within 1 month.

LACTO-FERMENTED GARLIC DILL PICKLES

Shannon Jones and Bryan Dyck, the organic farmers behind Broadfork Farm in River Hebert, Nova Scotia, are two of the most generous, hardworking people we've ever met. About halfway through our trip, we received an email from Shannon, who'd read about our project and invited us to their farm, enticing us with warm beds and fresh vegetables. Who could say no to that?

Life as an organic farmer can be a tough one, but Shannon and Bryan accept the many challenges with grace and perseverance. They're also active fermenters and were excited to share their knowledge of lacto-fermentation, a technique that creates probiotics and healthy bacteria. Consider yourself warned: these dills are a "gateway ferment," and you'll want to try many more after them!

MAKES FOUR QUART (1 L) WIDE-MOUTH JARS

- 4 to 8 large grape, tomato, oak, cherry, or horseradish leaves, divided
- 1 bunch fresh dill (flowering tops, dill leaves, and/or seeds are all great!)
- 2 Tbsp (30 mL) mustard seeds, divided
- 4 large garlic cloves
- 5 pounds (2.25 kg) pickling or other smaller cucumbers
- 4 Tbsp (60 mL) coarse sea salt, divided (see note)
- 4 cups (1 L) filtered water, divided

Line the bottom of each jar with one or two leaves. These will be the hardest ingredient to find, but you'll get a crunchier ferment if you use them. Try asking at your local farmers' market—there are bound to be farmers who can bring you some. To each jar, add four to five sprigs of dill and sprinkle in ½ Tbsp (7 mL) of mustard seeds. Peel and crush the garlic cloves and add one to each jar, or a few more if you want really garlicky pickles.

Divide the cucumbers and set them up vertically in the jars. Stuff the jars as full as possible, leaving 2 inches (5 cm) of headspace. Depending on the size of your cucumbers, you should be able to fit about 1¼ pounds (570 g) per 1 L mason jar. Having more or fewer cucumbers will not affect whether the fermentation works; it just may slow it down (if you have more) or speed it up (if you have fewer). The difference will be slight.

For each jar, mix 1 Tbsp (15 mL) of sea salt with 1 cup (250 mL) of water and dissolve. Pour the salt solution into the jar and fill it with more water, leaving 1 inch (2.5 cm) of headspace. Place a smaller canning lid, a small plate, or a clean rock into the jar to help keep the cucumbers under the brine. Loosely screw on a canning lid and ring, then set aside to ferment at room temperature, avoiding direct sunlight. Repeat this process for the next three jars.

Within a day, you should start to see some bubbles, and you may need to "burp" your jars by removing the lid for a few seconds to let excess gas escape. Taste the pickles after 3 to 4 days and decide whether you like the flavour and texture. By this time, the brine should be cloudy, the pickles will have sunk to the bottom, and white film may be collecting at the bottom of the jar (this is just excess yeast and nothing to be concerned about). At this point, it's entirely up to you whether the pickles are done! You can leave them 1 to 2 days longer or continue with the instructions below. We prefer whole cucumbers that ferment at room temperature (70°F/21°C) for about 6 to 7 days.

Once you are happy with the flavour and texture, transfer everything in the brining jars to clean jars and store in the refrigerator or a cellar. They should maintain their crispness at this cooler temperature for at least 6 months, and probably much longer. If the ferment becomes too soft for your liking, either during the initial fermentation or after the pickles have been in the refrigerator for many months, Bryan and Shannon suggest finely chopping them and eating them as homemade relish.

Note: You can choose to use more or less salt. Using more salt will slow down the fermentation process and produce a more sour pickle, and using less salt will speed up the process, creating a less sour pickle. The amounts provided in this recipe are a good starting point if this is your first time fermenting.

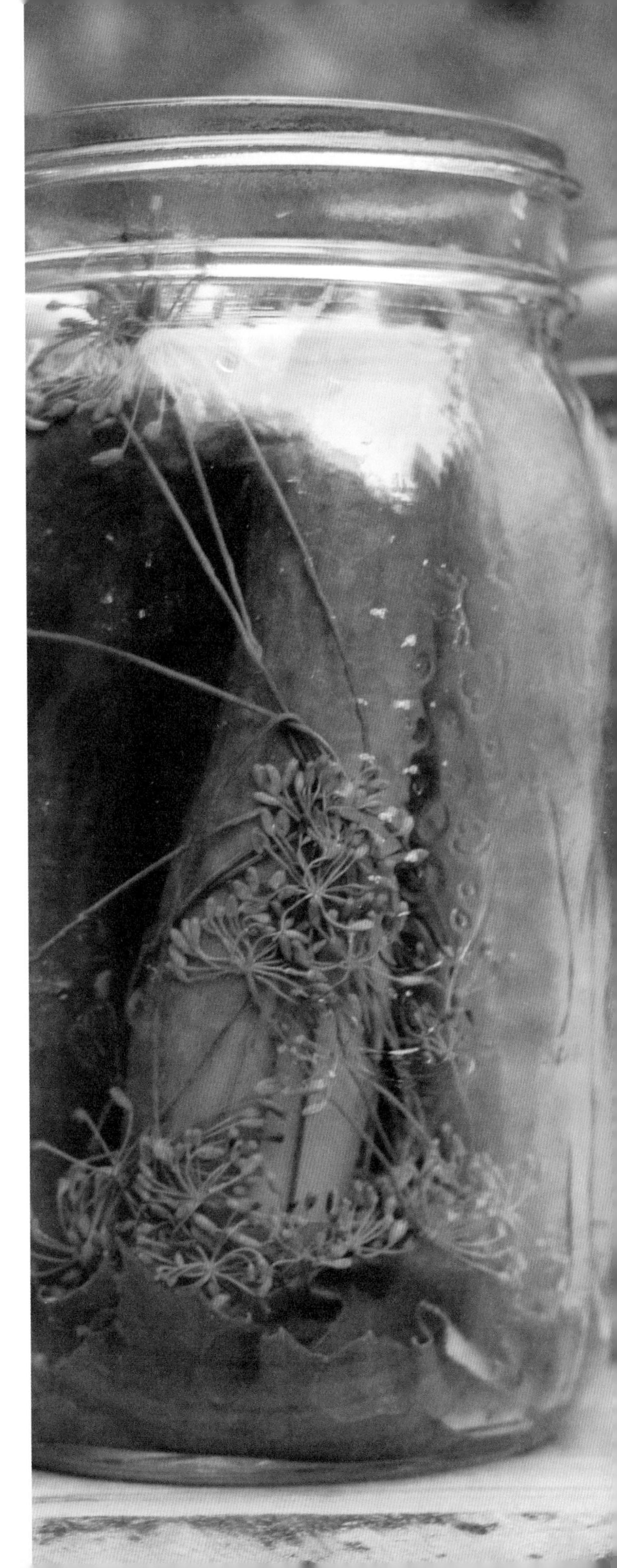

DIJON-STYLE GRAINY MUSTARD

WITH LABRADOR TEA

This is another recipe from our country's boreal food expert, Michele Genest. While we were in the Yukon, Miche took us on our first-ever foraging adventure just outside of Dawson City, where we discovered nearly 20 new-to-us edible plants. Labrador tea, an herb long valued for its medicinal properties, grows abundantly on that trail, and its leaves are often boiled to make—you guessed it—tea! In her second book, *The Boreal Feast*, Miche combines the leaves with freshly ground mustard seeds for an herbal, spicy version of the condiment. Labrador tea can be found at many health food stores or natural pharmacies, but if you can't find any, substitute dried sage or rosemary, 1 tsp (5 mL) at a time, until it suits your taste. The mustard seeds need to soak for two days, so plan ahead.

MAKES ONE HALF PINT (250 ML) JAR

3 Tbsp (45 mL) yellow mustard seeds
3 Tbsp (45 mL) black mustard seeds
1/3 cup (80 mL) white wine vinegar
1/3 cup (80 mL) dry white wine
1/2 tsp (2 mL) coarse sea salt
2 Tbsp (30 mL) birch syrup, or 1 Tbsp (15 mL) maple syrup + 1 Tbsp (15 mL) molasses
1 Tbsp (15 mL) finely chopped Labrador tea leaves (see note)

Combine the mustard seeds, vinegar, and wine in a small bowl or jar. Cover and let sit for 48 hours at room temperature.

Grind the soaked mustard seeds in the bowl of a food processor until thick but still grainy, about 3 to 5 minutes. Add the salt and birch syrup and pulse to combine.

Add the chopped Labrador tea leaves to the mustard mixture and pulse again to thoroughly combine. Transfer to a dry, sterilized screw-top jar and refrigerate. This is best if used within 2 months.

Note: Labrador tea is a health food in the right quantities (like in this recipe), but must not be used excessively. Miche has this caution in her book: "Use Labrador tea in low concentrations and in moderation, as it contains narcotic properties and can cause digestive upset in concentrated doses. Pregnant women and those with high blood pressure should be particularly careful."

THE SOURTOE COCKTAIL

In Dawson City, you can wander into the Downtown Hotel, purchase a drink from the bar, and *wait in line* to have a gnarly old toe plunked into your glass before taking the shot. It's a decades-long tradition in this northern Yukon town, one that started with an actual miner's toe. Over the years, various toes have gone missing or been swallowed (if you can believe it), but they're always replaced by new ones; these have been donated, preserved, and then stored over rock salt. Did we become the 50,697th and 50,698th members of Captain Dick's World Famous Sourtoe Cocktail Club? *Absolutely.* No trip to Dawson City would be complete without it.

CLOVE-SPICED LINGONBERRY SAUCE

This sweet/savoury sauce goes with Reindeer Meatloaf (page 86), both contributed by Yellowknife chef Robin Wasicuna. It's beautifully spiced, can be made with lingonberries or cranberries, and makes a great condiment for many different meat dishes, including a festive turkey dinner (page 117).

MAKES APPROXIMATELY 2 CUPS (500 ML)

2 tsp (10 mL) extra virgin olive oil
1 small yellow onion (about 120 g), finely diced
2 cloves garlic, minced
1/2 tsp (2 mL) ground cloves
2 Tbsp (30 mL) sherry vinegar
2 cups (250 mL) lingonberry or cranberry jam, or
  4 cups (1 L) fresh lingonberries or cranberries
2 Tbsp (30 mL) white sugar, or 3/4 cup (185 mL) if using
  fresh berries in place of the jam
2 tsp (10 mL) salt
1/4 tsp (1 mL) freshly ground black pepper

In a medium pot, heat the olive oil over medium heat. Once hot, add the onion and garlic and cook until the onion turns translucent, about 2 to 3 minutes. Add the cloves and cook for another 30 seconds. Deglaze the pot with the sherry vinegar. If using jam, stir in the jam, sugar, salt, and pepper and cook for a few more minutes. Remove from the heat and let cool. Transfer to a jar and store in the refrigerator for up to 1 month.

If using fresh berries, add them to the pot after deglazing it with the sherry vinegar and cook until they pop and become saucy, about 6 to 8 minutes. Once saucy, add the sugar, salt, and pepper and crush the berries with a potato masher or the back of a wooden spoon. Let the sauce thicken and reduce, about 5 minutes, stirring regularly. Remove from the heat and let cool. Transfer to a jar and store in the refrigerator for up to 1 month.

Lighting the Qulliq with Annie

There are few elders left in Rankin Inlet who speak solely Inuktitut, and we had the privilege of meeting one of them. Annie slowly climbed the stairs to where we gathered, her niece Veronica following with a heavy bag. It held a traditional lamp called the *qulliq*, a tool that women have used for centuries to keep their families warm and fed on the tundra.

Today, *qulliqs* are used only ceremonially, but Annie remembers when they were lit daily. About 60 years ago, she contracted tuberculosis and was sent to a hospital in Brandon, Manitoba, to recover. When she returned four years later, her baby had grown into a boy and *qulliqs* had been replaced by camp stoves.

The lamps are half-moon-shaped and carved out of soapstone; sometimes they are supported by three dowels, but Annie just rested hers on a small wooden box. Because it burns the brightest, whale fat was traditionally poured over the surface, but that day they used vegetable oil.

Annie pulled apart pieces of Arctic cotton and spread them along the front edge of the lamp. The fluffy white grass absorbed some of the oil and, when lit, acted as the wick, capable of burning slowly for long periods of time and adjusted now and then with a hook-shaped tool called a *taqqut*.

The *qulliq*, and Annie, provided us with more answers to one of our biggest questions in Nunavut: How have people survived for centuries in the Arctic? Even while wrapped in expensive gear and fed daily by others, we felt accomplished if we could manage a 10-minute walk around town. The thought of living solely off the land was incomprehensible to us, which made our meeting with Annie even more of an honour.

ROASTED TOMATO & FIG KETCHUP

This ketchup, by Newfoundland's Garry Gosse, was created to accompany his Maple Molasses-Braised Pork Belly (page 88), but it's an awesome condiment all on its own. This recipe is easily halved, but we find it useful to have a full batch on hand for barbeque season or as a dip for aged-cheddar grilled cheese sandwiches.

MAKES APPROXIMATELY 4 CUPS (1 L)

6 vine-ripened tomatoes (about 500 g), whole
1 medium red bell pepper (about 200 g), halved
1 medium green bell pepper (about 200 g), halved
1 large red onion (about 220 g), quartered
6 fresh figs (about 240 g)
1 to 2 sprigs fresh thyme, leaves removed
1 Tbsp (15 mL) extra virgin olive oil
1 tsp (5 mL) salt
1/4 tsp (1 mL) freshly ground black pepper
1 head of garlic (about 30 g)
1/8 tsp ground cinnamon
1/8 tsp ground allspice
1/4 tsp (1 mL) ground cloves

Preheat the oven to 400°F (200°C).

In a large bowl, toss the tomatoes, peppers, onions, and figs with the thyme, olive oil, salt, and pepper. Spread the mixture out onto a large baking sheet. Slice the top off the head of garlic so the cloves are exposed, wrap in tinfoil, and place on the baking sheet next to the vegetables. Place the tray in the oven and let roast for 1 hour, until the tomatoes are soft and the edges of the vegetables have blackened.

Once the vegetables and figs have roasted, remove the tray from the oven and cool slightly. Transfer the mixture to a blender. Unwrap the garlic bulb and squeeze out the softened cloves into the blender as well. Blend until smooth, then transfer to a medium pot. Add the cinnamon, allspice, and cloves and simmer over medium heat until reduced and thickened (similar to the consistency of ketchup), about 30 to 60 minutes.

Taste and season with more salt and pepper if desired. Let cool, transfer to an airtight container, and store in the refrigerator for 3 to 4 weeks or in the freezer for up to 3 months.

SWEET & SMOKY BLUEBERRY ALE BARBEQUE SAUCE

In Northern Ontario, we spent an idyllic summer day in Kenora, a small city that sits on Lake of the Woods. This massive body of fresh water earned its name from the hundreds of forested islands scattered across it. We spent the day boating around the lake with two new friends who expertly manoeuvred through these islands, showed us secret beaches, and fed us snacks like homemade deer sausage. Kenora is also home to a craft brewpub, Lake of the Woods Brewing Company, and we rounded out the day with a few great ales on their sunny patio.

This barbeque sauce is courtesy of the brewery. Use it as you would any barbeque sauce, but it's particularly good on ribs or grilled chicken.

MAKES 4 CUPS (1 L)

1/4 cup (60 mL) lightly packed brown sugar
1/2 cup (125 mL) apple cider vinegar
1/4 cup (60 mL) molasses
1/4 cup (60 mL) honey
1/2 cup (125 mL) Lake of the Woods' Forgotten Lake Blueberry Ale, or any other mild ale
1/4 cup (60 mL) Worcestershire sauce
1/4 cup (60 mL) dark rum
2 Tbsp (30 mL) yellow mustard
1 Tbsp (15 mL) liquid smoke
1 Tbsp (15 mL) chili powder
2 tsp (10 mL) freshly ground black pepper
2 tsp (10 mL) ground allspice
1/4 tsp (1 mL) ground cloves
1/4 cup (60 mL) fresh or thawed frozen wild blueberries
3 1/2 cups (875 mL) ketchup

Combine the sugar, vinegar, molasses, honey, beer, Worcestershire, rum, mustard, smoke, chili powder, pepper, allspice, and cloves in a medium pot and bring to a boil. Once boiling, lower the heat and simmer until the mixture reduces by about a third, about 40 to 60 minutes.

Add the blueberries and ketchup and let simmer another 30 minutes. Remove from the heat and let cool. In a blender or with an immersion blender, purée until smooth. Transfer to an airtight container and refrigerate for up to 1 month or freeze for up to 3 months.

HOMEMADE SEA SALT

First: Did you know Canada has the longest ocean coastline in the world? Second: Did you know making your own sea salt from some of that ocean water is so easy?

This was a recipe-testing mission we loved—we got up before dawn on a foggy morning, packed as many large mason jars as we could find, and headed to the beach (stopping along the way for breakfast doughnuts—an important, not-to-be-underrated part of the mission). For this recipe, you need access to relatively clean ocean water (you don't want to scoop it out of a busy marina, for example), some basic filtering materials, a pot, and a stove. We first did this with water from Boundary Bay just south of Vancouver, and then again in Tofino, where we boiled it down on a beach campfire. While this method won't provide you with pounds of salt, it will give you a great amount to keep on hand for finishing dishes.

MAKES 1/2 CUP (125 ML)

8 cups (2 L) ocean water
Organic coffee filters, finely meshed cheesecloth, and/or nut milk bag, for filtering
1/2 ounce (14 g) dried porcini mushrooms (optional)

Collect your water from a clean source, then filter it by pouring it through two or ideally three filters. We usually line a sieve with cheesecloth or a reusable nut milk bag (the kind used for straining homemade almond milk), put an opened coffee filter on top of those, and place the whole thing over a large pot. Carefully pour the water through the filter a bit at a time, replacing the coffee filters as they become oversaturated.

Once all the water has been filtered into the pot, bring it to a boil over high heat, then lower the heat slightly and let it simmer. Depending on how much water you have, it will take 1 to 2 hours to reduce down completely, during which time you can busy yourself with other tasks, like eating leftover doughnuts. Once the water gets very low, watch it carefully and listen for popping sounds. After about 45 to 60 minutes, the water will eventually turn into a milky white paste. Use a whisk to stir around the salt as it begins to appear, and remove from the heat once the salt looks only slightly damp. Break up the clumps with the whisk and let the water finish evaporating in the residual heat of the pot. Or, if the salt looks like it is drying out a bit too much, transfer to a bowl immediately. Once cool, transfer to a covered container and it's ready to use.

Different oceans vary in their salinity, but in general, you can expect a yield of approximately 1/2 cup of salt (125 mL) for every 8 cups (2 L) of ocean water you boil down.

If you want to add an umami twist to your salt, blend the dried porcini mushrooms in a food processor until they turn into a fine powder. Mix this into the salt, then sprinkle it on *everything*.

Cheers!

To Drink

THE HENDRICK'S KERRY

This vibrantly green cocktail is named for Kerry, the gin-loving friend of Prince Edward Island's the Pearl Eatery, who once won six rounds of *Jeopardy!* Featuring juniper berries and the cool flavour of cucumber, this cocktail by owner Maxine Delaney is an exceptionally refreshing summer drink.

SERVES 6

1 English cucumber (about 450 g), skin on

FOR 1 COCKTAIL

- Ice
- 3 to 5 dried or fresh juniper berries, crushed
- 1¼ ounces (38 mL) Hendrick's Gin (or a Canadian gin)
- ¾ ounce (23 mL) Lillet Blanc
- 1¼ ounces (38 mL) fresh cucumber juice
- ¾ ounce (23 mL) freshly squeezed lime juice
- ¾ ounce (23 mL) lime cordial
- 5 drops bitters
- 2 to 3 ounces (60 to 90 mL) soda or tonic water

Cucumber slices and lime wedges, to garnish

First, make the fresh cucumber juice. In general, you'll get about 1 cup (250 mL) of juice from one English cucumber, which is roughly enough to make six cocktails. If you don't have a juicer, simply cut the cucumber into 1-inch (2.5 cm) chunks and blend in a blender or food processor. Pass the mixture through a cheesecloth-lined sieve or through a fine mesh nut milk bag. Discard the pulp and keep the juice in the refrigerator (for up to 3 days) until you need it.

To make the cocktail, add some ice and the juniper berries to a tumbler. In a cocktail shaker, add the gin, lillet, cucumber juice, lime juice, cordial, bitters, and ice and shake well. Strain into the tumbler and top with soda or tonic water to taste. Garnish with slices of cucumber or a wedge of lime, if desired.

Be sure to cheers to Kerry when you drink it! Can you feel yourself getting smarter?

THE CAESAR

We are huge fans of this classic Canadian cocktail. It was created by Walter Chell in 1969 to celebrate the opening of a new restaurant, and it quickly became a national sensation. Clam juice—*the* ingredient needed to make a Caesar—is easy to find at the grocery store, so it's simple to make your own Caesar mix from scratch! While people tend to get creative with meal-sized garnishes, we prefer the traditional celery, lemon wedge, and/or pickle combo. Joy Road Catering's Pickled Asparagus with Lovage & Tarragon (page 254) is our ideal adornment.

SERVES 4

TOMATO WINE

The Caesar is, without a doubt, the most iconic Canadian cocktail, but there is another tomato-based Canadian beverage you should know about. In the quiet hills of Charlevoix, Quebec, Pascale Miche tends to a few acres of organic heirloom tomatoes, which he harvests, presses, and ferments into wine—yes, wine! The operation was inspired by Pascale's great-grandfather, who had an excess of tomatoes during WWI and turned them into wine to avoid food waste. When we visited Pascale's company, Omerto, in Baie-Saint-Paul, it was the first and only commercial operation in the world to make such a product. Perhaps the biggest surprise? Tomatoes can be made into wines that are just as interesting as those made from grapes. The acidic Omerto Sec tasted of lime and grapefruit, similar to a Sauvignon Blanc, and we loved it so much we left with several bottles.

INFUSED VODKA

1½ tsp (7 mL) celery seeds
1 cup (250 mL) vodka

CELERY RIMMING SALT

¼ tsp (1 mL) celery seeds
1½ tsp (7 mL) coarse sea salt

CAESAR MIX

3 cups (750 mL) tomato juice
¼ cup + 2 Tbsp (90 mL) clam juice
4½ Tbsp (67 mL) freshly squeezed lemon juice
1½ Tbsp (22 mL) Worcestershire sauce
½ tsp (2 mL) Tabasco
Salt and freshly ground black pepper

Celery stalks, pickled vegetables, and lemon wedges, to garnish

To infuse the vodka, combine the celery seeds with the vodka and let sit until fragrant, at least 1 hour or, ideally, overnight.

To make the rimming salt, add the ¼ tsp of celery seeds and coarse sea salt to a mortar and pestle or spice grinder and grind into a coarse mixture. Transfer to a small plate.

To make the Caesar mix, add the tomato juice, clam juice, lemon juice, Worcestershire sauce, and Tabasco in a spouted bowl or pitcher. Stir to combine, then add salt, pepper, and more Tabasco to taste. Mix in the celery-infused vodka and stir well to combine.

Moisten the rims of four pint-sized (500 mL) mason jars. Dip the rims in the prepared celery salt, making small circles until well coated. Fill each glass with three to four large cubes of ice. Pour the boozy Caesar mixture over the ice, garnish as desired, and enjoy with brunch!

MANITOBA MULE

This cocktail recipe comes from Steven Ackerman, drink enthusiast and co-owner of the Tallest Poppy, a popular restaurant in Winnipeg. It features sweet grass, a sacred plant for First Nations, Métis, and Inuit people that is most commonly found in the Prairies. Its signature sweet scent is intensified when it rains or when it's burned, as it often is for ceremonies. It can be found at some natural health food stores, or you can use Żubrówka Bison Grass Vodka and skip the infusion altogether.

SERVES 8

SWEET GRASS-INFUSED VODKA (MAKES ABOUT ENOUGH FOR 8 COCKTAILS)

- 10 inches/25 cm (1/4 oz or 8 g) braided sweet grass
- 1 1/2 cups (375 mL) vodka

GINGER SYRUP (MAKES ABOUT ENOUGH FOR 8 COCKTAILS)

- 1/2 cup (125 mL) water
- 1/2 cup (125 mL) white sugar
- 1/2 cup (125 mL) fresh ginger, peeled and thinly sliced

FOR 1 COCKTAIL

- 1 ounce (30 mL) sweet grass-infused vodka
- 3/4 ounce (23 mL) freshly squeezed lime juice
- 3/4 ounce (23 mL) prepared ginger syrup
- 2 ounces (60 mL) ginger ale or ginger beer
- 4 dashes bitters
- Lime wedge, to garnish

To make the vodka infusion, place the sweet grass in a jar, pour in the vodka so that it fully covers the sweet grass, and let sit until the vodka has turned a golden colour and becomes fragrant. This takes about 2 hours, or ideally can be left overnight.

To make the ginger syrup, add water, sugar, and ginger to a small saucepan and bring to a boil, stirring regularly. Once the sugar has dissolved, remove the mixture from the heat and let cool. Once cool, strain the syrup, discard the ginger, and refrigerate until needed.

To make the cocktail, put two large cubes of ice in a tumbler or a copper mug (the traditional Moscow Mule vessel), if you have one. Pour in the vodka, lime juice, ginger syrup, ginger beer, and bitters. Stir and garnish with a wedge of lime and/or a slice of ginger, if desired. Repeat until all your friends have a drink!

CRAFT DISTILLERIES

There was once a vibrant distillery culture across North America, with hundreds of mini-distilleries in Canada alone. None of them survived Prohibition, however, and the industry has been ever-so-slow in rebuilding, thanks in part to outdated liquor laws. At the time of our road trip, there were about 25 small distilleries across the country, though more continue to emerge each year.

Our first real education in craft distillery culture came from a visit to Lucky Bastard Distillery in Saskatoon. Their spirits highlight many important Saskatchewan flavours; their Gambit Gin, for example, is the only one in the world (that they know of) that lists Saskatoon berries amongst its botanicals. We purchased a bottle, as well as their sea buckthorn and wild flower honey liqueur, and left with a desire to seek out as many other distilleries as we could. Along the way, some of those included Last Mountain (also in Saskatchewan), Glenora Distillery on Cape Breton Island, and Ironworks Distillery in Lunenburg.

Next time you're buying spirits, try going local!

ROASTED CONCORD GRAPE MIMOSA

We love late summer, when Concord grapes reappear at the farmers' market. We consume as many of these dark purple gems as we can, and one of our favourite ways to eat them is roasted, blended into a syrup, and poured over/into everything—including cocktails! Beyond boozy drinks, this syrup is great with pancakes, crêpes, or yogurt and is a pleasing addition to salad dressings.

SERVES 5

ROASTED CONCORD GRAPE SYRUP (MAKES ABOUT 3½ CUPS/875 ML)

- 3 pounds (1.4 kg) Concord or Coronation grapes
- ¼ cup (60 mL) honey
- 1 Tbsp (15 mL) freshly squeezed lemon juice
- ¼ cup (60 mL) water

MIMOSA (FOR 1 COCKTAIL)

- 5 ounces (150 mL) dry Canadian sparkling wine or Champagne (1 bottle will be enough for 5 cocktails)
- 2 ounces (60 mL) roasted Concord grape syrup

Preheat the oven to 350°F (180°C).

Line a baking sheet with a layer of parchment paper and arrange the grape clusters so they completely cover the sheet without overlapping. Roast the grapes in the preheated oven until oozing and many of the grapes have split, about 45 to 55 minutes.

Remove from the oven, let cool slightly, and press through a food mill. Alternatively, you could remove the grapes from their stems, blend the grapes until smooth, and then strain through cheesecloth. Transfer the strained mixture to a medium pan and set to simmer. Add honey, lemon juice, and water and stir until combined. Remove from the heat, let cool, and store in the refrigerator. Best consumed within 2 weeks from the refrigerator or within 3 months from the freezer.

To make the mimosas, pop a bottle of sparkling wine, mix in the grape syrup, and sip with brunch!

Wilton.
38.7 x 26 x 1.91 cm

SPICED AUTUMN CHAI

We know fall has arrived when Dana makes a big pot of chai, her annual tradition. The original recipe came from a friend of a friend of a friend, and it continues to be adapted slightly each year. While it can easily be halved, it's a spicy, comforting, and much-beloved gift for friends, so we encourage you to make the full batch!

MAKES APPROXIMATELY 20 CUPS (5 L)

CHAI CONCENTRATE

- Fifteen 6-inch (15 cm) cinnamon sticks
- 1/2 cup (125 mL) whole allspice berries
- 1/3 cup (80 mL) whole cardamom
- 1/3 cup (80 mL) whole coriander seeds
- 3 Tbsp (45 mL) whole black peppercorns
- 2 1/2 cups (625 mL) fresh ginger, peeled and thinly sliced
- 24 cups (6 L) water

FOR 1 MUG OF CHAI

- 1/2 cup (125 mL) prepared chai concentrate
- 1/2 cup (125 mL) whole milk or nut/soy milk
- 1 to 2 tsp (5 to 10 mL) honey
- Cinnamon stick
- 1 bag black tea (optional)
- Whisky or bourbon (optional)

To make the concentrate, add the cinnamon sticks to a food processor or blender and pulse a few times to break them up—this will allow them to release more flavour into the concentrate. Add the allspice, cardamom, coriander, and peppercorns and pulse until all the spices are a coarse mixture but not a powder.

In a large pot, combine the spices, ginger, and water. Bring to a boil, then lower the heat and let simmer, uncovered, for about 2 hours. Once simmered, strain out the spices and transfer the chai concentrate to jars or containers, let cool, and store in the refrigerator. The chai will keep for about 3 weeks if kept cool.

To make a mug of chai, heat equal parts chai concentrate and milk in the microwave or in a small pot over medium heat. Once simmering, add the honey to taste and stir in with a cinnamon stick. Simmer with a black tea bag if you like and discard the bag once the chai reaches your desired strength. Enjoy hot, ideally wrapped in a blanket and lounging beside a fireplace. Add a splash of whisky or bourbon, if desired!

RASPBERRY & THYME CORDIAL

"I love bright red drinks, don't you? They taste twice as good as any other colour."
—From *Anne of Green Gables*, by Lucy Maud Montgomery

We could not agree more, Anne.

SERVES 4

3 cups (750 mL) fresh or frozen raspberries
½ cup (125 mL) white sugar
3 to 4 sprigs fresh thyme
2½ cups (625 mL) boiling water
3 Tbsp (45 mL) freshly squeezed lemon juice
Sparkling water, vodka, or gin (optional)

Add the berries, sugar, and thyme to a medium pot. Cook over medium heat for about 10 minutes or until the sugar is dissolved and the mixture is saucy.

Remove the sprigs of thyme and discard. If you have a food mill, press the raspberry mixture through it to remove the seeds. Mix the resulting raspberry juice with the boiling water and the lemon juice. Let cool, stirring occasionally, and strain through cheesecloth to remove any remaining seeds. Alternatively, use a blender to blend the hot raspberry mixture directly with the hot water and lemon juice, then strain through cheesecloth. Let the cordial cool and refrigerate (for up to 5 days) until you're ready to serve.

This is lovely poured over ice on its own, with sparkling water, or with a splash of vodka or gin.

Nunavut

Figuring out how to get to Nunavut was a puzzle we attempted to solve for most of our trip. The territory consists of 26 communities spread across approximately one-fifth of Canada's entire land mass, and each is accessible only by plane or boat. There's no way a person can get lost on a country road in Nunavut, because all streets simply end outside of town.

With a lot of strategizing, we hatched a plan, and after a two-day train ride to Churchill, Manitoba, and a short flight, we planted our feet on the frozen ground in Rankin Inlet.

In a culture that has changed rapidly, many people are only a generation or two from a life that was once completely centred on fishing, hunting, and day-to-day survival. Today, most people no longer live nomadically and instead are settled in communities with grocery stores stocked with imported foods. The overwhelming cost of fresh produce (a quarter of a watermelon for $13, for example) has meant that more processed foods have become the norm. People contend with the difficulties of these changes daily, working to preserve their culture's unique knowledge and traditions, while also innovating to bring their past, present, and future together in sustainable and culturally relevant ways.

In Nunavut, the emotional connections to traditional food were some of the strongest we've ever seen. We visited the Rankin Inlet Healing Facility—the territory's correctional facility for men—where a young Inuk man named Harry prepares country food once a week for the inmates. He said the emotional calm this meal provides to the men is remarkable. While country food is not as readily available as it used to be, it is of fundamental importance to the community.

During our time there, we found ourselves in many unique-to-Nunavut situations, like the time we were almost run over by a dogsled team zipping through the streets, or when we met Titaaq, a hunter who travels up to 16 hours per day, sometimes in temperatures below -76°F (-60°C), to hunt for his family. We ate whale blubber and tundra berry muffins with Annie, a highly respected elder in town, and sat on tanned seal hides while sampling frozen caribou fat with Monica and Michael Shouldice.

Nunavut gave us experiences we had never even thought possible, and a far better understanding of life in the true North. The perspective we gained there was essential to understanding this country as a whole, and as we headed back to the parts of Canada that are connected by roads, we felt grateful to live in a place so extraordinarily diverse.

The End of the Road . . .

And thus, with its frosty final days, our five-month journey was over. When we pulled into our friend's driveway in Vancouver (both of us were technically homeless, at that point), we turned off the car and sat still for a while. We were back where we had started, tired and proud of ourselves, but mainly full of disbelief that our idea had worked out. After all, not only had we managed to stay alive and well fed, but we were even better friends than when we'd started. We sat there thinking about just how far we had travelled in that little white car, knowing the trip had taught us far more than we could even comprehend at that point.

While we both longed to have a real home again and a bit of a routine, we also mourned the end of our time on the road. It had been difficult and euphoric and entertainingly diverse, and we had become accustomed to the perpetual change of view. Also, we had gotten kind of weird after hundreds of hours spent in the car, swearing like sailors and crying with laughter over jokes only the seriously stir-crazy would find funny. We often wondered aloud whether the real world would take us back in.

We readjusted soon enough, however, and set to work sorting through all the stories we'd gathered on the road, tucked away in our brains and in notebooks and in the thousands of photos we'd taken. Over the next few years, we had the chance to relive the trip all over again—such is the joy of blogging and writing a book—and we know that it will continue to feed us, and (we hope) you, for years to come.

Acknowledgements

It is impossible to express the gratitude we have for the people who've made this book a reality, but we'll do our absolute best. To Appetite by Random House and the lovely Robert McCullough, thank you for making this collective dream of ours come true and for welcoming us so warmly into the Appetite family. Robert, there hasn't been a single time we've left your office and not danced our way down Water Street. Thank you to our goddess of an editor, Zoe Maslow, who became a friend during our very first phone call and who guided us through this process with intelligence, humour, and warmth. Thank you to the incomparable CS Richardson and to the production team for designing the book and for making us look so damn good, and to our copy editor Lana Okerlund for being an all-around genius. We are honoured to have worked with all of you and to have had the rest of Appetite by Random House's talented team behind us.

If for no other reason, writing this book was worth it just for the opportunity to publicly thank our family and friends and to put our love for them in ink. We are in awe of you. Thank you for wrapping us up in your loyal arms and for your endless support. We love you more than the Yukon loves cinnamon buns.

Thank you to our dear friend Jillian Povarchook, who lent her paramount sense of style to this process. Nearly every weekend for an entire summer, she helped us shoot the book, assisting with everything from cooking and props to the consumption of at least 50 bags of potato chips. Your help was an incredible gift.

We are extremely grateful to all the people who recipe-tested for us—your comments and suggestions were invaluable. Thank you to Ina Anderson, Anne VanVeller, Brett VanVeller, Mark Anderson, Jillian Povarchook, Heather Jessup, Jacquie Jessup, Bart Jessup, Debbie Levy, Robyn Levy, Stephanie Levy, Sally McBride, Zoe Fitch, Heather Bartlett, Lauren Painter, Karen Hong, Caylee Hong, Nicole Hong, Mary Duck, Dave Duck, Angela Bennett, Lindsay Kwasnicia, Andrew Sutton, Keith Lennig, and Shane Trudell.

Thank you to Andrés Rodriguez Ruiz, Stephanie Adams-Jacobson, and Dymetha Hopping for answering all our Photoshop questions and lending your aesthetic expertise, and a special shout out to Andrew Sutton for "forgetting" you owned half of the *Feast* car for five months so we could explore the country.

Endless thanks to our readers. *Feast* could not exist without you. Had it not been for the generous donations of our Indiegogo funders in the summer of 2013, we wouldn't have made it on the road in the first place. Your enthusiasm not only made this project a reality, but also gave us the confidence we needed to set out. Thank you so much.

To the countless people across Canada who took us in and became a part of our project, we thank you. For two people living out of a car and suitcases, it was remarkable just how often we felt at home across this big country. We were fed, housed, and invited to experience the life and work of numerous talented people, many of whom shared recipes for this book. A full list of our recipe contributors can be found on page 290.

Finally, we'd like to offer a huge thanks to all the businesses, organizations, and tourism boards who sponsored us during the trip. Without your help, we'd have been sleeping in tents in November, eating canned beans, and clueless about who to talk to. Thank you to Destination British Columbia, Tourism Nanaimo, the Thompson Okanagan Tourism Association, Tourism Kelowna, Travel Yukon, Travel Alberta, Tourism Saskatchewan, Travel Manitoba, Parkland Tourism, Tourism Winnipeg, Tourisme Montréal, Québec City Tourism, Tourisme Québec, Tourisme Charlevoix, Tourism New Brunswick, Tourism Prince Edward Island, Tourism Nova Scotia, Destination Halifax, Newfoundland and Labrador Tourism, Go Western Newfoundland, Adventure Central Newfoundland, Legendary Coasts of Eastern Newfoundland, Destination St. John's, and Nunavut Tourism. We'd also like to thank Food Bloggers of Canada, Telus, Hootsuite, Via Rail, Calm Air, Thinkers Lodge, West Coast Expeditions, the Waring House, Kingsbrae Garden, Montréal en Lumière, the Bears' Den Bed and Breakfast in Churchill, Frontiers North Adventures, Marine Atlantic, and BC Ferries.

One final note: Lindsay would like to thank Dana for being so kind to her when she had a ~~major~~ wee meltdown over the humidity in Toronto, and Dana would like to thank Lindsay for being so kind to her when she had a ~~major~~ wee meltdown over the broken bike rack in Merritt. We are both so thankful for this friendship.

Recipe Contributors

Aimée Wimbush-Bourque, cookbook author, food writer, and recipe developer, www.simplebites.net, Quebec

Andrew Aitken, chef/owner of Wild Caraway Restaurant, Nova Scotia

Aviv Fried & Michal Lavi, co-owners of Sidewalk Citizen Bakery, Alberta

Bob Arniel, chef/owner of Chef to Go, Newfoundland

Bridget Oland, marketing manager and recipe developer at Crosby's Molasses Co. Ltd., New Brunswick

Bryan Picard, chef/owner of the Bite House, Nova Scotia

Chelsea Tunnell, pastry chef at Mon Petit Choux, British Columbia

Chris Aerni, chef/owner of the Rossmount Inn, New Brunswick

Claira Vautour, Acadian traditional cook, New Brunswick

Colin Metcalfe, chef at Sidewalk Citizen Bakery, Alberta

Connie DeSousa & John Jackson, co-owners of CHARCUT, Alberta

Dan Clapson, food writer and TV personality, www.eatnorth.com, Saskatchewan/Alberta

Dana Ewart & Cameron Smith, chefs/owners of Joy Road Catering, British Columbia

Debbie Levy (& family), cheese educator at Savour This, Ontario

Dominique Fortier, owner of Charcuterie de Tours, Quebec

Doreen Crowe, restaurant owner, Ontario

Elizabeth Baird, author of *Classic Canadian Cooking* and other cookbooks with a Canadian theme, Ontario

Eric Pateman, CEO of Edible Canada, British Columbia

Garry Gosse, chef/owner of Harbour Breeze Catering, Newfoundland

Gerri Robicheau, community maven and home cook, New Brunswick

Gilles Bernard, former chef at Auberge des Peupliers, Quebec

Giselle Courteau, owner of Duchess Bake Shop, Alberta

Greg Mazur, president of Kelowna Métis Association, British Columbia

Jackie Kai Ellis, owner of Beaucoup Bakery and the Paris Tours, British Columbia

James Power, manager at Raspberry Point Oysters, Prince Edward Island

Janice Beaton (& family), proprietor of Janice Beaton Fine Cheese, Alberta/Nova Scotia

Jennifer Heagle & Jo-Ann Laverty, co-owners of the Red Apron, Ontario

Jesse Vergen, chef at the Saint John Ale House and Smoking Pig BBQ, New Brunswick

Jessica Weatherhead, co-owner of Roots and Shoots Farm, Ontario/Quebec

Jillian Povarchook (& the late Mary Weissman), curatorial associate at the Museum of Vancouver and home cook, British Columbia

John Horne, executive chef at Canoe Restaurant & Bar, Ontario

Josh Michnik & Dustin Sepkowski, owner of (Josh) and manager at (Dustin) 33 Acres Brewing Company, British Columbia

Julian Armstrong, food writer at the *Montreal Gazette* and author of *Made in Quebec: A Culinary Journey* (HarperCollins, 2014) and *A Taste of Quebec* (Macmillan Canada, 1990 and 2001), Quebec

Julie Van Rosendaal, cookbook author and food writer, www.dinnerwithjulie.com, Alberta

Karen Anderson, owner of Alberta Food Tours Inc., New Brunswick/Alberta

Kat Romanow & Sydney Warshaw, co-founders of www.wanderingchew.ca, Quebec

Kathy Jollimore, food writer and blogger at www.eathalifax.ca, Nova Scotia

Katie Gorrie, poet, editor of the *Filid Chapbook* and home cook, Saskatchewan/Quebec

Kelly Lindell, owner of A & K Canteen and Catering, Nunavut

Kent Van Dyk, chef and high school culinary arts teacher, Ontario
Kimberley Phaneuf, owner of the Flour Shoppe: Bread and Pastry Studio, Saskatchewan
Lana Antonia Jules, cultural host at West Coast Expeditions, British Columbia
Lone Sorensen, owner of Northern Roots, Northwest Territories
Lyndsey Larson & Juliana Frisch, owner of Uncle Berwyn's Yukon Birch Syrup (Lyndsey) & mother-in-law to Lyndsey and Yukon resident (Juliana), Yukon
Maria A. Mancini, special needs educational resource worker and lover of *cucina casalinga* (home cooking) for the *famiglia*, Ontario
Mark Plouffe, chef/owner of MARKco Global Eats, Northwest Territories/Ontario
Matt & Angela Honey, co-owners of Honeybeans Coffee, Tea, and Treats, New Brunswick
Maxine Delaney, owner of the Pearl Eatery, Prince Edward Island
Michael Soucy, farmer and founder of Seed + Soil, Alberta
Michele Genest, author of *The Boreal Gourmet* and *The Boreal Feast* (Harbour Publishing, 2010 and 2014), Yukon
Moreka Jolar & Linda Solomon, authors of *Hollyhock Cooks* (New Society Publishers, 2003), British Columbia
Murray McDonald, executive chef at Fogo Island Inn, Newfoundland
Pascale Berthiaume, glacier, owner of Pascale's Ice Cream, Ontario
Patrice Demers, chef/co-owner of Patrice Pâtissier, Quebec
Peter Saunders & Sophie Ouellet, chefs/owners of EVOO, Quebec
Renée Kohlman, cookbook author and blogger at www.sweetsugarbean.com, Saskatchewan
Roary MacPherson, CCC, CFBE, executive chef at the Sheraton Hotel, Newfoundland
Robin Wasicuna, chef/owner of Wiseguy Foods and Twin Pine Diner, Northwest Territories
Roger Andrews, chef, instructor at the College of the North Atlantic, Newfoundland
Rose Murray, cookbook author, Ontario
Shane M. Chartrand, chef at River Cree Resort and Casino, Alberta
Shannon Jones & Bryan Dyck, farmers at Broadfork Farm, Nova Scotia
Shaun Hussey & Michelle LeBlanc, chefs/owners of Chinched Bistro, Newfoundland
Speerville Flour Mill (& community), New Brunswick
Stephanie & Andrea French, owners of the Pie Shoppe, British Columbia
Stéphanie Labelle, owner of Pâtisserie Rhubarbe, Quebec
Stephanie Le, blogger at www.iamafoodblog.com, British Columbia
Steven Ackerman, cocktail engineer/co-owner at the Tallest Poppy, Manitoba
Sue Asquith, co-owner of Two Whales Coffee Shop, Newfoundland
Suresh Doss, food/drink/travel writer, Ontario
Susan Ross, co-owner of Lendrum Ross Farm, Yukon
Talia Syrie, executive chef/co-owner of the Tallest Poppy, Manitoba
Tall Grass Prairie Bread Company & Grass Roots Community, Manitoba
Tara MacDonald, co-owner of Two If By Sea Café, Nova Scotia
Taras Manzie, president of Lake of the Woods Brewing Company, Ontario
Tim Davies, chef at the Willow on Wascana, Saskatchewan
Todd Johnson, general manager of Kivalliq Arctic Foods Ltd., Nunavut
Todd Perrin, chef/owner of Mallard Cottage, Newfoundland
Trisha Gordon, chef at the Pearl Eatery, Prince Edward Island
Tyler Kaktins, executive chef/owner of Foxtail Café, Manitoba
Valerie Lugonja, writer and owner of www.acanadianfoodie.com, Alberta
Vicki Emlaw, co-owner of Vicki's Veggies, Ontario

Index

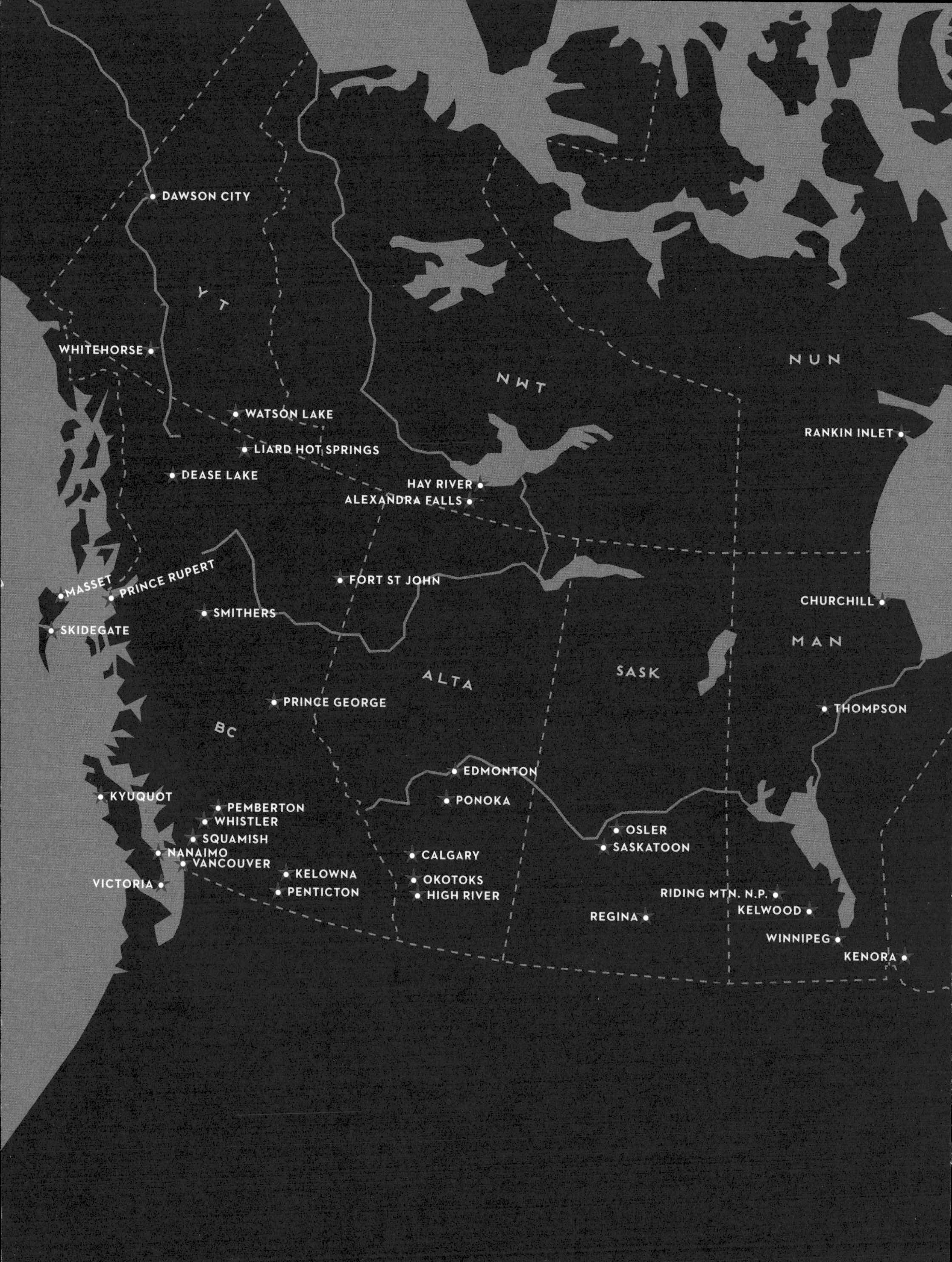

DAWSON CITY
YT
WHITEHORSE
NWT
NUN
WATSON LAKE
LIARD HOT SPRINGS
DEASE LAKE
RANKIN INLET
HAY RIVER
ALEXANDRA FALLS
MASSET
PRINCE RUPERT
FORT ST JOHN
SKIDEGATE
SMITHERS
CHURCHILL
MAN
ALTA
SASK
PRINCE GEORGE
THOMPSON
BC
EDMONTON
KYUQUOT
PONOKA
PEMBERTON
WHISTLER
OSLER
SQUAMISH
NANAIMO
SASKATOON
VANCOUVER
CALGARY
KELOWNA
VICTORIA
OKOTOKS
PENTICTON
HIGH RIVER
RIDING MTN. N.P.
KELWOOD
REGINA
WINNIPEG
KENORA